ALMOST A CENTURY

96 Years of Musings
from the Extraordinary Life
of a South Dakota Farm Girl

Jo Ryman Scott

Liberté Press books may be purchase for educational, business, or sales promotional use.

For information, please email the Special Markets Department at info@libertepress.com

NONFICTION / Memoir / History / Autobiography / Inspiration

First Edition: April 2025
Printed in the United States of America
ISBN: 979-8-9909388-3-0 (paperback)
Cover photo © 2025 Leon Unruh
Cover design by Liz Blume

LIBERTÉ
PRESS

Liberté Press San Francisco
558 Presidio Blvd. Suite B, # 29015
San Francisco, CA 94129-5710

Liberté Press New York
521 Jerusalem Ave.
N. Belmore, NY 11710

libertepress.com

DISCLAIMER

Dear Reader,

Welcome to a collection
of my thoughts and stories.
I was a teacher for more than seventy years
and I always paid attention to detail.
However, if you come across
any quirky mistakes,
I hope they will put a smile
on your face rather than
cause any concern.

Jo

Jo Ryman Scott

ADVANCE PRAISE FOR ALMOST A CENTURY

Jo has uncanny recall of nine decades of teachers, students, and Festival guests in this engaging book. Here, in her own words, is the story of her well-lived life.

Sue Matsuki
Cabaret artist, New York City

Jo Scott is unequaled in terms of her generosity, caring and kindness. This book encapsulates the essence of who Jo Scott is.

Gregory Buchalter
Retired Conductor, The Metropolitan Opera

Dynamo Jo Scott, a true force of nature, provided a spark for the Fairbanks arts scene. Her writing chronicles how she left a lasting imprint on the community that she loved.

Dermot Cole
Journalist and author, Fairbanks, Alaska

Jo Scott is a mover and a shaker, and a doer. Her dream of building the Fairbanks Summer Arts Festival became a magnificent achievement. I am so happy to have spent thirty summers of my life up there so far, working with her on this dream.

Greg Hopkins
Professor of Jazz Composition, Berklee College of Music

More Advance Praise

Jo Scott was the Grand Dame of music and the arts in Fairbanks. She had a dream for a music festival in this small Alaskan town and her dedication, leadership, extraordinary energy, and vision made it happen. Jo's excitement is infectious, and the world saw this every summer with guest artists and participants from around the world performing in Fairbanks, Alaska… all a result of one amazing lady's dream.

Jake Poole
Vice Chancellor Emeritus, University of Alaska Fairbanks

Jo Ryman Scott is one of my favorite people on the planet! What a life she recounts in this book. I feel blessed to have gotten to know Jo in her New York City era after she left Fairbanks, meeting initially when she hired me to play for of her big New York events. That led to shared holidays, parties, and a beautiful friendship.

Matt Baker
Jazz pianist, New York City

Jo Ryman Scott is one of those rare people who makes things happen and makes the world a better place to live.

Frederick Moyer
Pianist

DEDICATION

To the memory of my husband, Dick Scott, whose unwavering support and encouragement for my dreams were always a guiding light. A brilliant humorist and masterful storyteller, he had dictated an account of a unique engineering challenge in our early Alaska days. We delighted in helping each other fill in the quirky details. After his passing, it was *that* story that inspired me to continue writing my own.

ACKNOWLEDGMENTS

I want to thank my children, Julie, Bryan, and Shirley, who have contributed to this undertaking, each in their own way. I never imagined that I would tackle writing a book in my nineties, but it just goes to show that it's never too late to embark on a new adventure.

I am grateful to my publisher, Teresa Rodriguez and Liberté Press, for believing in my stories and helping to bring them to life.

To my dear friends who have answered numerous calls and e-mails as I researched different chapters, thank you. You've filled in blanks and clarified memories, sent photos, articles, and, once, even a thumb drive, which started me on yet another techie learning curve and paved the way to the fascinating world of QR codes.

I want to extend my gratitude to my Facebook friends and followers, whose likes and encouraging comments have given me the energy and motivation to keep writing. Your support has truly inspired me, and reading your own stories reminds me of the beauty of connecting with others, no matter our age.

I also want to express my deep appreciation to Monica and Alphonso Lascano, as well as Beckie and Scott Davis, for providing the solace of a writing haven at the beginning of the compiling process.

Finally, to the readers of this book, thank you for taking the time to join me on this journey.

FOREWORD

Some people dream dreams. Others have visions. Then there are those special few that do both. Jo Ryman Scott did both.

She dreamed about an arts festival at the top of the world in Fairbanks, Alaska, and she had a vision of how that festival would impact the citizens and artistic life of her beloved city and state.

In the beginning, it is doubtful that she or anyone else could visualize the real impact the Fairbanks Summer Arts Festival would have nationally and internationally.

Once her vision crystallized in her mind, she applied her seemingly boundless energy, unswerving determination, creative resources, and courage, which was born of a firm conviction of her mission to make the festival happen. And Jo Scott made it happen.

Aided by the encouragement and support of the love of her life, her husband Dick, and the advice of the Boston-based educator Edward Madden, she started to work. Those who know her know that Jo is a force to whom one cannot say "NO."

She recruited a body of influential and resourceful citizens and sold them on her dream, thereby organizing a board. She went to individuals and businesses and convinced them to underwrite her dream. She selected a body of local volunteers to aid in the production process.

All of these people "came on board" solely because they believed in her, and she believed in her dream. Jo loved her faculty and her students and was their most ardent cheerleader. To her, we were all equally special.

She encouraged, appreciated, and applauded us, and she was forever promoting us and our endeavors. Even in her retirement, she continues to cheer us on to new heights and follow our progress.

Countless former students of the Arts Festival continue to enrich the artistic lives of Fairbanks, Alaska, the nation, and beyond. The realization of Jo's dream and vision are hers. She willed it to happen, and she made it happen.

Most people want to make an impression; others want to make a difference. Jo Scott made a difference, and, WHAT A DIFFERENCE! Yes, some people dream dreams, others have visions, but...

...then there was Jo.

Byron McGilvray, DMA
Fairbanks Summer Arts Festival Guest Artist
1981 - present

INTRODUCTION

At the age of 96, I look back on a journey that began on the dusty plains of South Dakota during the Great Depression. It was a time when the world felt heavy, yet my childhood on a humble farm was filled with music and simplicity.

The rhythm of daily farm life taught me the value of hard work and the warmth of community, which laid the foundation for my future. I credit my mother for my range of music appreciation. She would tune in to jazz, opera, pop, gospel, country, big band, and classical music on the little wooden radio in our farmhouse kitchen. I heard it all.

I begin the book with a picture of my little brother Mike and I on our first day of school in 1938 just before we walked the two miles to our one-room country schoolhouse.

Join me as I recount the stories, the lessons learned, and the magic of the years since then that have defined who I am today. I'm excited to take you on this journey through time, filled with memories and a few surprises. My hope is that you will be inspired to begin writing your *own* life stories!

Jo Ryman Scott

CONTENTS

The 1930s

The 1940s

The 1990s

The 2000s

QR BONUS MEDIA

At the conclusion of each chapter, you will find a QR code that provides access to bonus media related to the chapter's content. This may consist of additional photos, videos, interviews, or other supplemental material designed to enrich your reading experience.

To access the bonus media, simply scan the OR code using the camera on your smartphone or tablet. While having a Dropbox account will streamline access, it is not necessary. It will give you the option to easily sign up for a free one, but just select *use a web browser* to view the bonus media without signing up.

Below is my QR tutorial to get you started.

Historical film clips in QR Bonus Media links are courtesy of the Alaska Film Archives at the University of Alaska Fairbanks.

Jo's QR Tutorial

Some Fairbanks Summer Arts Festival historical images in QR Bonus Media links are courtesy of the Alaska and Polar Regions Collections & Archives at the University of Alaska Fairbanks.

THE 1930S

CHAPTER 1

THE BAD MAN IN THE GREEN CAR

It was a hot, windy day on our farm in South Dakota in the late 1930s. Dust storms, drought, and grasshoppers plagued the countryside.

Our rather large kitchen was hot, too. My mother was baking bread in her big old Monarch wood-burning stove while listening to a Bismarck, North Dakota radio station. Each day, that station read police reports announcing criminals who had escaped imprisonment.

My interest was piqued that day when I heard a reward was being offered to the person who caught a dangerous criminal. He was last seen heading east in a green car.

My world as an eight-year-old was very small. I was naïve but determined in everything I did. My brother Mike, who was a year younger, always liked my creative ideas.

I knew of only one road: it was at the end of our long driveway. As luck would have it, it headed east!

I told Mike about the news report, and we carefully made our plans to catch this bad man and collect the reward.

We were fearless as we walked down our long, dusty driveway, carrying big sticks. We were ready.

We reached the end of our driveway and sat comfortably in the grassy ditch by the country road heading east.

We sat for a long, long time.

Eagerly watching.

Eagerly waiting.

It was a VERY quiet country road.

We didn't see a green car heading east. We didn't see any car heading east. In fact, we didn't see any car heading in any direction.

We waited longer. No one drove by.

Then we remembered Mother was baking bread! We hastily walked back up our long, dusty driveway, leaving our big sticks behind.

When we got back to the hot kitchen, Mother sliced the fresh-baked bread and covered it with butter that we had churned the day before. Mike and I forgot about catching the bad man with the green car because we got busy planning our next adventure.

CHAPTER 2

JIMMY, MIKE, AND OUR LITTLE WOODEN WAGON

We had no close neighbors on our farm in South Dakota in the 1930s. My brother, Mike, was my best friend.

My next best friend was probably my pony, Jimmy. I always said he was mine because no one else in our family was as crazy about Jimmy as I was.

Oh, the adventures I had with Jimmy! Of course, one needs company for a good adventure, so Mike was my perfect friend. He always liked my creative ideas.

Some of my ideas weren't very good. In fact, some were less than perfect, and they could have been seriously disastrous.

One of those ideas stands out in my memory. I was eight, and Mike was seven. We had a little old wooden wagon. We liked that little old wagon and played with it a lot.

One day, I thought it would be a great idea to hitch Jimmy up to it. I had to think carefully about how I was going to do this.

So, I searched the barnyard for ideas. I was in luck! I found a long, old hemp rope that would work perfectly.

I tied the rope to the wagon's handle and told Mike to get in. He obediently followed my instructions. I had no harness, but I thought I could tie the other end of the rope to Jimmy's tail. He was a patient pony, and I was sure he wouldn't mind.

After I got the rope tied to the wagon and the other end tied to Jimmy's tail, I picked up a 2 x 4 and gave Jimmy a gentle whack on his behind.

As I said, Jimmy was a patient pony, but he decided THIS idea was too much, and ran wildly down our long, dusty driveway just as fast as he could. I ran down the driveway after them.

Mike and the wagon were fine for a few seconds, but when the wagon hit a big old rock, it broke into hundreds of pieces. Fortunately, Mike wasn't in pieces! In fact, he had no broken bones and not a single scratch on him.

I can't imagine how I explained this situation to our parents, but that was the end of our little wooden wagon.

Jimmy knew that I meant no harm that day. I talked to him a lot and understood his horse language: he was ready for the next adventure with Mike and me!

CHAPTER 3

DRESS-UP DAY
AND THE OLD VIOLIN

It was too hot to play outdoors that day, so Mike and I decided to go to one of our favorite places in our farmhouse: the attic! Once we got up there, it was pretty hot too.

I remember that attic. You had to go upstairs and to the back of the east bedroom. If you looked carefully, you could find a little door. When you opened that door, you'd see all sorts of treasures!

We opened it and in we went.

We had gone to the attic several times, but there was one thing we had never explored. It was a big old trunk in a back corner beyond the boxes and crates. I don't recall Mother telling us *not* to get into that trunk, so when Mike and I discovered it, we thought we had found a treasure chest!

Instead of treasures, it was full of old dresses and ladies' accessories.

So, we started having fun by trying on the dresses. Mike tried them on, too. There weren't any men's clothes in that trunk, but Mike wanted to be a part of the dress-up day!

I remember finding some high-heeled black shoes. Of course, I had to try them on. They were comically oversized on me, but I practiced and could walk in them!

I found a fancy black taffeta dress with lots of lace and ruffles. Mike found a magnificent big black velveteen hat to match the dress, with a gorgeous black satin bow and a wide brim. What fun it was to dress up!

We thought we were finished digging to the bottom of the big old trunk when we found something else: Dad's old violin! Mike and I had seen it in another box the year before, and Mother had made us promise we would *never* play with it. We had promised.

Mother must have suspected that she needed to hide the violin deep in that trunk in the attic so Mike and I couldn't find it again.

But we found it. In his younger years, my dad played the fiddle for square dances in the hay mows in our and our neighbors' barns. A "hay mow" (which rhymes with cow) is the barn's second floor, where the newly harvested hay would be stored.

These popular barn dances were held in July or August, before haying time, when wagon loads of hay would be brought up to the hay mow with slings and pulleys.

The violin was a treasured keepsake. We forgot about our promise.

When I was all dressed up in my black high heels, the beautiful black taffeta dress with lace and ruffles, and the magnificent black velveteen hat with a satin bow and a wide brim, I thought I looked so stunning that Mother would be happy to see me make an entrance with Dad's violin.

She was working at her sewing machine on the floor below.

But first, I decided to see if I could find a tune on the violin. I had a perfect ear for music but had no training at all at the tender age of eight. I picked up the violin, and after a few tries, voila! I could play *Mary Had a Little Lamb*.

I was certain Mother would be proud of me if I showed her how beautiful I was in my dress-up finery and played her a tune on the violin.

So, violin in hand, I went back through the little door and started down the stairs in my fancy black dress, dramatic velveteen hat, and enormous high heels, ready to share my talent and beauty with my mother.

I didn't get too far when, suddenly, one of the high heels got caught in the lace of my beautiful black dress and I started tumbling down the stairs. I rolled on and on, all the way down, landing loudly in a pile at the bottom. The violin had slipped out of my hand and bounced its way down as well.

Mother rushed to see what had made such a noise.

She found me in a pile and the violin in pieces around me on the floor. My grand entrance did not go as planned.

I remember Mother's voice when she quietly told me that I would have to tell my dad what had happened when he came home from working in the fields all day.

I thought that day would never end, waiting for my dad to come home.

But when my dad did arrive from the fields, he had horrible news to share with my mother. Even though we had gotten considerable rain that summer, and it had looked like we might finally get a crop, a horde of grasshoppers had come to our fields that day and had eaten every last bit of the juicy tops of the grain.

It was disastrous. The crop was ruined.

Dad had something much more serious to contend with than a child who had broken not only a violin but her promise never to touch that violin again. I don't think I was even punished for being disobedient, but I learned a lesson on my own and truly felt ashamed of myself.

I was sorry that our family no longer had my dad's old violin.

CHAPTER 4

BEAUTY AND THE TWO-WHEELED CART

Sometime during the summer of 1938, my dad purchased a two-wheeled cart. He was looking for a nice, quiet horse to pull that cart and who would take my sister Jean, thirteen, Mike, eight, and me, nine, to school in the fall. He met up with a friend selling a big, beautiful white horse and was willing to deliver it to our farm.

I remember the day she arrived. My dad's friend had sent her over with some hired hands instead of coming himself. I was right there, and being the child who loved horses, I got to name her. I called her Beauty.

My dad looked her over and was shocked at Beauty's teeth and thin, bony frame. There was no question about Beauty's age. She was an old horse.

Indeed, Beauty was quite a bit older than my dad had been led to believe.

It turns out that my dad trusted the friend who sold Beauty to him. The man even graciously offered to deliver Beauty to our barnyard. My dad had never seen Beauty until that day, but he had paid him up front in good faith.

Despite my dad's disappointment, even though she was a bit skinny and had seen better days, I still loved Beauty! I constantly brushed her coat, combed her mane and long, beautiful white tail, and talked to her, affirming my love for her. Jean and Mike didn't like her.

One thing intrigued me about Beauty: Unlike our wonderful pony, Jimmy, Beauty *liked* being harnessed and hitched up to our new two-wheeled cart!

Finally, it was the first day of school in September of 1938, and we got to do just that: we harnessed and hitched Beauty up to the new two-wheeled cart.

Jean drove the cart, with Mike and me beside her. We traveled about two miles over the dusty farm roads to our little one-room country schoolhouse near Scatterwood Lake.

Jean was a very good driver. Every morning after we arrived at the school grounds, Jean unharnessed Beauty and put her in the little old barn in the schoolyard.

I don't recall any hay or water in the little old barn. That year, no other children drove or rode a horse to school. So, Beauty had the barn all to herself!

This story is short because my dad didn't keep Beauty long. It was a very sad day for me just a few weeks later when dad sold Beauty.

Not only was I going to miss Beauty and our rides to school, but I was sad as I did not know what happened to Beauty after she left us. Jean and Mike told me that dad sold Beauty to a glue factory!

I still treasure my fond memories of the few weeks we had Beauty, who happily pulled our two-wheeled cart so we didn't have to walk to school.

CHAPTER 5

WORKHORSE DOLLY AND HER COLT I NAMED QUEENIE

We still had workhorses on our farm in the 1930s. Tractors were too expensive for my parents during those years of dust storms, drought, and grasshoppers on our South Dakota farm.

My brother Mike didn't like horses as much as I did, so he wasn't actively involved in some of my horse escapades.

Dad had a workhorse named Dolly. She was a beautiful white mare with a long, flowing mane and a shimmering white tail. Oh, how I wanted to become friends with Dolly, but Dolly did not want to become friends with me!

Her name did not fit her temperament. She was not a sweet, loving, patient horse. Quite the opposite.

I remember Dolly had a companion workhorse who was less spirited and beautiful. One day, those two horses ran wildly up our long dusty driveway and into our barnyard, pulling a hayrack with a large load of hay. My dad was nowhere to be seen. They had run away from him in the hayfield!

When Dad arrived home later, Mother was happy to see that he wasn't hurt. He just had to walk all the way back from the hayfield.

One spring, I was particularly excited. Dolly had a colt! Dolly and her colt stayed in the barnyard that summer, never going out to the pasture. Every day, I would go to the barnyard and visit that cute little colt. I named her Queenie.

I curried Queenie and talked to her all summer long. Dolly didn't seem to mind that I was becoming friends with her colt. Queenie was cute, but not beautiful like her mother. But I loved Queenie, even though she wasn't beautiful.

My friendship with Queenie developed over that summer and into the fall and winter. By the end of the following summer, we had become solid friends.

When Queenie turned two in the spring of 1939 and our bond was strong, I had another one of my great ideas. Even though no one had ever tried to put a bridle or halter on Queenie, I felt confident that it was time for me to see if she would let me get on her back.

The perfect time came one day that summer when Queenie was at the water tank in our barnyard, drinking with all the workhorses.

The tank was built with cedar 2" x 12" planks and steel cables around it to hold it together. There was no wide ledge at the top of the tank. I observed the horses that day as they were drinking. Queenie was way over to the left of the tank, by herself.

I saw my opportunity. I carefully and quietly climbed up to the edge of the three-foot-high water tank. Then, I carefully started climbing onto Queenie's back, petting her, and quietly talking to her all that time. She stood still at the water tank, drinking the water with the other horses. She was as quiet as could be when I got on her back.

But suddenly, Dolly became upset about something and started moving wildly around the water tank, upsetting all the other workhorses! I wisely decided that it was time for me to carefully, quietly, and quickly get down from Queenie's back.

Queenie stood still while I climbed off her back and crawled down to reach the top edge of the water tank. Then I jumped safely to the ground and quietly walked away, feeling quite proud of myself. I had achieved my dream, Queenie let me sit on her back!

I have no memories of Queenie after that day's successful adventure. I don't know if Dad sold her, or if she went on to become a workhorse like her spirited, unfriendly mother.

I found out later that my dad had seen all this happening and didn't yell for me to get away from the water tank for fear of startling those wild-mannered workhorses. This experience made me realize I had to be very careful when taking on potentially dangerous adventures.

My parents must have realized that I would always be the child to explore dangerous happenings. I'm sure they remained prayerful that I wouldn't get seriously hurt. I believe their prayers must have helped me.

I had so many adventures on that farm in South Dakota!

CHAPTER 6

THE OLD SADDLE, THE ACCIDENT AND A LIFE-CHANGING PARCEL

An accident happened on a Friday in late September 1939. I was ten and in the fifth grade; my brother Mike was nine and in the fourth. Mike and I rode my pony, Jimmy, to our little one-room country schoolhouse near Scatterwood Lake each school day. I rode in the front on the saddle, and Mike rode behind me. Riding on Jimmy's back the two miles to and from school was fun.

Jimmy stayed in the little old school barn until school was out, and it was time for all of us to go home. I don't recall having any hay or water in the barn for Jimmy, but he seemed happy about being there, plus he didn't have to work.

I had problems getting Jimmy to stand still when school was out on one Friday while I cinched up his saddle. Usually, Jimmy was very patient about letting me bridle him up and put his saddle on. But on this day, he bucked and whinnied! He did NOT want me to put that saddle on his back! I persisted and finally got him saddled up and ready to head home. I helped Mike get on, and then I got on in front of him.

Oh, my — we had troubles right away!

We barely started down the dusty, one-lane road toward home when Jimmy began bucking. I was a strong ten-year-old, but I couldn't get him to settle down. Jimmy had bucked us off within a few minutes, and he ran wildly home without us!

Mike and I were okay, so we walked the short distance back to our schoolhouse. Our beautiful young teacher, Miss Virginia Harbaugh, was still there, correcting papers.

Telephones in our rural farm community were a luxury we didn't have. Mother must have been surprised when she saw Jimmy running back to the barnyard — without Mike or me!

Miss Harbaugh walked down the little hill to the Bierman home, where she was a boarder. She explained the situation to Mrs. Bierman, who graciously drove us home.

In those days, children walked to school or rode their ponies. Parents rarely gave their children rides to school, so being driven home in a car was quite a luxury!

Mother was happy Mike hadn't gotten hurt, but I was less fortunate, and she was concerned. When Jimmy bucked me off, I had landed on a rock halfway buried in the sandy soil. My left arm and shoulder really hurt.

It was late afternoon on a Friday. My parents decided to wait until Monday morning to see if I was better before taking me to the doctor.

I remember that weekend. The September sun was out. I was happy lying on the floor with my pillow while the sun shone through an open doorway into the house.

Looking back, I was a pretty patient little kid. My arm and shoulder really did hurt. I became very frightened when I heard friends who stopped by quietly whispering that perhaps my arm and shoulder were broken.

I had never heard of anyone breaking bones. In my naïve, country-style way of thinking, I imagined that once you broke a bone, that was that. It was broken forever.

On Monday morning, my parents decided it was time to take me to the doctor in Aberdeen, about 30 miles from our farm home. As soon as we got there, his kind nurse took an x-ray of my arm and shoulder. That was a new experience for me.

I froze when the doctor showed us the x-ray and confirmed I had indeed broken my shoulder. But then the doctor explained that it would heal in about six weeks! After I was assured that broken bones could heal, all this activity became a great adventure.

It was quite a serious break. I needed a large cast on my left arm and shoulder. It was called an airplane cast. My left arm extended outward and bent like a bird's wing at the elbow.

The doctor told my parents that I had to be kept quiet for six weeks until the cast would be removed. My parents understood that with my high energy level, keeping me quiet would require some serious planning. So, they put me in the hospital for the first week, where my activity would be monitored.

I had many visitors in the hospital, and I loved having delicious meals delivered right to my room. (Yes, I remember thinking those meals were delicious!) I must have driven those poor nurses crazy with all my questions, stories, and talking.

But I also wondered why Jimmy had made such a fuss when I was cinching his saddle that day.

Back home, Dad carefully looked over that very old saddle. Sadly, he found that a nail holding parts of the saddle together had come loose, and that nail was puncturing Jimmy's hide with every pull to cinch up the saddle. No wonder poor Jimmy was unhappy with me! Dad repaired the saddle so it would never hurt Jimmy again.

Beautiful October fall days were coming, and the corn harvest was about to begin. When I came home from the hospital at the end of that week, I followed the doctor's instructions: I had to stay home from school for five more weeks.

I remember spending countless hours in the barnyard talking to Jimmy, telling him how sorry I was that I didn't realize a nail was coming through that old saddle.

I gave him ears of corn. I was amazed to see him eat all the corn off the cob and then spit out the cob. I knew that Jimmy understood that I meant no harm, and I was sorry I had persisted in getting that old saddle on his back that day after school.

Jimmy and I had five wonderful weeks of fun together while waiting to get the cast off. Then, I could go back to school, and I was so happy to return. And yes, Mike and I rode Jimmy to school. The old saddle was fixed.

A significant thing happened because of the accident that affected my life forever. Mother's old maid sister, my Aunt Mary, lived in Chicago. I loved her very much. She evidently had a good job during the 30s and often sent nice gifts.

She seemed to have fun sending these packages, and we loved getting them. Whenever we received a gift, Mother taught us to sit down immediately and write a thank you letter, complete with original drawings.

When Aunt Mary heard that I had broken my arm, she sent me a package! I opened it with excitement and found two music books. I started right in, if only with one hand! They inspired my growing interest in music.

My cast eventually came off, and by age eleven, I had taught myself how to read music. I wasn't taking piano lessons, but I still recall learning Schumann's *The Happy Farmer* from one of the books from Aunt Mary. I treasured them; they changed my life!

Decades later they would be lost in a *hundred year flood* — but that is a story for another chapter.

CHAPTER 7

SAILOR SUITS, A BANDSTAND, AND SCATTERWOOD LAKE

Scatterwood Lake was about two miles from our old farm. It was still a lovely lake until the late 1930s, when it dried up entirely because of the drought.

For the big Fourth of July celebration at the Lake in the summer of 1935, it still had quite a bit of water. I was six and Mike was five.

Mother had made us cute little sailor outfits. The shirts had the traditional large white collars trimmed in red and blue. Mine had a little white skirt, and Mike's had white pants. I remember feeling rather cute wearing mine!

In the late 20s and early 30s, the Fourth of July was always a special celebration at the Lake. It was crowded with farmers and city folk alike. Wealthier people had built beautiful summer homes around the north side. I thought those houses were amazing, and I wished I could look around inside.

The Lake had a huge dance pavilion. At the front was a raised bandstand, perfect for the dance bands that came each year. Their bandleaders had them play for most of the day.

I made new friends wherever I went, and this day was no different. I remember meeting a new little friend about my age, Mary Voight. Mary and I danced to the band music in the big pavilion with the other kids.

In those days, farm parents didn't have babysitters. They brought their children with them to all these events. The children were there all day and into the evening. When they got tired, their parents took them to their car. The children had brought their pillows along with them, so they were ready to go to sleep comfortably. The cars weren't locked, but back then, it was safe for children to be left alone sleeping in their parents' cars.

Mother told me that Lawrence Welk was one of the bandleaders who brought his band to play at the Scatterwood Lake Pavilion. He was young and working hard to make it to the big time. Born in 1903, he was just five years younger than my parents. He was from the little German-speaking town of Strasbourg, North Dakota—not too far from Scatterwood Lake!

Years later, in 1951, I went to one of Lawrence Welk's big dances while working as a waitress at a summer resort near Chicago. I was sad when some people made fun of Welk's German accent. He worked hard, was sincere, honest, talented, and generous, and was a favorite of many people in my parents' generation.

Between 1951 and 1982, he produced over 1,000 TV shows, some of which continue to air on PBS. I still thoroughly enjoy watching his TV reruns.

Lawrence Welk will never be forgotten. For people like me from that part of South Dakota, neither will the stories of the dance pavilion, its big bandstand, and the musical celebrations at Scatterwood Lake.

CHAPTER 8

FARM FUN
AND LESSONS LEARNED

When my brother Mike didn't feel like joining me on an adventure, I invented new and entertaining things to do by myself.

At age seven, I loved all our farm animals and always tried to make friends with them.

One of my favorite games was trying to catch the attention of one of our mother hens, pecking away in the chicken yard and searching for bugs and worms.

I would lure a mother hen to follow me to where I had found an old board on the ground. I'd lift it, and she would be delighted with the easy catch of bugs and worms I'd uncovered. After that delicious find, that mother hen would continue to follow me, clucking happily. Then she would bring along more mother hens!

With every board I lifted, these mother hens would all be happy to find those delicious treats. What a joy to have ten or fifteen mother hens following me around the large chicken yard! The yard had endless boards for me to lift up and feed my flock of beautiful mother hens.

I didn't have the same love for our big white roosters that I had for the mother hens. Mike and I were both scared of the roosters. We would climb to the safety of an empty hay rack in our barnyard when the roosters would try to catch us. They had strong necks and beaks and could hurt us if we weren't careful. We would situate ourselves safely on the hay rack with a few rocks in our pockets and retaliate by throwing them at the roosters. They had a very short attention span and quickly left the bombardment, so Mike and I went on to other adventures.

An entertaining game that Mike and I invented was called "Spy." We played it in the barnyard. We would go off in separate directions and try to keep moving without being seen by each other. When one of us saw the other, we would yell, "SPY!" We could spend hours playing that game.

Another vivid memory is of my dad washing my mouth out with Palmolive soap when I was eight. I have no memory, however, of what I might have said to cause him to do it. I can say two things: I have never liked Palmolive soap, and I don't use swear words!

That same summer, Dad took Mike and me along when he drove to the Hanson's farm about two miles away. Dad told us to stay in the car and wait for him.

After sitting in the car for a while, I thought how terribly boring it was to do nothing while waiting for Dad. I suggested to Mike that we get out and walk over to visit Mrs. Price on the next farm.

Mike was more obedient than I was and declined the offer to join me, so I decided to visit Mrs. Price by myself.

I got out of the car and started walking on the dusty, gravel road to see Mrs. Price. No trucks or cars were in sight. It was at least a mile to her farm from the Hanson's farm.

When I finally arrived, Mrs. Price was so gracious. She asked me if I'd like a cup of coffee or a cup of tea. I said I'd enjoy having a cup of tea. I don't think I'd ever had a cup of tea before!

Then she told me I could go to her backyard and play with their son's tractors and other farm toys.

Somehow, Dad found me; I imagine Mike had told him where I was headed. He thanked Mrs. Price, and we drove back home together. I don't recall if I was scolded for not staying in the car to wait for my dad like Mike did, but I sure had loved those farm toys and enjoyed my cup of tea!

At the end of that summer, my dad's sister Magdalene, her husband Ray, and their five children arrived unannounced at our farm! Of course, Mother and Dad welcomed them warmly. We were thrilled to meet our cousins, and we liked them right away. They lived in a city in Iowa. The children had never been on a farm before and loved to see how we lived. They had never even ridden a horse. My wonderful Jimmy was perfect for their first pony ride. We had such fun playing with Jimmy and our cousins that summer.

Not long after they left, our parents went to Aberdeen without us one Saturday night. We usually went along with them—that was our entertainment! I don't know how it happened that Jean, Mike, and I stayed home while they went to town.

Later that night, Jean and I went upstairs to the west bedroom to watch out the window for the headlights of our parents' car. Our parents would be the only people coming east on that dusty, lonely, one-lane road that night.

While we waited, I seriously shared with Jean that I wouldn't mind getting married if only I knew my way around town.

Well, that comment tickled Jean, and like every big sister would do, she was delighted to tell my parents what I'd said when they finally made their way up our driveway. In fact, after that night, she would repeat that story to anyone who would listen!

Many years later, when Jean heard the news that I was going to be married, she wrote me a note and asked, "Do you know your way around Fairbanks?"

CHAPTER 9

TWO TEACHERS AND A QUOTE TO REMEMBER

I must have been a handful as a child. I was not particularly precocious, but I was a curious child. I didn't do bad things specifically, but I did things I thought sounded like fun, like getting on a horse that hadn't been broken.

My first five years of school were spent in a little one-room schoolhouse about two miles from our farm home, just a short distance from the north side of Scatterwood Lake. The school had grades one through eight, and seven to nine children were enrolled each year.

I met my third-grade teacher, Miss Ella Hartwell, at the beginning of the 1937 school year. I was the only third grader!

I remember reading stories about the South Dakota Indians. At that time, I had long, thick brown hair, which my mother managed by braiding. Miss Hartwell called me her little papoose. She made school fun.

Many years later, I realized that Miss Hartwell must have been a very intelligent, well-read young woman. She became a teacher during the Great Depression when teaching was almost the only opportunity for young women.

She introduced me to Longfellow's *Hiawatha*, and she read works by other well-known poets to me. I enjoyed memorizing many of those poems.

In those days, children had little autograph books for friends, families, and teachers to sign and share their thoughts.

Miss Hartwell wrote this beautiful quatrain in my little autograph book:

> *There is a destiny that makes us brothers;*
> *None goes his way alone.*
> *All that we give to the lives of others*
> *Comes back again into our own.*

Miss Hartwell had discussed many poems and authors with me, but we had never discussed this quatrain. I loved that quatrain, and I memorized it. She didn't include the author's name.

She probably never dreamed that I would memorize it and that it would become an important part of my life.

I was only nine in the spring of 1938 when she signed my autograph book! As an educator, it was rather remarkable that the quatrain so touched me.

I'll fast-forward to 1952 for an amazing coincidence. I had just transferred my credits from the University of South Dakota to the Education Department of San Jose State College.

One afternoon, while exploring the San Jose campus, I came upon a beautiful old building identified as the Edwin Markham house, built in the 1860s. The poet Markham lived there in the 1880s. In 1872, he graduated from San Jose State—then called the California State Normal School. I knew he was well-known, especially for his poem *The Man with the Hoe*, inspired by the French artist Millet's painting of the same name.

I was curious, so I read more. I noticed a listing of some of Markham's quotations, so I began reading.

Suddenly, to my surprise, there was the quatrain Miss Hartwell had written in my little autograph book fourteen years earlier! I was so excited. I had never seen it in print before. From that point on, that quatrain became even more meaningful to me.

I hadn't seen Miss Hartwell since that year in the third grade. As I grew older, I was determined to find her. When I visited my parents in South Dakota in the late 1950s, I looked in the local phonebook and found her name. She still lived in Aberdeen!

She was so surprised and happy to hear from me when I called. Indeed, she remembered me. I thanked her for being my wonderful teacher in the third grade. I reminded her of the Markham quatrain she had written in my little autograph book. She remembered that, too. I shared with her that she was the one who inspired me to love reading and memorizing poetry. We had a wonderful visit and were both happy to have connected again.

Now I'll rewind back to the 1930s. The teacher I had the year after Miss Hartwell also greatly impacted my life. Her name was Miss Bernice Wehr. She inspired me to want to learn.

I was nine years old in the fall of 1938 when she became my fourth grade teacher in that same little one-room schoolhouse. Once again, I was the only child in my class.

We had very few reference books in our little country school. Miss Wehr had made a trip to Washington, D.C. the summer before the school year started. When she shared her black-and-white photographs of our nation's Capital with us, it was the first time we had seen pictures of what it looked like! We were even more excited to hear Miss Wehr tell us stories about her trip to the Capitol.

I doubt she realized the impact her stories and pictures had on my life.

Miss Wehr loved music, and of course, so did I. I realized later that she must have had considerable musical training. We did not have a piano in our classroom, but we did have a pump organ. I was thrilled to hear her play it.

Miss Wehr taught us to sing many difficult songs. One song, *Oh, Columbia, the Gem of the Ocean*, was quite difficult, but she taught us to sing it. We learned Stephen Foster favorites and oldies like *There's an Old Spinning Wheel in the Parlor*.

She also had us perform a cute little mini operetta. I still wonder how she did it with only seven or eight children in our school! After more than eight decades, I still remember one of the songs from the show that I sang with my brother, Mike:

> SOLDIER: *I am a little tin soldier;*
> DOLL: *I am a doll from France.*
> SOLDIER: *Gun put upon my shoulder. I'll be a hero!*
> DOLL: *Dear, oh, dear, oh! When you're away, be careful.*
> SOLDIER: *Soldiers must take a chance.*

DOLL: *So I'll worry about my little soldier.*

SOLDIER: *And I'll think about my doll from France!*

I delighted in everything that pretty and dynamic Miss Wehr said and did.

For years, I tried without success to find Miss Wehr. I wanted to thank her for being such a positive influence. Recently, after getting help with an online search, I found Miss Wehr's obituary. She passed away in 2013.

Through information in her obituary, I was able to contact her relatives. I was happy to be able to let them know how much she had enriched my life that one year when she taught in our little one-room schoolhouse.

These two teachers each made a big difference in my life.

Jo's little autograph book can be seen at the University of Alaska, Fairbanks Archives.

CHAPTER 10

MOTHER WAS SICK, AND I WAS WORRIED

Mike and I usually walked to school together, or we rode Jimmy.

But on one particularly beautiful spring day, I walked home by myself.

Instead of walking the mile north and a little more than a mile west of our little schoolhouse, I took a shortcut across our pasture to get home.

The warm, energizing spring sunshine was wonderful. Charming little rivulets flowed gently from the melting snow, finding their way southward between small stones and sandy soil. I loved the beautiful blooms on the little cactus plants. They were so delicate.

I was in a hurry to get home that day because I was worried about my mother. She had been in bed for many days, and I wanted to be sure she was all right.

When I finally arrived home, I ran upstairs to where Mother was lying in bed. I remember giving her a fond hug and telling her I hoped she felt better.

I don't recall how long she stayed in bed. It may have been only a few days, but to me, as a little child, it seemed like she had been ill for a long time. I was so afraid she was going to die.

Fortunately, she got well with time and returned to being my mother. She had a strong body again, and her Norwegian ancestry shone in her pretty, fair-skinned face.

I realize now that she was only 39 years old at the time, and this time in her life, my mother had experienced considerable sadness.

Just a few years before I was born, my parents had lost three little boys within nine months.

They lost dear little four-year-old Courtney in April 1926, just a month before his baby sister Jean would turn one year old. Courtney had pneumonia, which was deadly in those days. It was especially troubling for my parents who lived way out in the country, far from a doctor.

Then, they lost twin boys, Nicholas and George, who were born prematurely on Christmas Day in 1926. George passed away a few days after his birth, while Nicholas passed away about a month later, in January 1927.

Like all their neighbors, my parents were suffering through devastating days during the Great Depression.

Furthermore, they had little rain for their crops, and when the rains did come, clouds of grasshoppers would crowd the sky, coming by the millions to bite off the tender tops of the heads of grain, destroying the crop. The hot, windy days were oppressive.

They were heartbreaking times.

Years passed. I never asked Mother or my sisters about the time when Mother was ill. I never found out what her illness was or how long she was actually bedridden. As I recall the situation now, I wonder if my mother might have been suffering from depression. No one discussed that in those days.

When visiting my mother in the mid-1980s, I asked her about the little boys. Mother couldn't speak and broke into tears. It must be heart-wrenching to lose a child; she had lost three. The pain never left her.

I never again pressed Mother for answers about the three brothers I never knew.

However, Mike and I discovered a charming little wooden trunk in an upstairs bedroom one day. Mother made it clear that we should leave it alone. Mike and I obeyed, and we never opened that little trunk, even though we often wondered what was in it.

In later years, I found out that some of Courtney's favorite little toys and a pair of his little shoes were in that small trunk.

Mother did share one happy story that day. She told me that she and Dad were excited because they were expecting a baby in April 1929.

They hoped so much that the baby would be a boy! They had even picked out that baby's name—his name would be Joseph!

Well, I was the one they were expecting in April 1929, and when I was a girl, they named me Josephine!

My two older sisters, Alice Ruth and Jean, were happy I'd joined the family. Alice Ruth claimed me as "hers." A year later, when my parents got their boy, Mike, Jean claimed him.

Mother was happy that Jean and Alice Ruth did so many loving things for Mike and me during childhood.

CHAPTER 11

THE CREAMERY ROOM AND OUR ELECTRIC LIGHTS

In our big old barn on our farm near Scatterwood Lake, there was a room set apart from the rest of the barn. That's where we had our cream separator. We called it the Creamery Room.

That was handy for Dad. He could milk the cows standing in their stanchions, eating grain or hay, then take the milk a few steps to the Creamery Room. He would pour the milk into the large container on the top of the cream separator and turn the crank. Thanks to centrifugal force, the cream would come out of one spout of the separator, and skimmed milk would come out of the other.

As a child, that was magical to me!

Dad took the skimmed milk to the house daily but saved the cream in a five-gallon can in the Creamery Room.

On Saturdays, my parents would take the five-gallon can of cream to Aberdeen and sell it to the creamery there. The money they received helped pay for groceries and other items they couldn't grow or produce on our farm. They were indeed subsistence farmers!

Also, in the Creamery Room, there was a wall with shelves. There were lots of large glass containers on those shelves. I never asked my dad about these containers, but I can still picture that wall of glass in my mind.

Many years after Dad passed away, I asked Mother what she remembered about those containers in the Creamery Room. She explained they were glass storage batteries for our 32-volt Delco Light Plant.

Growing up, I never considered that we had electric lights in our home while the neighbors did not. Mother said the glass containers of lead-acid batteries made up the plant. It provided enough electricity for our home's electric lights but not enough for appliances.

I recently searched for "32-volt Delco Light Plant" online to find out how farmers might have learned about this.

Charles Kettering was a mechanically minded Ohio farm boy born in 1876, 22 years before my parents were born. He patented many of his inventions. As Kettering grew up on his parents' farm, he realized farmers missed out on enjoying more effortless living because they didn't have electricity. Because of his ingenuity, the 32-volt Delco Light Plant became available for sale in 1916.

Though I don't remember seeing them, my reading reveals that a generator and engine set must have been sitting next to the batteries, keeping them charged.

Still wondering how Dad would have heard about them, my search also revealed that the light plants were advertised in farm magazines such as *The Farm Journal*, which we did get. It said Delco salesmen frequently visited farmers at dusk to show them how their barns and homes could be lit up if only they would purchase a 32-volt Delco Light Plant.

I discovered that the lead-acid batteries required periodic maintenance to ensure that the water and acid levels remained at the required specifications. I never saw my dad work on maintaining the batteries, and I cannot recall having any salesman come to our farm to do so. But however he did it, my dad provided a brighter life for our family because I also cannot recall ever losing electricity!

CHAPTER 12

MINA LAKE AND OUR OLD ICEBOX

On our farm near Scatterwood Lake, our kitchen had an old icebox that could hold a pretty large chunk of ice. Though we had electric lights, we didn't have electrical appliances like a refrigerator or an electric stove.

My dad would drive our big old truck six miles north of our farm to Mina Lake. He and other neighbors would go there in the winter months to harvest ice.

I never went with him, but now I wonder how they cut the ice out of the lake. I doubt that any of them had a chainsaw. Harvesting the ice must have been a huge job.

Dad drove the ice home and stored it in our ice cellar, about 15 feet from the house. The ice cellar was a big hole dug below ground with a trap door on the top. It had a couple of steps carved into the dirt. The large blocks of newly harvested ice were placed on boards on the dirt floor. Then, Dad would cover the ice with straw, which helped keep it from melting during the hot summer days. The ice cellar was a cool place in the summer!

When the icebox in our kitchen needed more ice, Dad would lift the ice cellar's trap door and walk down the dirt steps to the large pieces of ice covered with straw. He would use an ice pick to chip off as large a piece of ice as possible that would fit in the ice box and bring the chunk of ice to the house in a wheelbarrow. He made a sling to put around the ice for ease in getting it to the wheelbarrow and then to the kitchen to put it in the ice box.

Living on a farm involved doing lots of important work like this—if you wanted ice in the icebox, you had to harvest ice!

Life would become easier for my parents when we moved to a new farm in the fall of 1940. Rains came to that part of South Dakota, and the farmers in our area suddenly had good crops, a welcome relief after years of drought, crop failures, and grasshopper infestations.

In the 1940s, the country's economy would boom as World War II became a reality. More jobs were available, and people had more money. Times would be good.

So good, in fact, that with the new farm, we would have a telephone, an electric stove, and an electric refrigerator. The most exciting part? The refrigerator had a freezer!

Dad would never have to harvest ice again.

THE 1940S

CHAPTER 13

THE BIG MOVE AND A NEW FARM

November 11th, 1940, was a cold, snowy, windy day. I helped my mother gather about 100 of our cackling, frightened White Rock chickens and put them in crates on the bed of our big, old truck. Then, I rode with my mother when she drove the truck about 24 miles east to our new farm. I was 11 years old and wonder how much help I was that day.

Sure enough, after a decade of drought, grasshoppers, and the hardship of the Great Depression, the onset of the 1940s brought much better times. Besides the needed rain, the grasshoppers didn't return.

My parents had signed the mortgage for our old farm near Scatterwood Lake in 1925. By the end of the 1930s, the mortgage payments were more than the property was worth, so they decided to walk away.

Whether it's true or not, the story goes that they got one dollar when they gave the farm back to the bank.

Without a mortgage, they were free to look for another farm. Dad looked at one that he chose not to buy because it was covered with an invasive plant called Creeping Jenny. (Decades later, I would purchase Creeping Jenny plants, and I would chuckle thinking of what Dad would have thought of me putting them in my garden on purpose!)

My parents kept searching for just the right farm, and they were happy when they landed on a new one near Warner.

It was a small farm compared to nearby farms. It was three quarters of land, approximately 480 acres.

The house was much nicer than the one we left. It had a lovely big barn, two granaries, a garage, a large chicken coop, and a small brooder coop for baby chicks.

Mother and Dad were excited about the potential move. It was fun to hear them talk about things like getting the new farmhouse floors sanded and oiled. Mother's creative eye noted that the hardwood floors had been revarnished so many times they were no longer beautiful. A good sanding and oiling would make them look like new again!

But there were two things they talked about that were *not* fun to hear. The first was regarding the big old upright piano in our living room; I practiced on it constantly, wearing out the pages of the two music books Aunt Mary had sent me. My parents had remodeled the living room doorway a few years earlier. When we were ready to move, they discovered the piano would not fit through the remodeled door. Our big upright piano, which I loved so much, had to be left in our old farmhouse. This made me very sad.

The last thing that happened broke my heart. My Dad didn't want to bring Jimmy to our new farm. There was never any explanation, and our family never had another pony again. I *am* happy to share that we did get another piano.

We started the move when I had helped Mother crate the chickens, but when the family actually moved into our new home a week later, we were told that it would be a few days before the workers would be through refinishing the floors and we couldn't walk on them!

So, our family patiently huddled together in the basement, waiting for the floors to be finished. The basement was more like a cellar. It had a dirt floor, and the big furnace was right in the middle. My parents carried down three comfortable easy chairs to make things cozier for all of us. At ages ten and eleven, Mike and I thought this move was another exciting adventure. I can still picture Mike as he settled himself in a comfy, easy chair. He shouted, "I LIKE LIVING THIS WAY!" That remark lived with him all his life!

We were patient while the workers completed the job, and in just a few days, our family settled in our new home.

In the fall of 1940, my older sister Alice Ruth was living in Aberdeen. Jobs were still hard to find, but she got a clerking job at Kresge's Five and Dime. I was so proud of her. I remember going to Kresge's and watching her help her customers. I pretended that Alice Ruth owned the store!

She lived at our dear Great Aunt Amelia Hye's home on South Jay Street. Aunt Meal, as we called her, was a fabulous cook, and took in boarders.

We quickly adapted to our new home and community. We were happy with this new chapter in our lives.

The timing was just right for my parents to purchase this property. The cost of a farm was relatively low in 1940, and, with the war economy, my parents talked about being able to pay off that mortgage in just a few years. Things were looking up.

PUPIL'S
REPORT CARD
19_41_ — 19_42_

Name _Josephine Rymass_

Grade__7__   Age_12_

Township_Warner Ind_District No._23_

Teacher _Marie Schrimpf_

ATTENDANCE

PERIOD	1	2	3	4	5	6	TOTAL
Days Taught	30	30	30	30	30	30	180
Days Present	29½	29	30	30	27	30	175½
Days Absent	½	1	0	0	3	0	4½
Times Tardy	0	0	0	0	0	0	0

This card gives the school's appraisal of your child's development. Do you agree? What can we do to promote his development? Remember that sickness is the only excuse for absence. Your suggestions are desired and conference with the teacher is advised.

GENEVIEVE ARNTZ,
County Supt., Brown County.

CHAPTER 14

OUR NEW FARM AND A NEW SCHOOL

Our family immediately became involved in the community after moving into our new home that cold, snowy, windy week in November 1940.

Mike and I started school right away, even while living in the cellar of our new home.

My sister Jean had attended her freshman year of high school in Aberdeen. When we moved to our new farm that fall, she transferred to Warner, where she continued her high school studies.

Mike and I were in the fifth and sixth grades respectively. Warner School had grades one through twelve, so we were all in the same school building. The total enrollment was about eighty students.

We all walked the mile to school. There were no more two-wheeled cart rides with Beauty and no more pony rides with Jimmy. This school in town did not need a barn.

The Warner grade school system was a teacher training school for education majors at Northern State Teachers College (NSTC) in Aberdeen, now called Northern State University (NSU).

Mr. Colp from Northern was the professor in charge of the teacher training program. He visited our classroom quite often. All the kids liked him.

The first day he visited, Mike and I had just started school there. Our wonderful teacher was Miss Schrimpf.

I can still picture the two of them standing in front of the large windows in the classroom. They were whispering about Mike and me. I could hear them even though they were holding up notebooks to cover their faces.

I heard Miss Schrimpf whisper rather loudly that we had come from a little one-room school and probably did not know much.

Miss Schrimpf didn't realize that Mike and I had been listening to classes for grades one through eight for several years in our little one-room country school. So, indeed, we had accumulated considerable knowledge over all those years.

I did so well that when I passed a geography test with 100%, even high school students talked about it. No one else in my class came close to that score. Small school chatter!

From that point on, I was considered to be a good student.

Though we had only seven or eight students in our old school, Mike and I had no problems adjusting to a much larger class size. We liked school, excelled in our studies, and found new friends.

My first new friend was Betty Seaman. She was very pretty. Her dad was the banker in Warner, and her mother also worked at the bank. I thought they were an amazing family; I had never before known a mother who worked outside the home.

Our family enjoyed attending the St. John Lutheran Church in Warner, and we liked their Sunday school classes too. We had a vivacious and pretty Sunday School teacher named Nona Rehfeld. She also played the old pump organ in the Church and led the Sunday School kids to have fun singing. I liked that part of Sunday School.

Mother started attending the Ladies' Aid meetings at the church. She enjoyed getting acquainted with her new neighbors. The women in the Ladies' Aid decided to publish a cookbook of their favorite recipes. Mother was excited to be a part of this project. One of her new friends was well-known for her delicious white cake. However, this new friend was also well-known for NEVER sharing that cake recipe with any of her church friends. (This was 1941 before you could buy never-fail white cake mixes in a box!)

When the recipe book eventually came out, everyone was excited: there was the recipe for the famous white cake in black and white! Sadly, all the women who followed the printed recipe had disastrous results. Evidently, she purposely omitted some ingredients and changed the measured amount of others. As a result, she continued making the best white cake in town!

From what Miss Rehfeld was teaching us in Sunday School, I recall thinking, "That was not a very Christian thing for that lady to do!"

The first year in our new community was educational for all of us.

Jo Ryman Scott

CHAPTER 15

OUR NEW SCHOOL AND A WONDERFUL TEACHER

I was so excited on the first day of the seventh grade in 1941. I discovered that this year, we would have a dedicated vocal music teacher, Miss Harriet Finsand.

I loved all kinds of music, but I especially loved classical.

I had quite a few favorite classical piano pieces I had heard on the radio and knew by name, but I couldn't play them because I had not yet had piano lessons.

Besides the two music books from Aunt Mary, Mike and I found several books of classical piano pieces in our attic. My aunts, Laura and Magdalene, had left this music stored in our home. The music books eventually ended up in the attic for us to discover.

Miss Finsand was an accomplished pianist, and I started bringing music books to school. She played pieces from them for me on the only piano we had in our school, down in the gym. Taking the time to do this for me made such an impact. It would inspire my own teaching years later.

One day, during a singing lesson, she went around to every student's desk to listen to them sing. When she came to my desk, she quietly said, "You have a very nice singing voice, Josephine."

My heart leapt up! She didn't say I was the best in the class. That didn't matter to me. Rather, she gave me confidence that I had some talent. She believed in me, inspiring me to want to be better in every way.

Miss Finsand was beautiful, talented, and gracious. She joined Miss Hartwell and Miss Wehr as teachers who made a huge difference in my life—and in the lives of students that I would have one day as well.

CHAPTER 16

A Creative Match-Up and an Intriguing Challenge

I was so inspired by Miss Finsand at our new school. I knew even then that I wanted to be a teacher and thought maybe one day, I would have students of my own! Well, about 32 years later, I *did* have a classroom of students of my own! They were bright-eyed kindergartners. I'm going to fast forward to 1973 for two chapters and tell you about a creative match-up and a fun surprise before continuing the 1940s.

My talented friend and fellow teacher, Nancy Scofield, taught sixth grade at the same school. We had an idea. What if we matched every sixth grader with a little kindergarten friend?

It turned out to be a fantastic project and included fifty children. The sixth graders learned to enjoy being around the little kindergartners, while the kindergartners looked up to their older friends.

Once a week, we had the children work on an educational project together. We coordinated with the school librarian for one such project. When the day came, we lined up all the children and headed to the library.

They found comfortable places to sit with their partners. Our dedicated librarian had chosen several children's books and placed them on each of the little tables in the library. We invited the sixth graders to select one book to read to their little friend that day.

It was a wonderful experience, especially for a few sixth graders who had trouble reading. Reading to their kindergartners helped them expand their skills. The kindergartners were thrilled to have the one-on-one attention and would patiently wait as words were sounded out.

It was fun seeing all these groups of two children reading and listening to stories. The older kids also discovered that having fun reading little kids' books was okay!

When they returned to their classroom, Miss Scofield guided her sixth graders to share what they thought made those stories so enjoyable. The children caught on immediately: it was the repetition of parts of the stories, the use of rhyming words, and alliteration.

They noticed that only a few words were printed on each page. Perhaps an exciting part of the story was about to be revealed, leading the reader to turn the page and read some more.

With those guidelines for components of a children's storybook, Miss Scofield challenged each sixth grader to use their imagination to write and illustrate a storybook themselves and devise a creative book cover.

When it came time to connect again the next week, everyone sat in a circle on the floor. The kindergartners were amazed as the sixth-grade authors read their original stories, showing the pictures as they read! The library project was a success.

I had an idea for music appreciation, and soon, Miss Scofield and I were on to the next project.

We had the kindergartners and sixth graders listen to a recording of the beautiful piano piece *Clair de Lune* (moonlight) by French composer Claude Debussy.

In their minds, the children were guided to picture the feeling that the music gave them about moonlight.

They had fun sharing their ideas. Some mentioned a lake with the moon shining down beautifully. Someone else said they imagined some people enjoying canoeing on the lake. One of the kindergartners said they imagined mountains in the background. It was all fun because there weren't any wrong ideas.

The sixth graders had fun drawing and painting their feelings about moonlight. Their kindergarten friends enjoyed watching them paint their pictures; some even did their own with their older friends' help.

This project provided many learning opportunities. The sixth graders looked up Debussy in the encyclopedia. (Today's teachers could have them Google him!) They found pictures of him and the story of his life in France. Some drew a map of France. The lessons encompassed all areas of study.

Miss Scofield and I each had a recording of *Clair de Lune,* which we frequently played as quiet background music in our classrooms during the day. The children became familiar with the beautiful melody.

As a finale to this classical music project, I arranged for a school bus to pick up Miss Scofield and all fifty of the kindergartners and sixth graders. It would bring them on a field trip to my home, where I'd have a mini-concert and art show awaiting them.

On the permission slip that the parents had to sign, it was suggested that the children might have fun dressing up for the field trip. Miss Scofield and I dressed up, too.

Planning it was exciting. There were lessons in behavior at concerts. These children learned about the courtesies of selecting the cookies and lemonade that would be served after the concert.

The children were excited when they got on the bus, but they were also orderly and polite as they arrived at my home.

They had fun looking around our large living room. They liked my concert grand piano. They had never seen such a big piano before!

I had some surprises for the children. I had invited two of my favorite local artist friends, Enid Cutler and Margaret Boyd, to join us that day. I knew they enjoyed working with children, so I asked them to bring their art supplies to help with my idea.

I introduced the children to Margaret and Enid. I briefly explained that Enid would be painting a picture of the composer Debussy, and Margaret would be painting her feelings of what the calm music brought to her mind.

I seated Margaret so half of the children could watch as she painted her feelings about *Clair de Lune*.

I seated Enid so the other half of the children could watch her draw a charcoal portrait of Debussy.

Then I sat down and played *Clair de Lune* on the piano. By this time, the children had heard this music so many times they were familiar with the melody.

The children sat spellbound while watching the artists and listening to the music. They didn't make a sound. It was truly magical!

The piece is about six minutes long, and when I finished, I sat quietly as well while the artists took a little more time to complete their artwork.

The children were completely engrossed. They didn't say a word. After about ten minutes, Margaret and Enid quietly indicated they were through.

What happened next was amazing: Margaret and Enid picked up their paintings and traded places. Suddenly, the children cheered and clapped with delight, in awe of what the other artist had painted!

I have to say it again: It was truly magical.

After they quieted down, the children had the opportunity to visit with Margaret and Enid while enjoying their cookies and lemonade. They looked so cute, all dressed up.

It was another successful afternoon for our kindergartner-sixth grader match-up project! The bus returned to take the children and Miss Scofield back to school.

After they left, Enid, Margaret, and I talked excitedly about this very magical afternoon. We all agreed that even if only one child was influenced by this art and music appreciation project, all of the time and effort involved was worth it.

I felt nostalgic about the afternoon and thought about Miss Finsand. I shared with Margaret and Enid how, 32 years earlier, Miss Finsand had made such a positive impression on my life when she was my seventh-grade vocal music teacher in 1941. From playing sheet music I would bring from my attic to encouraging my talent, everything Miss Finsand had done cultivated music appreciation, and certainly motivated my future teaching in creating afternoons like this one.

I casually said, "Someday, I will try to find Miss Finsand."

At that, my usually quiet friend Margaret piped up excitedly and said, "Jo, why don't you start right now?"

Wow. Well, why not?

I took Margaret up on her challenge!

CHAPTER 17

A CHALLENGE ACCEPTED, a DILIGENT POSTMAN, AND AN EXCITING REUNION

I was excited to take on the challenge of finding Miss Finsand after 32 years. But how would I begin? This was decades before the internet, so an instant search was out of the question.

I knew that Miss Finsand was from the little town of Lemmon, South Dakota, in the western part of the state. I began writing a letter to Miss Finsand, telling her how much she had meant to me when she was the vocal music teacher at Warner School in 1941. I reminded her that I was the child with the long curls who kept bringing classical piano music to school for her and how gracious she was to play them on the old piano down in the school gym.

After I had composed that letter and sealed the envelope, I thought carefully about how to address it. I remembered that she was to be married, but I had no idea of her married name.

This is what I wrote on the bottom of the envelope:

> *To the former Miss Harriet Finsand*
> *Lemmon, South Dakota*
>
> *Dear Postman: I hope you can find someone in Lemmon who remembers Miss Finsand and has her current mailing address so this letter can be forwarded to her.*
>
> *Thank you for your help.*
>
> *Jo Ryman Scott*

I mailed it.

This was in the summer of 1974. The last time I had seen Miss Finsand was in the spring of 1942. I waited and waited. I checked for a reply daily.

Incredibly, after about three weeks, I checked the mail, and there was a letter from Miss Finsand! I was so happy I was in tears. I ran to the house and showed it to Dick. We read it together.

But how did it finally get to Miss Finsand?

A kind postman in Lemmon had evidently asked around and found an older lady who knew Miss Finsand and had her current address. He himself addressed a new envelope and put a stamp on it and then he put my letter inside the envelope and mailed it again.

It made its way to Miss Finsand's mailbox, and she wrote back immediately.

She wrote that she was so happy to receive the letter that had found its way to her. She and her husband, Paul, now lived in Gettysburg, Pennsylvania.

Indeed, she remembered me and my long curls, the sheet music I would bring, and how much I loved music! Then she wrote something that shocked me—she had felt that she had been a complete failure that year in Warner! She was pleased to read my letter, which confirmed this was not true.

Miss Finsand and I continued writing, and in 1977, we got to visit in person. We were both excited about seeing each other, and I was happy to meet Paul. They lived in a charming old farmhouse near Gettysburg.

We reminisced about her year of teaching in Warner. Besides teaching vocal music to elementary school children, which she loved, she was also assigned to teach high school band. She said she felt inadequate teaching instrumental music. I told her that I knew those students loved her too.

I was right to appreciate her talents when I was so young. She was modest and reluctant to reply to some of my questions, but I persisted. She was a gifted musician, starting piano lessons when she was young. She graduated with honors from St. Olaf College in Northfield, Minnesota, a prestigious music school, before taking the teaching job at our little school.

Our reunion so impacted a friend of hers that they contacted The Gettysburg Times, the local newspaper, who sent a reporter to interview us.

The story was published the next day, and we saw that the reporter even contacted the postal clerk in Lemmon, who remembered the situation. He said that after reading the note on the bottom of my envelope, he felt he just had to find someone who knew her and could provide an address so the letter could be delivered.

Finding her brought about one more special thing: a few years after our meeting, she flew to Alaska to teach at the Junior High Fine Arts Camp that Dick and I had established there. She was still a wonderful teacher! The campers loved her and loved hearing how she had been my teacher when I was about their age and how we had reconnected after so many years. She was inspiring yet another generation of students, and maybe future teachers.

I'm incredibly grateful to my friend Margaret Boyd for challenging me to find Miss Finsand.

The Gettysburg Times *original article can be found at the University of Alaska Archives and in this chapter's Bonus Media.*

CHAPTER 18

A USED UPRIGHT AND MY FIRST PIANO TEACHER

In the summer of 1942, I was about to begin eighth grade at Warner School. World War II was happening, and sugar, gasoline, and tires were rationed.

I was still missing my big, old upright piano, which we had to leave in our house on our farm near Scatterwood Lake.

And I still missed my pony, Jimmy.

I heard some unexpected news that summer: I found out that our wonderful Miss Finsand would not be returning as our vocal music teacher at Warner School. In fact, we wouldn't have a vocal music teacher at all.

With all that in mind, I asked my mother if I could start taking piano lessons. I was so happy when she said yes! She knew of a popular piano teacher named Miss Bernice Remde. My mother told me that Miss Remde's father and my grandfather were young homesteaders together in the 1880s on land in Brown County before North and South Dakota became states.

None of us in the Warner community had telephones in our home in the early 1940s. However, the lovely Olwin Angell department store in Aberdeen had a nice ladies' lounge on the second floor. The lounge had a courtesy phone for customers to use.

We made the trip to Aberdeen to call Miss Remde. Sitting beside my mother in the lovely lounge, I could hear much of their conversation, as Miss Remde spoke rather loudly. Miss Remde asked my mother several questions about me and my interests. I heard my mother tell Miss Remde, "Yes, she said she will practice."

At that point, my mother smiled, and I could hear Miss Remde say she would accept me as one of her piano students in the fall of 1942! I was excited beyond words.

But there was one problem. We no longer had a piano. Mother rose to the occasion to help me. We couldn't afford a new piano, so Mother looked at ads in the Aberdeen American News. She found a used piano for only $50. It needed to be refinished, but my mother liked refinishing furniture, so she bought that piano.

As soon as we got the piano home, Mother assessed how she would begin. It was a plain piano with no fancy carved wood overlays, so that would make it easier. Mother got busy and worked on it for days, sometimes into the night. The morning, I woke up and saw the finished product, it looked like a new piano! I thanked my mother for all she had done. We had it tuned, and it sounded beautiful. I sat down immediately, playing pieces I had learned by ear. One of the first songs I figured out the chords for was *Shine on Harvest Moon*.

I couldn't wait to start piano lessons in the fall! I had taught myself to read music and enjoyed playing hymns. I was trying to learn pieces on my own from the music books my Aunt Mary had sent when I broke my arm. I was so happy to have those books.

When I finally started piano lessons with Miss Remde, I was ready to learn. I liked Miss Remde right away; she had an enthusiastic personality. My piano lessons were fun! I progressed quickly because I practiced several hours each week after my inspirational Saturday piano lessons.

I was sick during my sophomore year in high school and had to discontinue lessons, but happily, I started again in the fall of my junior year.

I loved classical music. Miss Remde taught me several Chopin Preludes and Nocturnes, which I enjoyed playing. But my favorite piece I worked on that year was Rachmaninoff's *Prelude in C# Minor*.

Then something exciting happened: Miss Remde entered me in the Regional Music Competition! It would be held in Aberdeen in the spring, and I would play that piece. This was a life-changing opportunity for me, and I was grateful to Miss Remde for her efforts.

I was the only student from Warner participating in the competition. I was excused from school for three days to attend the various piano master classes and workshops held in conjunction with it.

I was a farm girl, but not many of my farm girl friends shared my passion for music. For the first time in my life, I met other students my age who also loved classical music.

They had all been taking piano lessons for several years but welcomed me into their musical circle. I was thrilled to attend piano master classes and workshops with them. I had never done anything like that before.

There were about twenty of us in that year's Regional Music Competition.

Finally, on the third day, the competition began. I enjoyed hearing all the students play their competition pieces on the beautiful nine-foot Steinway concert grand piano. Then, it was my turn. I was excited! As planned, I performed Rachmaninoff's *Prelude in C# Minor.*

The judges' results were announced, and a boy named Arnold was the first-place winner. He played a Chopin Prelude beautifully.

When they announced the second-place winner, imagine my surprise when they said my name! I was happy but thought many other students were much better pianists than I was, but Miss Remde talked to me about the judges' comments. They all said that I played beautifully with considerable feeling, and they recognized my potential talent. She guided me to be a gracious winner. Those three days were a wonderful experience, and I was inspired to practice even more.

Later that summer, however, Miss Remde had news that left me heartbroken: she had decided to move to Menlo Park, California, with her aging father. The South Dakota winters were hard on him. I understood, but I was crushed. I didn't resume piano lessons after Miss Remde moved. It was a sad time for me.

Miss Remde gave more than just piano lessons. She helped me develop poise and self-confidence, inspiring me to work hard and always strive to do my best. She was cheerful and fun to be around. She believed in me and was a great mentor.

She joined Miss Wehr, Miss Hartwell, and Miss Finsand as another wonderful teacher who made a positive difference in my life!

CHAPTER 19

HIGH SCHOOL, APPENDICITIS, AND A CARING NEIGHBOR

I began high school in Warner, South Dakota, in the fall of 1943. My best friend Betty Seaman and I were cheerleaders for our basketball team during our junior and senior years of high school. There were only three of us on the squad. We wore short white pleated satin skirts with long-sleeved red satin tops. We made them ourselves.

It was fun for us, even though we weren't terribly talented, but the cheerleaders from the other schools weren't all that great either, so it all balanced out. Betty and I had only three other students in our graduating class.

The war was going on, so it was a sobering time. No one in our immediate family was in the service. We were all farm people and were needed at home to produce the crops and food.

In spite of the War, there were still dances in Warner and Aberdeen. I was all dressed up and ready to go to a dance one Saturday in my junior year. I had been having severe pain attacks in my side, but I didn't want to tell my mother because I was afraid she wouldn't let me go to the dance. Finally, it hurt so much that I had to tell her.

We went right to the hospital's emergency room, and it turned out I had appendicitis! I had an appendectomy that very night.

In those days, patients stayed in the hospital for about ten days after operations like that. I didn't return to school for another two weeks. It was fun going back to school. Mother had bought me a new dress, and I felt cute!

I never got hooked on drinking or smoking when I was in high school, which in those days were the years that teenagers started those habits.

I had two reasons to stay away from both of those habits.

First of all, my dad was a heavy smoker. I hated the smell of it, and I disliked having to clean up all the dirty ashtrays around the house.

And regarding drinking, one of my dear older friends had a wonderful husband but he drank liquor constantly. In those days, nothing was done to try to help drinkers learn how to stop that habit.

Sadly, he was frequently named in the local newspaper for being arrested for drunk driving. I saw how terribly sad and embarrassed this made my dear friend.

I decided then that I would stay away from liquor. Also, I was afraid that I would like it. So, when I was dating in my junior and senior years of high school, I never went out with anyone who felt we had to drink or smoke to have a good time.

I won't mention names, but I had several wonderful boyfriends over those last two high school years! We had fun roller skating and going to dances.

A highlight of the summer after I finished my freshman year of high school was getting better acquainted with my mother's new friend, Julia Kienow. That summer, I would hurry to finish my chores for the day. Then, I would let my mother know I was riding my bike to go visit Julia. Julia and her husband Henry lived about a mile west of our farm.

Julia was about ten years older than my parents. I never knew my grandmothers, but Julia was what I imagined a real grandmother would be like. She was a beautiful, classy-looking Norwegian lady who spoke with a distinct accent. She wore beautiful dresses, and she had lots of gorgeous hats!

I had so much fun learning a lot of different things from Julia. I especially liked helping her weed her garden and clean her house. I also helped her during the hectic harvest time in late July to mid-August.

We baked cinnamon rolls and prepared sandwiches and other goodies to take to the hired men in the fields for their 2:30 p.m. break. Everyone worked long hours during harvesting time on the farm. Julia and I worked long hours too.

Of course, I didn't get paid, and I didn't expect to. Julia was providing me with more learning opportunities than money could buy. She believed in me. She trusted me. She encouraged me. She praised me. And she loved me. She helped me develop my sense of self-worth! She was supportive of me. She called me her little Jo. She was good for my life.

I believe these things are what kids need to be on the path to success.

One Saturday, after the busy days of harvesting were over, Julia invited me to go to Aberdeen with her. I remember it as if it were yesterday. I was thirteen years old and felt so proud to be with Julia. She had planned our trip to Aberdeen as a surprise for me. We went into Olwin Angel's department store. Julia helped me pick a beautiful beige skirt and a lovely brown sweater, and some costume jewelry. She paid for everything and told me this was a small way to thank me for all I did to help her that summer. I was thrilled!

I will always treasure my memories of Julia. Dick and I named our first child "Julie" after her. Julie's middle name is Ruth, after my mother. I made a trip in 1956 to visit my parents, and for Julie to meet her namesake. Sadly, Julia Kienow passed away just a few days before Julie and I arrived. I was so sad. Her children gave Julie one of her antique mustache cups as a keepsake, and she still has it today.

CHAPTER 20

FROM A PUMP ORGAN KEYBOARD TO A ONE-ROOM SCHOOLHOUSE

Our family attended St John's Lutheran Church in Warner. I was the organist, playing an old-fashioned pump organ for five years, from 1945 to 1950. I had also started teaching Sunday School there when I was about 15. I loved kids, and I knew even then that I wanted to be a teacher!

A life-changing conversation happened to me in April 1947, one month before I graduated from high school. Mr. Erv Rehfeld spoke to me after church one Sunday. He congratulated me on my dedicated work as the church organist and Sunday School teacher. He was the clerk of the school board of a charming one-room country school named Wright School. It was about three miles south of Warner on US 281. He said that his school board was looking for a dedicated teacher for their school that coming fall.

He knew I planned to take teacher training courses at Northern State Teachers College (NSTC) in Aberdeen that fall, but he wanted to see if I might be interested in teaching at Wright School instead.

It might seem funny that I could teach right out of high school! The explanation was simple: teachers were desperately needed in the little one-room country schools. The South Dakota State Department of Education realized that the State had a severe problem, so special provisions were established, and Mr. Rehfeld walked me through what I would have to do.

First, I would need to take courses in teaching reading, math, and social studies at NSTC that summer. After passing those classes, I would have to take a State Test, which was like a general knowledge IQ test.

When I passed, I would have a Second Grade Teacher's Certificate, and I could then accept the offer to teach at that charming little school.

Mr. Rehfeld told me that besides teaching, my duties would include getting to school early enough during those cold, windy winter mornings to get the furnace fire going so the schoolroom would be warm by the time the children arrived. I would also be the janitor, supervise lunch hour, and play games with the children at recess. Oh, yes, and, of course, I would need to prepare each day's lesson plans for all the children, grades one through eight!

I was so excited and told Mr. Rehfeld that I was interested.

I took the required classes, passed the test, and got the Second Grade Teacher's Certificate! I signed my first contract in the fall of 1947. My salary was $1,440 for the nine months.

I loved Wright School and all the children and their parents. It was one of our area's few one-room country schools with electric lights. We also had a chemical toilet and a large multi-purpose area in the basement where the large furnace was located. It was very modern compared to many.

I lived at home while teaching there. My parents bought a new car in 1946 so I could use our family's 1937 Ford to drive to and from school.

A friend had quit teaching when she got married and gave me three huge boxes of decorations for the different seasons and art materials to brighten up my classroom. I was thrilled! I went to my classroom a week before school started that fall and had fun decorating and getting it ready to welcome my students to their first day of school with me!

After all these years, I can still picture all my students that fall in 1947: first graders Bonnie Munger and Keith Rehfeld, second grader Rodney Schoen, fifth grader Bill Fuhrman, sixth grader Mervin Nilsson, seventh grader Shirley Fuhrman, and eighth grader Lois Rehfeld. Dwayne Rehfeld enrolled in kindergarten for the last six weeks of school. They were all smart, well-behaved children, and I loved being their teacher.

My students and I decided to put on a school carnival in October 1947. I was pretty bold to think I could pull it off, but we did! The parents were all wonderful helpers. I learned to recognize and thank everyone who helped.

We carefully organized everything for the carnival. I purchased several small items as prizes for the winners in the fish pond, the bean bag toss, and the fortune-telling booth.

They were all fun and even brought in some money. Parents made cookies and candy, so we sold those as well.

The entire Warner community was invited to our big carnival, and we had a huge crowd. Activities were going on in our large classroom and the multi-purpose room downstairs.

The results: besides having fun, we cleared about $150 that night.

We decided to use the money to buy a modern record player and some children's records for the classroom. I refinished an old table to make a nice place for it. The children especially loved the charming musical recording of *Peter and the Wolf* by the Russian composer Prokofiev.

I had a very successful first year of teaching, and the school board asked me to return the following year.

I had planned to teach for only one year and then fulfill my dream of attending college. I had used my teaching salary to purchase a new-to-me small grand piano and wanted to earn more for college. I loved working with my students, so I decided to teach another year and accepted the board's offer.

I went to summer school at NSTC again, got good grades in all my classes, and learned a lot. I took another State test, and when I passed, I received a First Grade Teacher's Certificate.

My salary for my second year was $1,530 for the nine months.

All of my students returned except for Lois Rehfeld, who had graduated from eighth grade and was a freshman at Warner High School.

I enjoyed doing some all-student projects with the children that year. One project was presenting a basic introduction to the presidents of the United States. Harry Truman was the President during this 1948 school year.

My little second grader Keith Rehfeld became quite interested in the project and went home one night and memorized all 33 presidents in order!

This amazed me, and I realized that I had better keep up with my young student. The next night, I went home and memorized all the presidents in order, and also the dates they served. (I am happy to mention that sixty-two years later, Keith and his wife Lee came to visit me in Alaska! I bragged to Lee about Keith's memorization feat in second grade. Keith said how much all of my music appreciation exercises stuck in his memory. He remembered me telling the story, then playing the music, of *Peter and the Wolf, HMS Pinafore*, and *Carmen*. He attributes this fun early exposure to his love for classical music. This touched my heart; this is what I was hoping would happen!)

I made our one-room classroom as attractive and cozy as possible. I sewed short curtains for all the windows on each side of the large classroom. They added a little class to our surroundings. Luckily, even with all those windows, our trusty furnace kept the classroom warm and cozy. I had to keep adding coal to keep the fire going all day.

On cold winter mornings, I got to school by about 6 a.m. to get the furnace fire going so the schoolroom would be warm when the children came at 9 a.m. Once I got it started, I would sit with my feet on the front of the furnace while reading my students' lessons for the day, trying to stay warm.

I thoroughly enjoyed my second year of teaching, and when the school board asked me to return for the third year, I accepted.

I went to summer classes again, but this time at the University of South Dakota (USD) in Vermillion. Again, I got good grades and passed another State test. I received what was called a State Teacher's Certificate. Combined with my other summer studies, I had the equivalent of one full year of college. I was teaching but still working on my goal of college graduation.

In those days, a contract wasn't signed until school started in the fall. By then, the results of summer school classes and the State tests would be available. I was at the schoolhouse one afternoon before the semester started, preparing my room for the new year. I knew that the school board would have their monthly meeting that night and would be deciding on my contract. They always met in our school room. Since I now had a State Teacher's Certificate, I decided to write a note to the school board and leave it where they would see it when they came to their meeting that evening. This is what I wrote:

> *Dear School Board members: I attended USD classes this summer and got good grades. I also passed the State test, so now I have a State Teacher's Certificate. I think I deserve a raise!*
>
> *Sincerely,*
>
> *Miss Ryman*

The next morning, I found this note on my desk:

> *Dear Miss Ryman,*
>
> *We are proud of you for your accomplishments this summer. And yes, we think you deserve a raise, too. Thank you for your dedicated work.*
>
> *From your School Board*

That was my introduction to negotiating for a raise in salary; I presented the facts and asked for what I thought I deserved.

My salary that year was $1,935 for the nine months. I was thrilled!

Jo Ryman Scott

Our Christmas program was Dec. 22. Bill was behind the curtain.

CHAPTER 21

MEMORY ANNUALS, A DOUBLE QUARTET, AND A TRIP TO THE SYMPHONY

I had a wonderful time working with my students during the last year at Wright School from 1949 to 1950.

Lois Rehfeld and Shirley Fuhrman had completed their eighth-grade studies at Wright School and were now attending high school in Warner. I still had all seven from the previous year: Mervin Nilsson was in the eighth grade, Bill Fuhrman was in the seventh grade, Rodney Schoen was in the fourth grade, Bonnie Munger and Keith Rehfeld were in the third grade, Dwayne Rehfeld was in the second grade,

Charles Fuhrman was in the first grade, and Jimmy Rehfeld joined later in kindergarten.

In olden times, farm families didn't have many entertainment opportunities. Community Clubs were organized across the country specifically for these families. They would hold monthly meetings in the one-room country schools. They provided entertainment and fellowship for the entire family.

When I started teaching at Wright School in September of 1947, I was told that our Community Club was one of the very last still active in that part of South Dakota.

Entertainment might feature adults performing humorous skits, or students from the community performing everything from magic tricks to musical selections. Many good singers were in the group, and I created a Men's Double Quartet, taking advantage of the talent. They were featured often!

This bit of history helps to explain why we had such a huge crowd at our carnival in the fall of 1947. Since meetings were held at our school, members were especially supportive, and actively promoted it.

I enjoyed organizing field trips for my students and would send informative permission slips to the parents. In March 1949, I dreamed of taking the whole class to Aberdeen for a special afternoon children's concert I had heard about. It was featuring the Minneapolis Symphony Orchestra. Special student prices were available for that concert, and the Community Club helped to make it happen. In the permission slip, I asked the parents to have their child dress up for the occasion.

I prepared my students for the concert by telling them about the music to be performed and the composers' lives, showing them pictures of each one. We gathered at the school that

Saturday, and a parent and I drove all the children to Aberdeen. Sure enough, everyone dressed up to attend the concert!

I wanted to meet the Greek conductor, Dimitri Mitropoulos. He quietly walked by me after the concert, but I was too shy to get his attention, and I didn't get to meet him. The children enjoyed the concert, and we took them to ice cream afterward. Then we drove back to school, where the parents were waiting. It was a remarkable musical field trip.

I created a little library corner in our classroom. Rodney Schoen's grandfather gave his time to build bookshelves for us. It was a cozy, welcoming area where the students could go to read after finishing their lessons. Money from the Community Club covered the cost of materials for the bookshelves.

The County Superintendent of Schools, Ruth Johnson, visited one day. She was a dedicated educator who enjoyed visiting our area's little one-room country schools, and this was a special occasion.

I spent considerable time presenting music appreciation programs and plays. The children enjoyed Gilbert & Sullivan's *HMS Pinafore*. I gave all my students basic piano lessons during the last month of school.

Before the end of the school year, I had fun preparing a memory book for each student. I called it an annual. It contained many pictures of the children throughout the year. It also included spelling words written by each child, showing their excellent writing skills. Also included in the annual was a picture of the Wright school board members: Willie Fuhrman, Earl Schoen, and Irv Rehfeld, as well as a picture of me.

The children loved having their own annual and bit of their history at Wright School. Decades later, I reconnected with Dwayne Rehfeld, and he showed me the annual I had made for him—he had kept it all those years!

It was another busy year. I loved Wright School and all of my students.

The school board asked me to return that fall. I was tempted, but I wanted to finish college. I had read enough to know that teachers with a four-year degree and outstanding references could get excellent teaching jobs anywhere in our country or even at army schools in foreign countries.

It was a bittersweet time for me. I loved my life there but wanted to get that four-year degree. I thanked them, but told the school board that I couldn't return to teach another year.

There would never be another time quite like the three years I taught at my little one-room schoolhouse. It was my first teaching position, and I loved that charming farming community of Warner, South Dakota.

My friends thought I was so brave to go off by myself, and off I went!

Pictures of Dwayne's Annual and the Annual Jo made for herself are both in the University of Alaska, Fairbanks Archives and in this chapter's Bonus Media.

THE 1950S AND 1960S

CHAPTER 22

A Bad Semester, a Summer Job, and My First Long-Distance Phone Call

My first year of college in 1950 at the University of South Dakota (USD) Vermillion was a transition time for me.

Though I had taken summer classes at Northern State Teachers College NSTS in Aberdeen and the University of South Dakota in Vermillion USD, the students in those summer classes were primarily older.

When I met students at the University that fall, they seemed so young. Though I was essentially a first-year college student, I was about three years older than the first-year students.

Students at the University were relatively sophisticated. I was amidst a bevy of beautiful city girls who looked and dressed like models.

I simply didn't fit into their social circles.

I thought back on my youth. My friends and I were probably very naïve when I was growing up in our farm community. But we didn't think we needed to spend money on drinking and smoking to have a good time!

My friends at Warner thought I was brave to travel the 250 miles south to attend the University. But when I became acquainted with various students that fall, I began to think I had made a terrible mistake leaving my comfortable community. Indeed, I began to feel that my dream of finishing college was a dumb idea.

However, I had decided to finish college and was determined to overcome my challenges that fall. I always knew I wanted to be a teacher—a good teacher! That was my goal, and I needed my four-year degree to accomplish that.

My childhood education classes weren't as inspiring as I had hoped they would be. I looked forward to expanding my knowledge beyond what I had learned during the three years I taught at Wright School.

I lived in one of the dorms at the University. Leslie and Gloria were two freshman girls who lived in the same dorm. We became good friends. When spring came in 1951, we discussed what we wanted to do that summer.

We had been reading ads about summer jobs for college students. We were intrigued by the idea of seeking employment at a summer resort.

Gloria, Leslie, and I sent our applications to two places. One was a rather large, luxurious resort in Estes Park, Colorado, and the other was a smaller family-style resort at Lake Como, Wisconsin, not too far from Chicago.

The three of us were delighted when we were all offered jobs at Lake Como! That was a good match for the three of us.

We loved waitressing at Lake Como. The resort was a cozy, friendly place. The guests enjoyed swimming and boating on the beautiful lake.

This resort catered to city parents eager to have a country-style summer place for their children. Mothers often came with their children for the entire summer, and dads would come on weekends and holidays.

I still remember one family in particular. The Mother played easy-to-listen-to songs on the piano. She sang too. We all enjoyed hearing her perform. Her children were well-behaved, and I enjoyed playing outdoor games with them during my time off. (The teacher in me was showing!)

Leslie, Gloria, and I worked hard and enjoyed serving our guest families.

At age 21, I was the oldest of the waitresses—so I was assigned to work nights in the resort's bar! I had never BEEN in a bar before. It was a quiet family bar. I didn't have to mix drinks, but I did have to learn their names. I thought *Grasshopper* was a funny name for a drink! It was a pretty, mint green.

I had fun playing the piano and singing in the bar. The guests enjoyed hearing me perform. The owners even put a tip jar for me on the piano!

Each summer the management named a delicious fruit salad after one of the waitresses. I was very surprised when I saw the menu for the first time: the salad was called *Jo's Salad*!

Working as a waitress at the resort was an excellent experience for me. My room and board were provided so I could save $500—which was quite a bit of money in those days. When I added the $500 that I borrowed from my parents, I covered all my expenses for my junior year of college. I again worked in the University's cafeteria, which covered the cost of my meals. The cost of dorm housing was minimal. It's amazing now to consider how little it cost for me to go to college almost 70 years ago!

I had a busy junior year. I found pleasure in volunteering at KUSD, the public radio station on campus. I did various tasks at the station.

I cherish one memory of my KUSD job that year. I became acquainted "remotely" with a young girl who had had polio. She had restricted use of her arms and legs. She had a children's story-telling time on KUSD radio.

My job was to arrange for someone on staff to go to her home once a week to tape her reading that week's stories. I never got to meet her, but I enjoyed helping her in this small way. And I loved hearing her read her stories over the radio.

I finished the school year in June of 1952.

I decided to sign up for a six-week summer school class at USD. I was grateful to take the class to ensure I had enough credits to complete my four-year degree. However, I was unhappy with the USD class I'd have to take.

When I returned home early August, I decided to call Miss Remde. I had missed her. It was the first long-distance call I had ever made. Through tears, I shared that I had been disappointed with my classes at USD. I told her I had just one more year of classes and would graduate in June 1953.

Miss Remde listened intently. She had some ideas.

CHAPTER 23

SAYING *NO* TO USD, VENEZUELA, AND STANFORD

There I was, talking to Miss Remde on my first EVER long-distance phone call.

I listened carefully when Miss Remde gave me some exciting learning opportunities. Spending the last year of college in California sounded exciting.

She told me there were three colleges near her home in Menlo Park.

All we had to do was call the USD's Registrar's Office and ask them to send my college transcripts to these three colleges: San Jose State, San Francisco State, and Stanford University.

Miss Remde realized that this was something new for me to do. So, she lovingly helped me make the call to USD. That office immediately sent my transcripts to those three colleges.

It was only two weeks before the fall classes started. Students didn't usually change colleges that late. It was my hope that my USD credits would be accepted in one of those schools so I could begin classes in September and graduate in June 1953.

Here is what happened:

> *I never heard from San Francisco State.*
>
> *Stanford accepted me, but for the second semester since they had already closed the fall registration. I turned down Stanford because I didn't want to wait until the second semester to start my studies. (I had no idea that being accepted to study at Stanford was prestigious and years later, my children would think it was funny that I had turned them down.)*
>
> *I received another acceptance letter, this one with some good news. San Jose State accepted all my USD credits, and I could start classes in September and graduate in June 1953.*
>
> *I chose San Jose State!*

I arranged to take the train from Aberdeen to San Francisco. Miss Remde would meet me there, and we'd drive to her home in Menlo Park.

Miss Remde and I had discussed that she had three bedrooms she rented out. She had a comfortable bedroom in her basement where I could live. I could work off my living expenses by cleaning her large home once a week, and we would share in the costs of groceries.

I could catch the bus early every morning for the one-hour ride to the San Jose State Campus. I was on campus in classes or studying in the library all day each week.

When I left Warner that August, my friends thought I was brave to move to California alone. I told them I was fortunate to have Miss Remde's guidance and help.

I had fun getting settled at Miss Remde's. I liked my cozy, quiet room in the basement. I had a safe place there to study and do my schoolwork. I was happy with my new surroundings.

But there were many things I had to do to get settled in my new school.

I arrived at Miss Remde's just a week before classes began. I caught the bus to the huge San Jose State campus. Some caring staff helped me register for my classes. I felt comfortable there.

I was happy with my childhood education classes.

Getting acquainted with Dr. William R. Rogers the day I registered for classes was helpful. He was one of the popular professors in San Jose State's Education Department. He must have had at least 150 students in his classes. But he made each of us feel like we were his most important student!

Dr. Rogers was especially interested in hearing about my background. No one else in his classes had taught in a little one-room country school for three years. He was intrigued that I had even served as the janitor, keeping the school room warm on those cold, snowy winter days in South Dakota. In addition to music appreciation stories, plus entertaining the children with "kittenball" and other games during the noon hour and recess, I had prepared all the lesson plans for the seven students in grades one through eight!

It meant a lot that he appreciated what I had done at such a young age. Dr. Rogers was the fifth teacher who made a huge difference in my life when I needed help and encouragement.

I took several classes from Dr. Rogers that year and kept learning so much from him. I enjoyed other classes I took, too, including an English literature class and several other music appreciation classes.

In January 1953, all the graduating seniors in the Department of Education were called to a meeting to receive guidance in preparing their resumes and deciding where they wanted to apply to teach the coming fall.

Though I enjoyed San Jose State and living with Miss Remde, I had decided I didn't want to stay in California to teach. Nor did I want to return to South Dakota to teach.

My first choice was to teach in a United States Army School in Germany, but I discovered that I was a year too young. They had so many applicants that they wouldn't consider making an exception.

Some of my USD friends were accepting teaching positions in Venezuela. The United States government was interested in the oil fields there, and there were openings for teachers in the Army Schools. They really needed teachers and had eliminated the age requirement.

I almost signed a contract to teach in Caracas! But after thinking more about it, I decided it wasn't a good choice for me, and I didn't sign that contract.

I met a lovely teacher from Cordova, Alaska when I was working in the USD cafeteria. She made Alaska sound interesting to me. I went to the school's library and read everything I could find about these four Alaska communities: Anchorage, Cordova, Juneau, and Fairbanks.

I liked what I read and sent my resume to each of those four school districts. Within a few weeks, I had job offers from all of them!

The Superintendent of Schools in Fairbanks, Dr. James C. Ryan, wanted me to choose Fairbanks. He even called me long distance in California to see if I had further questions about the Fairbanks schools. I was interested in Fairbanks because the University of Alaska was located there.

I was impressed with Dr. Ryan's enthusiasm for the Fairbanks community and the school system. So, in March 1953, I chose to accept the teaching position in Fairbanks, Alaska!

I finished my school year at San Jose State as planned and graduated with honors in June 1953.

I was deeply grateful to Miss Remde for all she had done for me that year. I had worked hard studying and cleaning her house. I was sad to leave her and her father, who had recently had a stroke. They were like family to me.

I returned to my parents' farm in South Dakota and started planning my trip to Fairbanks.

California was one thing, but my Warner friends *really* thought I was brave to venture off to Alaska by myself!

On August 17th, 1953, I took the *Chicago, Milwaukee, St. Paul, and Pacific* train from Aberdeen to Seattle. My dear Aunt Laura and family met me at the train station.

After visiting them for a few days, they took me to board the Alaska Steamship Company's vessel bound for Alaska. What a trip that was! I enjoyed sailing up the Inside Passage to Ketchikan and Juneau, then sailing across the beautiful Gulf of Alaska to Seward.

From Seward, I took the Alaska Railroad north through Anchorage and Mt. McKinley National Park (now called Denali National Park) and even further north on to Fairbanks.

Dr. James C. Ryan and his lovely wife, Irice, met me at the train station.

I stayed with them and their son, Dennis, for a few days. Then I got settled in my apartment in the new Fairview

Manor Apartments. It was an easy walk to Denali Elementary, where I would teach.

What a year that had been! In August 1952, I moved to Menlo Park, California. In August 1953, I moved to Fairbanks, Alaska. I never regretted choosing Fairbanks.

CHAPTER 24

ITALY, PANAMA, AND A LAGUNA BEACH HAMBURGER STAND

Once upon a time, in the late 1940s, there was a handsome young man named Richard Scott-Fanelli who lived with his mother in Laguna Beach, California.

His mother, Irene Scott, was Scotch-Irish and was born in 1898.

Richard's father, Salvatore (Sully) Fanelli, was born in 1899. Sully had 13 brothers and sisters. The Fanelli family had left their little mountain village of Laurenzana, Italy in 1878 to live in New York City and nearby New Rochelle.

While serving in Panama in the US Army in 1918, Sully met Irene. She was a modern dance teacher and performer there. When she was on tour in Panama, Irene studied with the famed pioneer in modern dance, Miss Ruth St. Denis, and subsequently with Miss St. Denis' husband, Ted Shawn.

Sully was honorably discharged from the Panama Canal Zone in 1918, and they were married. Irene was ahead of her time and incorporated her maiden name into her married name: Irene Scott-Fanelli.

After they were married, they went back to New York City. They had a darling daughter, Marci Scott-Fanelli, in 1921. Richard was born in 1927. The siblings adored each other.

They lived in a brownstone apartment with the extended Fanelli family on Manhattan's Upper East Side. Richard attended Catholic School close by. There was no playground, but the children would march to the gym to the music of John Phillip Sousa. One year for Christmas, Richard got a little pair of skis from Santa and was thrilled one morning when it finally snowed in the city. The family walked west a few blocks to a hilly part of Central Park, and he got to try out his new skis.

They spent summers in his early childhood years at the Fanelli home in South Hampton with the rest of the Fanelli family.

Irene continued to study seriously with Miss St. Denis in the 1920s, and she took Marci and Richard with her to Florida for a time while she taught Denis-Shawn dance classes at Rollins College in Winter Park in the late 1920s and early 1930s.

Richard enjoyed a privileged life in Florida during the early years of The Great Depression. His mother was teaching and performing in Florida, and his dad was a successful legal secretary with a well-known law firm in New York City.

In 1934, Irene took Marci and Richard with her to Southern California. Sully would send the family money from New York City and he arranged to buy them a car. Irene took the children on some fabulous trips to several National Parks in that car.

When Richard would ask when he would see his father again, his mother kept telling him that his dad would eventually join the family. Sadly, that never happened. One afternoon when he was nine, he was waiting in the car for his mother to come out of the store. He was bored and saw an envelope on the dashboard. He opened it to find official looking paperwork, with the words "Divorce Decree" at the top. That's how he found out that his dad would not be joining the family.

Up until this time, his name was Richard Scott-Fanelli. However, Irene got a terse long-distance phone call from Sully on the day before he was going to marry another woman in New York. He said he "didn't want there to be two Mrs. Salvatore Fanelli's in the world," and asked that Irene drop Fanelli from her hyphenated name. She complied but went one step further: she dropped it from her children's names as well. After the divorce, Richard's name became Dick Scott.

Dick attended the elementary schools in Santa Monica until age twelve when he went to stay with Irene's parents on a small farm in Sullivan, Illinois, while his mother was working on her dance degree at the University of Illinois. He liked living there and had fun picking fresh asparagus, gathering eggs, and going to the sixth grade in a little one-room schoolhouse.

Later, they returned to California, but this time Irene chose Laguna Beach. He loved it there. He enjoyed surfing in the ocean and beach life during his High School years.

After graduating Laguna Beach High School in 1945, Dick began taking classes at a nearby junior college, especially enjoying the good teachers he had for economics, advertising, and finance.

Irene was a Rosie-the-Riveter during the war. She worked with her good friend, Lita Lyle. Lita's husband had passed away, and so had her son, who was a few years younger than Dick. Lita treated Dick like a son. Dick tried to sign up for various military branches when WWII broke out, but he had a bad knee and could not pass the health exams.

He was figuring out what he wanted to do for a living. He loved surfing and his time at the beach with his longboard. His dream became to continue that lifestyle by making enough money to buy his own hamburger stand on Laguna Beach. He needed to figure out how to make that money.

Out of nowhere, an exciting opportunity became available for Dick … in Alaska!

CHAPTER 25

A Means to an End, a Steampipe Crab, and a Change of Plans

Dick's dream of buying his own hamburger stand had him thinking about how to earn enough money to make it happen.

To that end, Dick worked for the United States Geological Survey (USGS) for two winters in California, working with engineers to update their quadrangle maps, many of which hadn't been revised since 1937.

An engineer on that job, Bob, usually worked summers in Alaska. He had recently married, and his wife would not be allowed to accompany him to Alaska.

Although Dick was not a graduate engineer, he had been a responsible worker for USGS and Bob offered Dick the opportunity to take his place in the summer of 1948 as a surveyor's aide with the USGS in Alaska.

If Dick would take this job, Bob could stay home in California with his wife and continue with the USGS there.

Dick's Laguna Beach life as a handsome young guy was filled with enjoying everything from surfing to swimming to sailing, and yes, meeting girls! He hesitated to accept Bob's offer. He was in the middle of negotiating to purchase a teak sailboat and was not excited about spending a summer in ice-cold Alaska.

Bob really wanted Dick to accept, so he encouraged him to go to the library and read up about Alaska, saying he might be surprised. Dick followed the suggestion and did considerable research. He learned about the beautiful flower and vegetable gardens, the midnight sun, and the warm summer temperatures in Fairbanks, where they would be headquartered.

Bob gave him an overview of what the job would entail:

The Air Force had just made overlapping high-altitude photographs of that area that included at least ten miles on either side of the highways there in central Alaska. The USGS survey crew received this data.

The Air Force photographs overlapped because each photo was taken at a slightly different angle when shot from a moving plane. These photographs were sent to the Denver offices, where they were viewed through a device that the viewer could use to create highly accurate contour maps.

In 1948, many returning GIs were interested in homesteading in Alaska. Maps were needed to file for a homestead. The person who wanted to homestead had to survey the proposed claim and mark all the corners.

Since many Alaska homesteaders wanted to create farmland, south-facing properties were sought after because they got more sun.

The United States government was interested in attracting more people to come to Alaska after WWII and realized that the 1938 pre-war maps of the Territory were out-of-date and rarely contained the luxury of showing the contour of the land.

USGS's assignment for crews like Bob's was to obtain data missing or outdated on the existing maps, and it was a good paying job!

Dick still had his goal in mind and thought this could be the means to an end. He calculated that after two summers he would have saved enough money to buy his hamburger stand. Dick accepted the job in Alaska!

He booked his passage on the Alaska Steamship Company. Once onboard, he made friends with the crew. One night, a couple of buddies from the engine room invited him to try an odd delicacy: Alaska King Crab! He followed them to the engine room and saw a huge crab wrapped around a steam pipe with twine! They had thrown a line with bait overboard, caught the crab, wrestled it down to the engine room, and lashed it onto the steam pipe to cook. It was already turning bright red and pink, and in no time, they were eating a delicious feast. At the time, crab had not yet become the sought-after Alaskan delicacy that it became later. Dick had never had a more delicious meal!

Once off the ship, he made his way to Fairbanks on the Alaska Railroad. The USGS had dorm-style housing for him, and he started working right away.

Decades later he related this memory:

"There were many unnamed lakes scattered throughout our project area. Our party chief

would interview Native residents to determine their local names for nearby lakes. He soon realized that the Native name for many lakes was Lily Lake. He figured out that any lake that was populated with flourishing water lilies was identified as Lily Lake. From our helicopter, I remember seeing huge bull moose standing at the edge of these lakes with their heads and antlers completely submerged, feasting on the lush water lilies. When they came up for air, their antlers would be draped with lily plants, with water streaming off the leaves."

The summer went so well that he decided to come back the following summer. After that second summer, he was thinking about staying through the winter and went about looking for winter work. He found a job at the municipal utilities department with the city and braced himself for his first Alaskan winter.

Even though Dick wasn't in the service, the Fairbanks USO was a welcoming place to go. Dick met several Ladd Air Force Base jet pilots there who became his buddies. They encouraged Dick to join the choir at the First Presbyterian Church where they sang. The choir director was a fiery redhead named Shirley Calnan. He did join, and as it happened during the rehearsal, someone mentioned that the church needed a sexton.

Housing was scarce and expensive in Fairbanks, and the sexton would receive a place to stay as part of the pay. Dick applied for the job and got it. He was happy to live in a little room on the second floor of the original 1904 church building and not pay rent or utilities all winter. It was connected to the new 1931 church building, and his job was to take care of the little church and the new building as well.

Dick ended up loving Fairbanks and exploring Alaska. After two summers of saving his money flying around Alaska in a helicopter and one winter working for the city while living in the little white church, he gave up the idea of returning to Laguna Beach and buying his very own hamburger stand.

Instead, he used his savings to buy a little 1930s era log cabin on a small lot at Six Mile Old Richardson Highway. Beginning in the fall of 1951 Fairbanks became his year-round home.

Dick flew his mother up from California in June 1952 and they traveled around central Alaska together. He was happy to show her around.

In 1952, while Dick was at an event at the USO, he noticed there were phone books for many cities in the United States. He found a phone book for New York City. He knew his dad had lived there when his parents were divorced in about 1936. He never saw or heard from his dad after the divorce.

So, he picked up the New York City phone book and looked for Salvatore Fanelli. In those days, not only were phone numbers listed, but addresses were also listed. Dick found his dad's home address, and he wrote him a letter. A few weeks later, he received a letter back! It was a congenial letter but made no mention of a possible reunion. Dick was disheartened but kept the letter.

In August 1953, Dick was the best man for one of his jet pilot buddies, Wayne Ketch, who married a lovely girl named Frances Tonseth. It was a beautiful wedding.

Little did he know, Dick's turn would be right around the corner!

The original 1904 church structure is now at Pioneer Park in Fairbanks. People refer to it as The Little White Church.

Visitors can go up the steps to the left of the altar to see Dick's tiny room that had enough space for a small cot and a little table for his typewriter.

CHAPTER 26

SAYING *YES* TO ALASKA, A PIANO ON WHEELS, AND A HANDSOME YOUNG MAN

I arrived in Fairbanks the third week in August 1953. I had a roommate, Helen, a new teacher at Denali Elementary. We shared the expenses of our one-bedroom apartment at Fairview Manor, which was two hundred and fifty dollars a month, and included utilities.

Dr. Ryan wanted to be sure that I met the band teacher, Shirley Calnan, who also lived in Fairview Manor. I immediately found her in her apartment, and introduced myself. She was a cute, vivacious little redhead, and we became friends immediately.

She invited Helen and me to a "before school starts" party in her apartment to meet her roommate, Edie, and other teachers. It was a great gathering with about 25 guests, some new to the school system and some long-time Fairbanks teachers.

Shirley was a gracious hostess. She had everyone introduce themselves, tell what they taught, and then tell what they did during their summer vacation.

I was amazed to hear about the exciting travels each person had experienced that summer. I thought back to my old friends in Warner who thought I was so brave to go to Alaska by myself. It's good I didn't brag that I was doing something so brave, as many of my new friends had already traveled the world!

Over the Labor Day weekend, Helen and I were included in a gathering of friends that made the 50-mile drive to Harding Lake. One of the teachers had a cabin there. I saw many interesting home sites along the Richardson Highway. About six miles from Fairbanks, I noticed an old wagon wheel hanging from a large beam, a creative driveway sign to someone's property.

Harding Lake was beautiful, but it was cold. I remember we were all surprised to see Edie jump in. She was the only one who had the nerve to swim that day.

I was particularly interested in walking around Harding Lake's nearby woods. Alaska was so far north it was about the same latitude as the Scandinavian countries. I enjoyed seeing all the beautiful plants, including low-bush cranberries.

In Norway, they were called lingonberries. I picked quite a few that day, and Shirley gave me the recipe for Alaska Low Bush Cranberry-Banana Jam. I made some. It was delicious. Over the nearly 60 years I lived in Fairbanks I continued picking those cranberries and making that jam.

School started the day after Labor Day. I was assigned to teach a sixth-grade class. I immediately loved my students, two of whom, Phil Pope and Andy Bachner, I am still in touch with years later!

In the third week of school, Dr. Ryan came by my classroom to ask me to consider leaving that sixth grade class to become Denali's first general music teacher. I had a music minor but hadn't thought about being a general music teacher. Dr. Ryan thought I had the talent and the personality for the job. He assured me he could find another teacher for my sixth-grade class.

After considerable thought, I decided to accept the challenge. I was sorry to leave those sixth graders, but I would see them twice weekly for their music classes. The new job would be fun. There was a catch, though! The school's classrooms were overcrowded that year, so there wasn't a dedicated music room. They gave me a small portion of the school's kitchen for an office.

There was a beautiful new Baldwin spinet piano on wheels in the hallway of each of the school's two floors for me to use. I rolled the pianos down the hall and got skilled at carefully maneuvering them through the classroom doors and into the room. I would teach up to twelve half-hour classes daily, so I got very good at rolling that Baldwin!

The school was new and as such, didn't have a school song. I set up a little contest for each class to submit a poem about Denali that I could put to music. Many classes submitted poems, and our principal, Mrs. Haggard, chose the winner: Miss Thompson's fifth grade class wrote *Denali of the North*. Part of the charm of the song was that the littler kids could join in for the chorus, even if they couldn't memorize the verse. Forty-eight years later, I was invited to the school's

50th anniversary celebration to direct *Denali of the North* with many past teachers and students present singing along.

Denali of the North

Verse:

Way up north
Where the northern lights glow
With dancing colors on ice and snow
Where the huskies look at the moon and howl
And malamutes bare white fangs and growl.

Where it's cold in the long winter night
And the stars shine down sparkling white
There stands Denali to be our guide
And on her we look with pride

Chorus:

Oh, Denali
We're proud of you
To your colors
We'll be ever true
Long may they wave
The gold and blue
We'll forever
Sing praise of you!

Besides meeting people at school, Shirley and I enjoyed hosting gatherings, getting acquainted with many interesting new people in the Fairbanks community. We were always the ones in our crowd who loved to organize parties.

Shirley was the choir director at the First Presbyterian Church. She thought I should meet one of the members of her choir, a handsome young baritone whose name was Dick Scott. He made the best Mexican dinners and "has his own deep fryer," she added. She would ask him to come to her place to prepare dinner, and we would have all the necessary groceries on hand to make it happen.

So, Shirley invited Dick to meet Helen, Edie, and me on the last Saturday in September of 1953. Sure enough, he showed up at the door with a big deep fryer in his arms, and proceeded to prepare dinner for all of us. It was delicious! Afterwards, the five of us went dancing at the Saturday Night Folk Dance Club.

Dick was a nice guy, and we had an excellent time together that evening. But he had plans to return to Laguna Beach and open his hamburger stand, and I planned to teach only one year in Fairbanks and then apply for the U.S. Army School position in Germany.

Dick and I did see each other at various dances, however, which were popular in Fairbanks at that time. There were two dance groups: The Sourdough Dance Club and the Saturday Night Folk Dance Club. Both groups involved square dancing as well as folk dancing. These clubs alternated Saturday nights at The Carpenters Hall.

The USO continued to be very important to the Fairbanks community as well. Ladd Air Force Base, now called Fort Wainwright Army Base, was located just outside of Fairbanks, and Eielson Air Force Base was 25 miles away.

The club's director was a vivacious, classy middle-aged lady named Madge Haney. She had just the right personality for her job! Madge organized many activities for the service men and women, and the Fairbanks community was welcomed to all their events, which also included dances.

Several of us young teachers had fun attending, and I would see Dick at these dances as well.

The new First Methodist Church building was completed that fall. Shirley had been a Methodist all her life and was eager to leave her position at the Presbyterian Church and accept that church's invitation to be their choir director.

Shirley knew I had experience in directing church choirs and was happy when I agreed to take her old position. That's how I became the choir director at the First Presbyterian Church at Seventh Avenue and Cushman Street in downtown Fairbanks!

From that time on, I would see Dick at Wednesday night choir rehearsals and at church on Sundays. We started to have fun together, but our relationship was nothing serious.

During that time, Dr. and Mrs. Ryan became very dear friends of mine. They had become my Fairbanks family and were included in many of my gatherings.

I started having fun giving dinner parties in our apartment. I became known for my homemade dinner rolls.

I remember my first Christmas in Fairbanks in 1953. Chickenpox had been spreading to many students at Denali Elementary. During the Christmas break, I came down with chickenpox. That was not a fun time for me to be sick.

One day Dick came by to see me. He had a huge box all wrapped up beautifully. It was heavy! I would never have guessed what was inside: a twenty-five-pound bag of flour and an electric hand mixer. Dick liked my homemade dinner rolls, and that was his hint that he liked me, too!

We started seeing more of each other after the holidays. We weren't teenagers. We were ages 24 and 26 that year. After several dates, we decided to put aside the plans we each had: teaching in Germany, and owning a Laguna Beach hamburger stand. Instead, we agreed that we loved each other, were meant for each other, and should just get married and make new plans together!

My friends in South Dakota were happy to hear the news. They were beginning to think I would be an old maid; after all, I was 24 years old and still not married.

In those days, young people had few or no marriage counseling opportunities. I observed married couples who argued a lot. They didn't seem to have much in common with each other.

I wisely observed that it was too late to attempt to change a person's lifestyles and habits after marriage. I had quietly figured out five requirements for a prospective husband before I would even date someone:

1. I would not date anyone who smoked.
2. I would not date anyone who had a drinking problem.
3. The man I dated had to go to church with me.
4. The man I dated had to go to concerts with me.
5. The man I dated had to be smarter than I was. I didn't want a *dumb dumb* for a husband.

I had decided that if I didn't happen to meet this *Mr. Wonderful,* my students would become my family. But here was this terrific young man, Dick Scott, who wanted to marry me.

He didn't realize it, but he met all my requirements. I said *yes*!

CHAPTER 27

QUESTIONING CHATTER, A CHARMING REQUEST, AND TWO LOVELY CAKES

On Saturday, January 23rd, 1954, Dick and I invited 35 friends to my apartment for a gathering. After the meal, we brought out a lovely cake decorated with the words "We're Engaged!" We told our friends we would marry at the First Presbyterian Church on Saturday, February 27th. Shirley Calnan would be my bridesmaid, and Dr. Ryan would give me away.

Dick and I treasured some great memories during the month between when we announced our engagement and the date we were married. My sister Jean was happy to hear the news. She mailed me a note asking, "Do you know your way around Fairbanks?!" (Chapter 8 provides the history of this wry comment.)

Dick and I were unaware of concerned conversations that were taking place about us before our wedding.

Madge from the USO and some of her friends were worried that I might not be good enough for Dick. At the same time, the Ryans and some of their friends were concerned that Dick might not be good enough for me!

Dick and I were amused when we heard about this. We hosted social gatherings with Madge, the Ryans, and their many friends. They all came to realize that we were indeed a good match.

As the general music teacher at Denali, I loved all my students. They were excited to see me roll the Baldwin piano into their classrooms twice a week and seemed to love me, too. They were tickled when they heard that I was getting married.

One day after school, three dear fifth-grade boys, Pete Haggland, Dick Webb, and Phil Smith, came by my office. I lovingly greeted them. They sort of looked at each other and were whispering, "No, you ask her. No, *you* ask her."

Finally, Pete said, "We want to know if we can be the best men at your wedding!"

Their request touched me, and I graciously thanked them for being so thoughtful. I explained that the groom always selects the best man. But I told them I'd be happy if they could attend the wedding, and sure enough, they did!

Pete gave me a book about Beethoven and a charming little metal tea box filled with Constant Comment for a wedding present. I treasured these! I kept in touch with Pete and sent him a note in 2001 saying that I wanted the little tea box to go to his darling daughter, Kris, who was turning

16. She had heard her dad's best man story and was happy to receive it. She now treasures that little tea box herself, almost seventy years later.

Fairbanks was a small town in 1954. There were some chic ladies' dress shops, but none carried a selection of wedding gowns.

The owner of one of the shops graciously helped me order a beautiful gown over a month before our wedding. We waited and waited for the gown to be delivered. I was getting concerned because the gown still hadn't arrived a week before the wedding!

My maid of honor, Shirley, told me that her friend Jane had married Chuck Behlke in November. Jane wore a beautiful ballerina-length gown. Shirley asked if I could borrow it if my dress didn't arrive on time, and Jane agreed. I tried it on, and it fit beautifully. I was not as tall as Jane, so while it was ballerina length for her, it was floor-length for me! By the day of the wedding, my dress still hadn't come, so I was grateful to be wearing Jane's gown for my special day. She and I became good friends.

It was a brisk forty-five degrees below zero for the evening ceremony, but the weather didn't keep people away; we had a church filled with our older friends and my young students. The reception was held at Bud and Emma Grill's home on College Road, and we served a lovely three-tiered wedding cake made by the popular baker of the time, Ann Shiek.

My gown never did arrive at the dress shop!

Our wedding pictures were taken at The Fisher Photography Studio in the beautiful two-story log building on Cushman Street. That building would later become Claire and Joe Fejes' Alaska House Art Gallery.

When Dick and I celebrated our 50th wedding anniversary in 2004, besides our family, we were happy to have Shirley Calnan Swanger and Jane Behlke join us. We had fun reminiscing about her wedding gown!

CHAPTER 28

A Parcel of Land, a Crazy Idea, and How to Move a Ten Thousand Pound Cabin

In early March 1954, after Dick and I returned from our honeymoon at Mt. McKinley National Park, we were ready to make our home together. It was spring, and we could start building immediately at Six Mile Old Richardson Highway, the land where Dick had his little bachelor cabin. It was on the way to Harding Lake, and the first time he took me to see the property, what a fun surprise it was to see the very wagon wheel I had noticed on the Labor Day trip marked *his* driveway! It seemed pretty far out of town.

Then we thought of a crazy idea. What if we could MOVE that little log cabin to a property that Dick had bought at Three Mile College Road, which was closer to town? That lot was a little over an acre. I was a farm girl, and I liked the idea of having a large piece of land. However, I was particularly excited about this option because it was just a mile from the University of Alaska campus.

Dick went along with my wishes and set about the daunting task of preparing to relocate a ten thousand pound cabin. It was about a ten-mile trek.

Dick thought carefully about who we could hire to help move the cabin. We didn't have a lot of money, but Dick knew he couldn't do it alone. So, he started to look for professional help.

He had heard positive comments about the young Bobby Mitchell, who was considered one of the top contractors in Fairbanks. So, Dick called Bobby.

After reviewing the job, Bobby told Dick that for his crew to do the necessary prep work in moving the cabin, the cost would be close to a thousand dollars. (That would be about ten thousand dollars today.)

However, Bobby graciously recognized that Dick was on a budget. He must have also recognized that Dick was intelligent and ambitious.

So, Bobby explained how he could lower the price to only one hundred and fifty dollars if Dick would do all the preparatory "grunt" work.

Bobby said he would even loan Dick the four hefty mechanical jacks and the necessary timbers he would need to raise the cabin above ground level in preparation for the move.

It would be tedious work.

Dick would have to jack up each corner of the cabin and place timbers, one corner at a time until the cabin was three feet off the ground.

When Dick finished this prep work, Bobby would come with his truck and driver along with the steel beams and wheels assembly, which would be pushed underneath the middle of the cabin.

The front of the steel beam assembly would be hitched to the truck. The rear wheel assembly would be rolled underneath the cabin and attached to the rear. At this point, the cabin would be ready to move because the cabin would be resting on the steel beams, not the timbers. The timbers would be cleared away and put on the truck.

It would be a tremendous amount of work, but Bobby had given us an extremely generous offer. Dick thanked him and agreed to the deal.

He did all the work himself. He carefully followed Bobby's instructions, working nights and weekends throughout March and April. It turned out to be a laborious one-person job.

When Dick finished, he called Bobby.

Bobby was impressed. He suggested doing the move very early on the second Sunday morning in April 1954, when there would be very little traffic on the Old Richardson Highway.

There was a problem that Bobby had to consider: The telephone service lines crossing the highway were relatively low, below the roof height of the cabin when on the truck.

When Bobby contacted the telephone company for help on what to do, they said they could do it, but they would have to charge three hundred dollars to disconnect and reconnect each telephone line on this move. So that was out of the question.

Bobby creatively solved that problem by straddling the front ridge on top of the cabin roof during the 10-mile journey.

Bobbly lifted each telephone line using a board so the cabin could safely move under the lines. He successfully helped the cabin make every one of the lines crossing the highway transparent. Fortunately, the service lines inside the city and onto College Road were high enough to clear the cabin.

As hoped, they encountered very little traffic and no more problems, making the move to our new property on College Road and Caribou Way successful!

Dick had marked exactly where the cabin had to be placed in our new yard. Bobby put the cabin down right on the mark. It was right next to where the basement would be dug.

Dick again used the four hefty mechanical jacks Bobby had loaned him and several cedar blocks. Bobby showed Dick how to place a jack under each corner of the cabin, then jack up a corner of the cabin and place two or three cedar blocks on top of the jack. He told Dick to continue doing this one corner at a time until the cabin reached the desired height of about three feet off the ground, so it would be ready for its final twenty foot move once the basement was ready.

The move was complete by late Sunday afternoon, and Bobby and his driver headed home.

Dick kept working into the night, following Bobby's directions to finish getting the cabin securely up on the cedar blocks.

Whew, what a day that had been.

I missed watching the move because I stayed in our Fairview Manor apartment all that day, packing our things so we would be ready to move into our cabin that week. Even though it was just on its temporary footings, we would move in as is and unpack all of our things. (This reminds me of my family moving to the cellar of our new farm in 1940 while they were finishing work on the floors. Moving the cabin to College Road and not living way out on the Old Richardson

Highway made me feel almost as excited as my brother Mike at the time: "I love living like this!")

Bobby Mitchell was our hero for getting the cabin moved and, indeed, charged only one hundred and fifty dollars. He was the perfect person for the job, and his guidance was invaluable. He knew exactly what needed to be done to have a successful move and was willing to share all of his know-how with Dick.

Building a home in Alaska took a lot of energy, ambition, and nerve.

We were always grateful for the insight we received from many old-timers who seemed to find pleasure in helping us. Thanks to their help, we were able to do much of the work ourselves to build our home over all those years.

The first expressway in Fairbanks, The Mitchell Expressway, was named in Bobby's honor. Bobby was a contractor with the Ghemm Construction Company. They were all wonderful people who did so much for the Fairbanks community.

Over the years, Bobby would check in with Dick to see the progress we had made in building our home and grounds. Throughout our lives, Dick and I sought to follow Bobby's example of helping others whenever we could. No one ever asked us how to move a ten thousand pound cabin, though. If they had, Dick would have been ready.

CHAPTER 29

A NEW FRIEND
AND A FUN TWIST

In September 1953, I was enjoying my new position teaching general music, rolling shiny Baldwin pianos down the halls of Denali Elementary from classroom to classroom. I taught all grades except kindergarten. Teachers had been talking about some cute little kindergarten twins. I got to meet the darling twins Judy and Jan, and I already knew their brother, Greg, as he was in my second-grade music class. I was happy to meet their mother one afternoon. She was an attractive, vivacious, classy-looking young parent named Mary.

When school was out in late May 1954, Mary invited me and another teacher to have lunch in her beautiful new home. I can still see cute little Judy and Jan peeking around the dining room door to see what was going on. Dick and I had been living in our little dry (no plumbing) log cabin for two months, so it was fun being in a house with running water and an indoor bathroom!

Mary was delightful, and we became good friends. One day during that summer, Mary and I were at a gathering with several friends. We were all talking about how we met that year.

Finally, the conversation focused on me. I said that I had just gotten married in February, and my husband and I were living in a little dry log cabin on College Road. I told them that Dick had been so fortunate to have found an amazing man named Bobby Mitchell to engineer moving our cabin from his faraway property at Six Mile Old Richardson Highway to our new lot closer to the university.

At that moment, Mary spoke up excitedly. "Oh, Jo! Bobby Mitchell is my husband!" Of course, a lively conversation of joy and laughter erupted. Mary and I hugged and knew then that our friendship would last a lifetime. We were both excited when we finally made the connection. It was a fun moment. I told all my friends that day what a tremendous help he had been.

The twins took piano lessons from me when they were older, which I taught at home in that little log cabin. They loved hearing the story that their dad had engineered the ten-mile move of the very house they were sitting in every week for their lessons!

CHAPTER 30

PERMAFROST, POINT PIPES, AND A WISH FOR A WELL

This chapter will be crucial for anyone needing to pound down a well, with information specific to doing it in a cold climate like Fairbanks, Alaska!

In 2019 Dick went to great lengths to describe this process to me as we started writing our stories. Some old-timers had given him instructions, and I took careful notes on every detail he described. It almost felt like more than I needed to know. This chapter will also shed light on bulldozing a basement, digging a water line, pouring concrete, laying a course of blocks, and building a septic system. I will share his explanation down to the minute details here if you contemplate taking on any of these tasks!

If you are near the latitude of Fairbanks, your first step is to check to see if permafrost is prevalent in the area. Permafrost is permanently frozen ground, typically below a forest of spindly spruce trees and spongy wet moss covering the ground.

Early old-timers knew about permafrost, and one of them warned Dick to be watching for it. Even after a lovely warm summer, the ground under the thick blanket of moss will only thaw down a few inches. They showed us pictures of beautiful homes around Fairbanks whose owners never hit gravel and built their homes there anyway. The heat from the house itself thawed the soil beneath them, and they would start to sink!

Dick had a long list of things to do before moving the log cabin from its temporary spot. The first thing was to dig a basement and create the foundation. When excavating in this area, the hope is that you will hit gravel when you reach six or seven feet. That means you should be able to build safely there, and your new construction will not sink.

Our new lot was full of spindly trees and spongy moss, which was not a great sign. We hired our neighbor Charles to clear the moss and spindly trees with his bulldozer. Then he started digging the hole for the new basement. He would shave off the frozen top layer of ground and return a few days later as the next few inches thawed to repeat the process.

In the meantime, Dick started the preparation for the second thing on the list: Pounding down a well! (Here comes the very detailed information I warned you about.)

He bought several five-foot lengths of heavy-duty two-inch water pipes, which were screwed together with couplings. He also purchased a well-point pipe, about five feet long, which looked different from the other pipes: It had screened holes all around it and a point at the end.

He got started on the first set with the coupling. Then he added another five-foot length. Now, he had a fifteen-foot length of pipe.

Next, he rigged up a tripod and hung the double pulley to the top of the tripod. He pulled one end of the rope through the pulley and brought the rope down to the pipe that had been installed.

Then, he attached the rope to the handle of a hefty concrete weight. Dick made the weight by pouring concrete into a two-gallon paint can. It had a two-inch hole from top to bottom, so the pipe could easily go through this heavy concrete weight. Dick cut out the bottom of the can after the concrete cured so the weight could slip over the pipe.

Picture the pipe assembly set up on the ground where Dick planned to pound down the well. This pipe assembly sticks UP above the ground.

Now picture Dick putting the concrete weight through the two-inch hole on the TOP of the pipe assembly. As noted above, the rope from the pulley was tied to a handle on the heavy concrete weight.

Dick had the other end of the rope coming down from the pulley, wound around twice, so he could control moving the heavy concrete weight by pulling down and up on the rope, making the concrete weight go down and up.

By controlling the rope, Dick could make the weight bang down on the coupling. This would drive down the pipe that was attached to the well-point pipe. He would keep pulling on the rope to make the heavy concrete weight bang on the coupling, driving the point even further into the ground.

What a tremendous job that was.

Dick was hoping to find water at about eight to ten feet. Unfortunately, he never had to screw more lengths onto the original pipe with the coupling. He hit permafrost every place on our property that he tried to pound down a well! He'd give up on that spot and set up the whole rig on another part of the property to try again.

Before long, he had set the rig up more than nine times, and each time, he hit permafrost and had to choose another location and begin again. Dick was getting discouraged.

He was eyeing a lot adjacent to our property. An extensive excavation had been started, and the lot was abandoned. The bottom of the excavated hole was already about eight feet deep. The property belonged to our good neighbor, Jack Bovee. Dick made a visit to Jack and told him about his problems in trying to pound down a well on our property. He told Jack he kept hitting permafrost and having to try again. He asked Jack for permission to try to pound a well at the bottom of that excavation on his vacant lot. Jack said yes!

Dick set up his tripod rig once more, dragging the pipes, pulley, and concrete weight down to the bottom of the hole. Once it was all set up, he started pounding. Suddenly, after pounding the well-point pipe down just two feet, he hit water!

Dick was overjoyed! He asked Jack if he would be willing to sell us that lot. We would be so happy to have a well on our own property. Jack agreed! This was a considerable task to mark off Dick's list. Dick arranged stones to walk up the mound around the well, and I finished it off by planting poppies and other perennials. Our wish for a well was granted!

Meanwhile, Charles continued to bulldoze what would become our basement. Finally, after four weeks and digging down over eight feet, Charles hit gravel! That was wonderful news. It meant it would be safe for us to build our home there. He continued to excavate the basement site.

After digging to the proper depth, he smoothed out the sand and gravel on the basement floor so it would be ready for the cement finisher to pour the floor. When he finished, Charles could drive the bulldozer up the ramp and out of that basement hole! Another job to tick off Dick's list!

The next project on the list was to dig a nine-foot-deep trench for a water pipeline that would run from our new well to the cabin's basement floor, more than 50 feet away. What a job that was!

When that was accomplished, we needed to build the septic system. We had to do some digging to construct a timber crib for drainage. The septic system had to have a four-inch sewer pipeline deep enough to go fifty feet away from the well to the level of the cabin's new basement floor.

My ability to help was limited for a short time when I got the mumps. Dick didn't think he had ever had the mumps, so we tried to isolate ourselves from each other in that small three-room cabin. He kept forging ahead, knowing that winter was coming. Thankfully, he didn't get the mumps!

It was time to start laying blocks for the new basement walls. Dick put in an order for a truckload of cement blocks with Fairbanks Block Company. Each block cost seventy cents. He and I had briefly attempted to make them ourselves, but time was of the essence, and that would have to wait. He hired a young fellow who said he had considerable block-laying experience and started the work. Sadly, when Dick checked out what he'd done at the end of the first day, he discovered that the wall was listing inward two inches in the first few courses. Dick had to quickly remove all of the blocks except for the bottom course before they hardened in place. He scraped off the cement to salvage those blocks. He had to let that young man go and was back at square one.

Then Dick met a truly experienced contractor, Ancel Johnson. Dick hired him to finish laying the concrete blocks for the basement walls. We liked Ancel. He was honest and trustworthy. We became friends with his wife and family. Their darling daughter, Wyan, attended Denali and was one of my students. The small basement measured 18' x 20', and Ancel finished the job perfectly in no time!

Next on the list was plumbing. Dick projected the location of all the basic plumbing needs in the new basement. He hired a professional plumber, Glen DeSpain, to install all the sewer and water lines on the basement floor and the plumbing up to the cabin's main floor. Glen did an excellent job for us, and we enjoyed his family, too. After Glen finished the plumbing, the final project on the list was to pour the basement's concrete floor. We got it done!

Warm summer days were precious, and chilly fall days were coming. We were grateful and relieved that we had finished everything on our list by the end of summer!

This concludes my notes on Dick's detailed instructions for that summer's list. They may serve to encourage (or even discourage) my readers to take on projects like these. I understand the mixed-feeling sentiment completely.

Every once in a while, working so many hours every day that summer, we thought about our friends who were buying homes in the newly established Westgate Subdivision. Their homes were lovely. All they had to do was sign the mortgage papers, pick up their keys, and move into their finished home! Instead of working on building projects on weekends, they headed out to Harding Lake and relaxed. I'll admit, we were tempted!

But we weren't ready to sign mortgage papers, and we liked the idea of working together to build our home on a few acres of land in the country.

I was a farm girl. I loved land, and I dreamed of having a horse or two. As a California boy, if not his beachside hamburger stand, Dick still had dreams of building a swimming pool! But we didn't have time for dreaming at that point in our adventure together. Winter was coming. Dick was already making plans for the next crucial project: Moving our little log cabin onto the newly built concrete block basement.

CHAPTER 31

ARMISTICE DAY, A TRUCK WITH A WINCH, AND A TRICKY TWENTY FEET

The first story Dick and I had fun recalling that winter 2019 was this one detailing how he and his friend Rob Hall had moved our little log cabin onto the new basement foundation at Three-Mile College Road and Caribou Way. I had Dick read what I'd written to be sure I had correctly recounted the facts. We googled "temperature in Fairbanks, Alaska on November 11th, 1954" and discovered that the high was twelve degrees above zero Fahrenheit, and the low was four above, with eight-mile-an-hour winds. What Rob and Dick did that chilly day

was miraculous. I'm happy to share this story that I treasure;
Dick is here in spirit!

We had worked hard during the seven months leading up to November 11th, 1954. That was the day Dick and his friend Rob Hall chose to move our little log cabin onto its newly finished basement. They picked that day because it was Armistice Day and they both had the day off from work. At 12 degrees above zero, it was a lovely winter day in Fairbanks.

Rob and Dick were young, smart, and determined. They had carefully made their cabin-moving plans ahead of time, and they had everything they needed on hand that morning, completely organized.

Rob arrived with his WWII surplus truck with all-wheel drive and a heavy-duty winch on the front of the truck. While Dick and Rob were very familiar with everything a winch like that could do, neither of them had ever used one to move a cabin onto an open basement. But they had thought it out and believed they could.

Picture this: A little log cabin next to an open block basement. The blocks extended about one foot above the surrounding ground.

Dick and Rob rolled a hefty 22' timber across each end of the open concrete block basement. They spaced these two temporary timbers to line up with the three permanent timbers attached underneath the cabin that extended about a foot beyond the cabin's side walls. These timbers supported both the weight of the cabin and the floor.

In April 1954, when Bobby Mitchell set the cabin down on our lot, he showed Dick how to place the four hefty jacks on cedar blocks under each corner of the cabin.

Using these same hefty jacks, Dick and Rob raised the cabin to the height of the temporary timbers across the ends of the cabin.

The plan was to solidly brace the front wheels of the truck across the basement from the cabin. Once they successfully did this, they had to attach the cabin to the winch. They pulled on the winch cable and looped it completely around the cabin and hooked the cable onto itself.

Now that the winch's cable encircled the cabin, the challenging plan of pulling the cabin onto the open basement could be carried out.

The two temporary timbers served as tracks for the 2" diameter pipe rollers that were under the three permanent timbers. The truck's winch cable would pull the cabin on the rollers until it reached its destination of being safely placed on the top of the open basement.

All of these components were crucial and had to work together. Rob had control of the winch inside the truck, and Dick was following alongside, watching the cabin's movement carefully. The move was going smoothly. Suddenly, one roller stalled while the others rolled merrily on, and the cabin began to twist! That roller may have caught on something -- perhaps a knot in the timber.

The cabin gave a lurch. It pivoted around, dangerously out of control! Rob immediately spotted the trouble, and calmly reacted, stopped maneuvering the winch, and the cabin stood still. They assessed the situation, and together, worked to pry the rollers back to where they belonged so the cabin would be back on the right track to roll forward again. Rob and Dick realized how lucky they were that the cabin didn't fall in.

They had no more problems and soon the cabin was properly rolled into place over the basement, not into it!

The next step was to use Bobby's jacks to raise the cabin enough, corner by corner, to take the steel pipe rollers and the two temporary timbers out from underneath. It was a tricky maneuver to carefully slide each one out. When they finished that part of the job, they slowly lowered the cabin directly, again corner by corner a little at a time, onto the concrete block basement.

WHEW!

Dick and Rob had succeeded!

What was I doing when they were moving the little cabin onto the new foundation?

Well, I was working, too. I stayed *inside* the cabin baking bread and preparing dinner. Dick had left the long electric line hooked up during the twenty-foot move, so the kitchen stove and all the outlets worked. I *did* feel when the cabin lurched, but I wasn't concerned. I was sure that Dick and Rob had everything under control.

After the job was done, Rob drove his truck back home to his family, and Dick enjoyed the dinner and homemade bread I had prepared. It was a productive day!

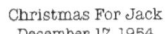

Christmas For Jack
December 17, 1954

Denali Elementary
Third Grade Class

CHAPTER 32

A Christmas Play, a Toy Soldier's Visit, and a Touching Reunion

I started writing a little Christmas operetta in the summer of 1954 for my third graders to present in December. My story allowed all 65 children to participate.

I called the show *Christmas For Jack*.

THE CAST: Besides the kind, elderly toy shop owner, Mrs. Hill, there were beautiful dolls and handsome toy soldiers. There were also customers, Christmas carolers, and a grumpy old jack-in-a-box.

THE PLOT: The kind, elderly toy shop owner, Mrs. Hill, didn't realize it, but every night when she closed her toy shop door, all the toys came to life.

I know this doesn't sound like an original theme, but my story ended with a fun twist that I think you'll like, so please read on!

The beautiful dolls and handsome toy soldiers danced and marched happily around the shop every night. They dreamed about being sold together and being under one big Christmas tree.

Jack, the very old, grumpy jack-in-a-box, didn't believe in Christmas. He found his joy by teasing the dolls and soldiers, and his song declared that no one would come to buy all of them.

Sadly, I have lost my original script and the songs that I wrote. I don't recall all the songs now, but I do remember Jack's teasing song:

> *I am a jack-in-a-box. I've never been sold.*
> *Nobody likes me, I'm shopworn and old.*
> *I've been around here many years. Listen to me:*
> *You'll never be under one big tree!*
> *Ha, Ha! Wait and see!*

One night, Jack was still wide awake when the dolls and toy soldiers were sound asleep. He heard singing from far, far away.

It kept coming closer and closer—until Jack could see carolers come right up to the toy shop's window. They saw Jack and began to sing directly to him!

Jack quietly listened to the words the carolers were singing. After he had heard their stories in song, he finally caught on to the true meaning of Christmas! Jack joyfully waved goodbye to the carolers and returned to sleep.

The next morning was the day before Christmas. Jack woke up happy for the first time in his life!

That morning, customers came filing into the toy shop. One customer was delighted to see so many beautiful dolls and handsome soldiers. She told Mrs. Hill she had a lovely orphanage for children and wanted to purchase ALL of them! The dolls and soldiers were elated that they really would all be under one big Christmas tree!

Then the customer saw Jack, who was SMILING.

Guess what?! She decided to purchase Jack, too!

And as if by magic, Jack began singing happily:

> *I am a jack-in-a-box! I have been sold!*
> *Everyone loves me, though shopworn and old.*
> *I've been around here many years. Listen to me:*
> *We'll all be under one big tree!*
> *Ha, Ha! Wait and see!*

Everyone was so happy. Mrs. Hill boxed up all the toys, and the orphanage owner sang happily all the way home.

THE END

of *Christmas for Jack*

Jack was played by a talented little boy named Kent Chandler, and Richard Gadbury played one of the handsome toy soldiers.

It was a cold week in Fairbanks, with temperatures reaching forty-five below zero. The Gadbury family lived on their homestead beyond the town of North Pole. It was at least twenty miles from the school. Richard's mother told me that they wouldn't be able to get him to the performance because of the long night time drive in the bitter cold.

Richard had a beautiful singing voice, and I wanted him to be able to be in the show.

I told Mrs. Gadbury this, and offered to have Richard stay with Dick and me the night of performance. She was happy he could still be in the play and said it would be fine.

The children performed beautifully, and the crowd loved the musical story. Richard came home with us after the show. He was a smart, polite, and talented child, and we loved having him as our first overnight guest. We made him a little bed on the davenport.

Like his parents, we had no running water or indoor bathroom. Since we had no heating system, I had to keep adding wood to our enameled parlor stove throughout the night.

Richard felt right at home. That's what his parents had to do, too!

A touching follow-up to this story from many years later, in the summer of 1999. I needed a new self-propelled lawn mower, so I picked one out at our local John Deere store, Craig Taylor Equipment Company.

Imagine my surprise when I was checking out and saw the clerk's name tag, Richard Gadbury. I hadn't seen Richard since 1954 when he was a handsome toy soldier in my little operetta, *Christmas For Jack*.

Richard told me he was the manager of the store. He had fun memories of being in the play. We were happy to have found each other again after so many years.

Later that summer, I heard that Richard was very ill. He'd had to quit his job, and his family cared for him in their North Pole home. I called Richard's wife, and we arranged a time when Dick and I could visit him.

Indeed, Richard was very ill, but he had a positive spirit and was happy to see us. We reminisced about the time he had stayed with Dick and me after the 1954 performance of *Christmas For Jack*. We enjoyed a wonderful afternoon together.

Sadly, a few days after our visit, Richard passed away at the young age of 52. I treasure the memory of seeing my handsome toy soldier again.

CHAPTER 33

A Retiring Angel, a Modernized Cabin, and a Visit from Mother

With the cabin finally moved onto its new concrete block basement foundation, Dick knew he had to get the plumbing and heating systems completed as soon as possible. Our first baby was on the way, and we needed to modernize our little cabin before the arrival.

Until this time, the cabin was heated by a porcelain enameled parlor stove that burned coal and wood. It was rather attractive and quite efficient. It even had a stack robber in the chimney with a fan that blew warm air into the room.

However, no one was home during the daytime to keep the fire going, so we would come home from work to a very cold cabin. I remember times when I couldn't scrub the kitchen floor because the floor was below freezing and it would ice up.

Dick had various projects that needed to get done, but the priority now was heating the cabin. Dick was resourceful and smart. Once again, many long-time Fairbanks contractors were happy to help him learn how to do the work that needed to be done.

Dick became acquainted with a dear older plumbing and heating contractor, Booker T. Baggett. Mr. Baggett was trying to retire, so he hesitated to officially take on working with Dick to install our cabin's heating system. But Mr. Baggett admired Dick's ambition and offered to just give his time to help guide him through the various steps of installing the heating system. He became our retiring angel!

Dick bought a new boiler connected to a fire pit. It had large cast iron water heating passages. Dick read ads in the *Fairbanks Daily News-Miner*, and he found a used Iron Fireman coal stoker in good condition at a price we could afford. Mr. Baggett gave excellent directions regarding how to get the stoker and boiler system up and running. The stoker had an auger in a steel tube, which would turn and bring coal and air from the outside coal bin to the fire pit.

Mr. Baggett's guidance was a generous gift. Dick would often call on Mr. Baggett for help on nights and weekends. He was always available. He never came over to guide Dick's work in person but explained things so well over the phone that Dick successfully caught on to all he was directed to do.

Dick built a coal bin outside the end of the basement adjacent to the furnace room with the stoker and the boiler. We had a small utility trailer which Dick loaded up at the coal yards on Illinois Street. The coal came from the Usibelli Coal Mine in Healy, near Mount McKinley. It was a very soft coal, but it worked. Dick would pull the trailer home with his car and shovel it from the little trailer into the coal bin. WOW! Lots of muscle-building work went into heating that little log cabin. In earlier days, not only did he have to shovel the coal into the coal bin, but he would have to then shovel it into the fire pit. It was life-changing to have the stoker's auger automatically do that job for him!

This heating system came together in the spring of 1955. Mr. Baggett explained how to install finned baseboard heaters around the floor of the outer walls of the cabin's interior. A small pump controlled by the living room thermostat circulated hot water from the boiler in the basement through the baseboard heaters. Copper piping needed to be soldered together to connect the baseboard heaters with the heated water from the boiler in the basement. Glen DeSpain taught Dick how to solder the piping. It took some skill to do the job correctly, but Dick became a pro at soldering.

When it was all done, we could set the thermostat on our living room wall to our desired temperature, and the stoker's auger would automatically start working and raise the temperature in the room. That was amazing and magical!

Occasionally, a rock or something would be included in the coal. The auger couldn't handle those things and would shear the pin. So, Dick had to learn how to fix that, as he had to learn how to fix many things.

Dick built a roof on the coal bin to keep out the rain and snow. However, there were times when the coal's top layer got wet, and that moisture would freeze.

Imagine this: The auger kept feeding coal from the outside coal bin to the boiler's fire pit. If some top coal had gotten wet and had frozen, it would make a frozen bridge of coal over the auger. When no more loose coal was on the auger, the fire would go out, and the cabin would get cold.

When that happened, poor Dick would have to crawl down into the coal bin and jump up and down to break up the bridge of frozen coal. When the auger was free of the ice bridge, Dick would hear a loud WHOMP, which meant the auger was ready to work again. This was not a fun thing to do on a cold winter night. But he did it, and the house would magically begin to warm up again.

What else did Dick do to modernize our little home that winter? Lots!

He hooked up the plumbing so we would have running water in the house. He installed a toilet in the cabin's tiny closet. He insulated the spaces around the cabin between the log frame and the concrete blocks. He built a flight of stairs to the lower level to replace the trapdoor and ladder we'd used until then. And finally, he helped me paint the kitchen cupboards! WHEW!

We were happy with the result of all of his work: a modern cabin with heat, running water, and indoor plumbing, ready for company and a new baby!

My mother, Ruth Ryman, arrived the second week of June 1955 for the birth of our little Julia Ruth, her namesake. She had seen pictures, but this was her first visit to Alaska. She was amazed at all Dick had accomplished in a little over a year. I was amazed, too, and I was very proud of him. It was a joyous time for us.

In later years, when friends asked me if I liked to go camping, I would explain that I had already done all the camp-style living I ever wanted to during the year we had lived in our little dry cabin.

Jo Ryman Scott

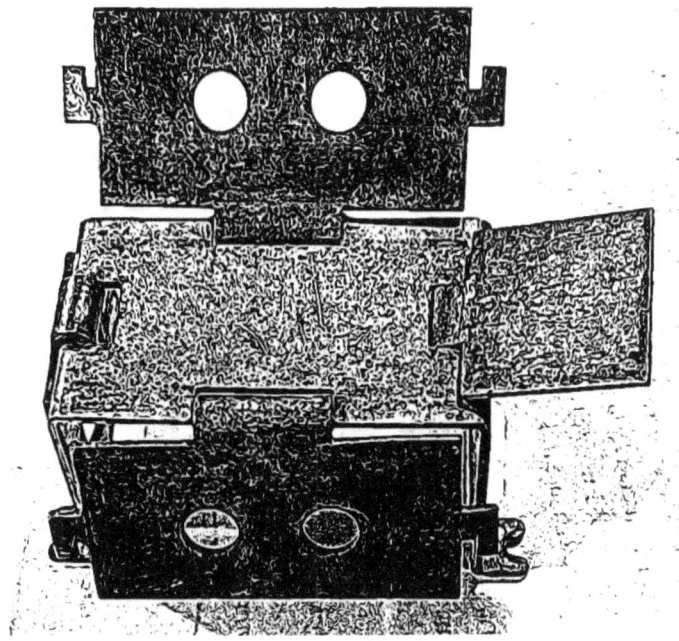

CHAPTER 34

SAND, CEMENT, AND BLOCK-MAKING 101

I always liked Dick's creative spirit. I was a good organizer, and we made a good team. He thought up the creative things to do, and I kept things organized until we completed them.

During that first summer in our little log cabin in 1954, Dick had the idea in his head that we could make our own concrete blocks for the basement foundation. He found a fellow with a used mold who had given up trying to make his own blocks. The fellow practically gave the mold to Dick while asking him if he was sure that he wanted it. But Dick, ever the optimist, looked at the potential project as an interesting challenge.

When he brought the mold home, we got right to work. We started making blocks using sifted sand from our basement and a bag of cement. The fellow was right; it was very labor-intensive. We had many more urgent things to do that summer, so we gave up as the fellow had, and placed an order for blocks with the Fairbanks Block Company. We carefully washed down the old mold and put it in a corner of the garage.

Two summers later, in 1956, we got our nerve up to try again. This time, we were intent on succeeding. We wanted to finish the basement extension project we had started and would need hundreds of cement blocks.

Our cement block-making center was a few feet from our cabin's back door. Dick bought a long water hose with an on/off attachment to run water from the outdoor faucet. He purchased a cement mixer from his good friend, Paul Baker, and set it up next to a pair of sawhorses with a large piece of plywood on top. This made a perfect surface for a pile of sand and the bags of cement.

We splurged on commercial sand this time, and the Fairbanks Block Company delivered it, along with ten forty-pound bags of cement. We were committed! With this setup, Dick could easily measure the right recipe of sand, cement, and water to put into the mixer and make the mud. Then he could dump the mud from there onto the plywood again. He placed the mold alongside, and I used a short-handled shovel to fill the mold with mud. My job was to firmly pack the mud into the mold. I used a stick to try to pack it down.

This was hard for me to do.

We were about ready to give up again when Dick happened to interview a cement finisher at the Employment Service where he worked. Dick shared that we were trying to make our own concrete blocks. He told him I was using a stick to compact the mud into the mold.

Dick explained that that concrete block mold was built into a sturdy metal frame. The man listened intently and finally said, "What you need to do is hook up a vibrator on the bottom of the mold's frame." He further explained, "When your wife puts the mud in the mold, all she has to do is turn on the switch to the vibrator, and it will instantly compact the mud as she adds it. After she turns it off, she just has to smooth off the top of the block."

Now it was Dick who was listening intently! He sincerely thanked his new friend and understood what he had to do. (Dick was able to help him find a job, too.) Dick was so excited when he came home from work that day. He immediately got busy.

Somehow, he had everything he needed in our garage to construct a vibrator assembly, and he attached it under the base of the mold, just like his new friend had told him to do.

The next morning, we tried it out, and it worked like a charm! Now, we felt energized to get busy mass-producing as many blocks as we could. We carefully thought it out. Each cement block we made needed a wooden pallet to hold it while it cured.

We figured we would have the energy to make fifty blocks at a time, so Dick sawed up fifty plywood pallets. We set up beams that could accommodate fifty blocks, each on its own pallet. When I would put the sides of the mold up to begin a block, I would place a pallet in the bottom, fill it with mud, and turn on the vibrator.

I would keep on adding more mud to the mold until it was full, and the mud was firmly compacted. I used the side of a stick to smooth off the top of the block and would yell, "OK!" so Dick could hear me over the sound of the cement mixer, where he was busy mixing the next batch of mud. He'd come and carefully release the sides of the mold. Then, he'd carry the finished block on its pallet over to the beam to cure.

We had quite a system and were excited with our success.

Dick had the block company test our blocks to be sure they were as strong as the ones they sold. Our blocks got an A+ rating! We started making blocks at around five a.m. a couple of mornings a week before Dick went to work.

My job during the day would be to spray the new blocks with water often so they would cure properly. Not counting our labor, we could make blocks for about seventeen cents apiece. If we bought blocks commercially, each block would cost seventy cents. It was worth our time to make them!

One beautiful morning when we had just finished making that day's fifty blocks, and they were all lined up on the beam, a Fairbanks Block Company truck rolled down the driveway with the next order of cement.

The delivery man got down from the cab and stared with amazement at our setup and the beautiful blocks lined up on the beam. "MY GAWD! I heard you guys were doing this, but I didn't believe it!" This gave us a chuckle. He must have shared this with others because the story made its way around town.

Overall, we had a wonderful experience making our concrete blocks that summer. We worked hard, but we saved money. We calculated that we made over five hundred cement blocks. They were used in the addition to the original basement and in the sunken Japanese garden I was creating at the end of the basement, with its windows giving light to the lower level.

Someone who'd heard about our setup came over, wanting to buy the concrete mixer, block mold, and pallets. Not only did we sell them everything, but we also gave them all the

Block-Making 101 directions with all of the hints we had learned along the way. They took it all happily.

CHAPTER 35

A Tarmac Sprint, a '56 Chevy, and a Five Thousand Mile Trek

In the middle of that block-making summer, baby Julie and I traveled by plane and train to South Dakota to visit family and friends. Dick would join us there ten days later.

To keep up the cement block production, Dick hired two college boys to help him make a batch of fifty concrete blocks. That was when Dick realized that the two of us could make concrete blocks faster than he could with two college boys!

Dick closed up our little cement block factory before his trip, washing down the cement mixer, the block mold and the plywood mixing table thoroughly. He arranged for a friend to come by every day for a week to sprinkle water on the last batch of newly made blocks so they would cure properly. Finally, he was ready to pack his suitcase.

Dick was late getting to the airport the morning of his flight and was rushing to get into the small Fairbanks terminal.

The gate agent saw him coming and checked him off the manifest; he was the only person missing on the flight. She told him the plane was about to take off, but he could run across the tarmac and try to get the pilot's attention to make the flight. In those days, there wasn't radio contact between the terminal and the plane so she couldn't alert the crew.

Dick ran as fast as he could across the tarmac and dashed up the airstairs. When he reached the top, the plane's door was closed!

Dick was not about to be left behind, and he pounded on the door of the plane. Miraculously, the door opened. Just then, a ramp guy ran over to roll the stairs away for takeoff. He made it! A gracious stewardess let him onboard, and Dick quickly took the first empty seat he saw. He made it to Seattle in time for his train connection to Aberdeen, where Julie and I were waiting for him.

This was the trip I mentioned in an earlier chapter when I had hoped to introduce my dear neighbor Julia Kienow to her namesake, our little Julie, who had just turned one before the trip. Sadly, Mrs. Kienow passed away shortly before we arrived. We were able to visit with her daughters, though, and that's when they gave Julie the antique mustache cup as a keepsake from their mother. Julie still has it.

Earlier that spring, Dick had pre-ordered a 1956 Chevy Bel Air from Lust Chevrolet in Aberdeen. When he arrived, we went to pick up our new car. It was a beautiful two-tone color scheme. They called it Grecian Gold/Calypso Cream.

It cost a little over two thousand dollars, and would replace the train and plane tickets for the trip back!

After visiting for a few more days in the Aberdeen area, Dick, Julie, and I drove our new car to California. It was over sixteen hundred miles, about twenty-four hours' worth of driving. We made a stop or two along the way.

Once there, we spent time with Dick's mother, Irene Scott, in Capistrano Beach. We took her to dinners and enjoyed being in her charming home, and meeting many of her friends.

We had another exciting visit to make, too.

After we were married, Dick had told me the story about finding his dad's address in the New York City phone book at the Fairbanks USO. He had lost touch after his folks divorced. He told me about writing a letter and even getting a cordial reply from his dad, but with no mention of a reunion. This touched me.

So after Julie was born, I encouraged Dick to write again to let him know he was a grandfather. Dick received another letter from his dad, and this time he was very much interested in seeing Dick again and meeting me and his baby granddaughter.

He told us he would be visiting friends in Capistrano in late July, so we arranged to visit him there while we were at Irene's. Dick and his dad saw each other for the first time in more than 20 years! It was an emotional visit. We called him Dad Fanelli.

The reunion with Dad Fanelli sparked many visits to New York City. We came to know and love his wife, who we lovingly called Auntie Florence.

We'd had a wonderful trip to see our families, and it was time to head back to Alaska. After the scenic drive up the coast through California, Oregon, and Washington, we continued north through Canada to the Alaska Highway.

We made it to Fairbanks without a single flat tire. We were happy to get back home. When we rolled into the garage, the new car's odometer read over five thousand miles!

CHAPTER 36

An Opportunity, a Challenge, and a Valentine Kiss

In the fall of 1956, I relished being a stay-at-home mom to our darling one-year-old daughter Julie. I loved being a wife, a mom, and a homemaker. I loved our little cabin with its cozy kitchen, small bedroom, tiny closet that housed the toilet, and combined dining and living room.

For the second year in a row, I was grateful we would go into winter in a modernized home! Though we had endured many challenges to get to that point, life in our little log cabin was a wonderful learning experience.

Our first gathering that fall was our Thanksgiving Day dinner with about twenty friends. They all marveled at all the work that Dick had done since Bobby Mitchell had moved the cabin from Six-Mile Richardson Highway to our lot on College Road in April 1954. We enjoyed a wonderful day together.

The next day when Dick and I were nibbling on leftovers, the phone rang. It was my school superintendent, Dr. Ryan. He asked if I would consider finishing that year's school term teaching English classes at the new Lathrop High School. He explained that the teacher was ill and had to quit. He wanted to fill that position as soon as possible. He knew I had a minor in English and hoped I would accept the opportunity to finish the school year.

Yes, I did have a minor in English, but I had never considered teaching high school English to juniors and seniors. Dr. Ryan believed in me and urged me to accept the offer. He thought I would enjoy my work with those students.

When he sensed that I might prefer to just substitute until a replacement could be found, he said he would try to find a permanent teacher by the next semester. When Dr. Ryan ended his phone call, he suggested that Dick and I discuss this new opportunity.

So, we did.

It so happened that just a few days before Dr. Ryan called, Dick heard that an acre of land adjoining our property on College Road was up for sale. I was a farm girl and loved the idea of more land!

The asking price of $2,200 was a good offer. That's about how much my salary would be if I took the teaching position at Lathrop.

I found a dear babysitter who would come to our home to look after Julie. With all this in mind, Dick and I agreed I should accept Dr. Ryan's offer.

I'll admit that I was a bit nervous when I went to school and met my students the following Monday.

However, I got my students to start sharing their life goals and what they hoped to get from my class, and my nervousness vanished. We all had a good time except for one student I'll call Dan, who didn't participate.

The rest of the students latched on to this dialogue, so I gave it to them as their first assignment: Go home and write about your life goals and what you hope to learn from this class with me. Everyone turned in their assignment except for Dan.

I was happy with the responses I did get. I read many interesting life stories, one of which was very sad. I shared that one with the school counselor, and she was able to have a meaningful conversation with the student and help him out as a result.

That assignment turned out to be an excellent idea. In addition to our classes in English Literature, my students wanted to zero in on developing their talent, leadership skills, and social skills, such as learning to get along with others.

I felt like I was helping every student except for Dan.

Dan liked me, but I knew I was failing to help him develop his talents and understand the importance of developing his social skills, specifically kindness to others.

Dan was bright and very good-looking, but he was cocky and believed he was always right, an egotist with little compassion for others. He liked playing hurtful pranks on the other students.

Dan did have some friends, but they all recognized his lack of kindness. I kept thinking about how I might get Dan to acknowledge his shortcomings while helping him realize his many talents.

By this time, all the students liked me, and at the end of the semester, Dr. Ryan was happy that I had the classes under control and that he didn't have to find a new teacher. I was even doing many things outside of class time that my students showed up for.

I invited the seniors to our home one Saturday. Everyone came but Dan. I introduced them to the story of the opera *Carmen*. Then, we listened to a recording of the opera using librettos to follow along with the words. We had a delightful time. I had cinnamon rolls baking in the oven, and they all had one before they left.

But I was still worried about Dan. I finally had an idea.

On Valentine's Day, as soon as the students were seated quietly, waiting for class to begin, I put on a dramatic air and said, "Good morning, class. In honor of Valentine's Day and showing our love for others, I want to tell you how much I appreciated your kindness when I took over as your teacher last fall. Now, to show my love for all of you, I will give each of you a great big kiss – and I will start with *you*, Dan!"

Now, picture this: Dan's desk was way in the back of the classroom. I started sauntering slowly toward his desk with outstretched arms.

At that moment, Dan's face turned all shades of red. For the first time, his aloof demeanor was stifled.

I stopped in front of Dan's desk and slowly reached into a bag I was carrying. I plucked out . . . a Hershey's Chocolate Kiss! I held it up, showed it to the class, and placed it in front of Dan.

The class roared with laughter.

I was thrilled to see that Dan was laughing, too. This time, he was on the receiving end of a joke, which was a new experience for him.

Fortunately, this little episode opened up the opportunity for us to communicate. I am happy to share that by the end of the school year, Dan began interacting more with others and became quite a thoughtful student. It just took a good-natured Valentine prank to get him moving in that direction.

I am also happy to share that by the end of the school year, we used my salary to purchase the acre of land next door that the farm girl in me had hoped for.

CHAPTER 37

AN EPIDEMIC,
A FAITHFUL TEAM,
AND A RADIO SHOW

My friendship with Jo Anne Wold began when I met her sister, Bonnie, in the fall of 1954. Bonnie was a fifth grader in my music class at Denali.

Bonnie's mother, Eleanor, was widowed in 1946. Her husband was a gold miner, and when he passed away, he left Eleanor with three darling little girls. Eleanor was constantly cheerful, optimistic, and helpful.

At school, I had heard about Bonnie's amazing older sister, Jo Anne.

In the fall of 1950, the Fairbanks community had been hit with a disastrous polio epidemic. It was so devastating that Fairbanks schools closed soon after the school year started that September.

Jo Anne was twelve years old at the time. She came down with a high fever. Eleanor feared the worst. Jo Anne complained to her mother that her whole body hurt.

The family doctor made a house call. When Dr. Weston saw Jo Anne, he immediately arranged for her to get to the hospital. She was having trouble breathing and was put on an iron lung. Eleanor's worst fear came to be: Jo Anne had polio.

She became completely paralyzed from her neck down, and the prognosis for her recovery was not good. She was not expected to live. They were told that if Jo Anne caught so much as a cold, her fragile body would not be able to recover.

With time, Jo Anne regained her ability to breathe but remained paralyzed. Eleanor cared for her at home once she was released from the hospital. Eleanor was determined to do all she could to help her precious daughter recover. She spent countless hours massaging Jo Anne's lifeless limbs, trying to bring living energy back into them again.

The Christian Science Church reached out to the family. Jo Anne enjoyed Bible study with a caring reader from the church, who would visit the home a few times a week. Through this, the family connected with church members Rosamond Weller and Mildred Nerland, and they became an important part of Jo Anne's life.

Jo Anne faithfully studied the Bible every morning. A creative solution was devised for her to turn pages by attaching a flat circle of rubber about the size of a quarter on a segment of hard plastic surgical tube, the size and shape of a pencil. On the other end, they slipped on a red school pencil eraser. She could bite down on the flat rubber end and manipulate the eraser end to turn the pages of a book. Jo Anne called it her *stick* and kept it in a glass on the desk of her wheelchair. It was an excellent invention because she loved to read. She literally wore out one Bible using her stick to turn the pages.

I was looking forward to meeting Jo Anne and had an idea of how I might help her. I arranged through Bonnie to visit Jo Anne and her mother in their log cabin home on First Avenue. I was immediately touched by the loving, kind, and joyful atmosphere in the Wold family's home. I was excited to share my idea.

In addition to my studies at the University of South Dakota in Vermillion in 1951, I volunteered for KUSD, the public radio station on campus. One of my duties each week was to arrange to have a qualified staff person drive recording equipment to the home of a young girl with polio who had become completely paralyzed.

That staff person's job was to record a week of five children's stories, which would be aired the following week on KUSD. Though I never met that young storyteller, I remember how much I enjoyed listening to her read her stories on the radio! I was touched to know about this young girl's life challenges.

Jo Anne was excited to hear that my idea was for *her* to become Fairbanks' story lady!

My next step was to reach out to the popular Don McCune, the general manager of local radio station KFAR. Don listened intently to my idea, and he liked it. I arranged for Don to visit the Wold home to meet this amazing girl and her caring mother.

Don immediately sensed the love in that family's home and listened to Jo Anne read a children's story that she had been practicing. She sounded like a pro already, and Don was impressed. He promised on the spot to do everything he could to help.

Don brought all the necessary recording equipment to their home and showed me how to use it. The best part was that he left the whole setup there, so I wouldn't have to transport it back and forth to the station. I arranged to go to Jo Anne's home once a week to record a story. I would deliver the tape to the station, and it would air the following week.

Don named the program *Jo Anne Wold and Her Magic Storybook.*

Don had a deep, rich, beautiful radio announcer voice and recorded an imaginative introduction to begin her program each week. It created the right mood to catch the children's attention. He included exciting background music and sound effects while he talked about adventuresome times and places. This was before television, and listeners could use their imaginations with the fun sounds. It was a perfect introduction to Jo Anne's stories each week, and her show caught on!

I would check out several children's story books from Denali's library, and Jo Anne would select her favorites to practice reading for the next recording session.

I arranged for *The Fairbanks Daily News-Miner* to run a story and picture which helped promote the show and also for Jo Anne to visit some Fairbanks schools so children could meet her. It was in the days before the Americans with Disabilities Act, so she couldn't visit many of them. Most had lots of steps and no elevator, which made it impossible to maneuver in a wheelchair. The children in the schools we did get to visit were delighted to put a face to the sweet voice they heard on the radio!

This was a happy time for Jo Anne. She got the story lady job at age sixteen. She was good at what she did and got paid for her work. I did the recordings with her for two school years. After our daughter Julie was born, I had my hands full. I taught Bonnie how to do the recording, and she took over my duties so *Jo Anne Wold and Her Magic Storybook* could continue.

Jo Ryman Scott

CHAPTER 38

A College Degree, an Innovative Genius, and a Book Deal

Besides doing her radio show, Jo Anne Wold completed her high school studies by taking correspondence classes. Polio kept Jo Anne from attending in person. The teachers and students tried to help her attend Lathrop, but she was in a wheelchair, and there was no elevator.

After graduating in the early 1960s, Jo Anne took writing classes at the University of Alaska Fairbanks. Jo Anne was grateful to two professors in the Journalism Department who were especially helpful to her: Jimmy Bedford and Chuck Keim.

Jo Anne was determined to become a writer. She devised a new adaptive tool to this end! Medical tape was wrapped around the lead end of an unsharpened pencil various times, leaving the eraser end intact. She could hold the taped end in her teeth and direct the eraser end to actually type the keys on a typewriter. It was extraordinary. It took a lot of patience, typing one letter at a time, but she became quite proficient. A Fairbanks service group gifted Jo Anne with a brand new Selectric typewriter. The action of the keys was so much lighter than her old one, and with the speedy rollerball head, the return key took a fraction of the time. The new technology made getting her ideas on paper even easier. This facilitated her UAF writing classes.

Around this time, Jo Anne's mother, Eleanor, married a gracious, kind man named Glen Buchanan. He loved the Wold family and was a blessing not only for Eleanor but also for Jo Anne and her sisters.

They had fun talking about going on a trip together, and one year, Glen, Eleanor, and Jo Anne spent eight glorious weeks traveling throughout Europe.

One of Jo Anne's favorite travel stories involved laboring over whether to purchase a charming little vase she found while shopping in Italy. After much deliberation, she finally decided to buy it. When she returned to Fairbanks, she saw the same vase at Nerland's Home Furnishings, at a lower price than she had paid. She continued to treasure her little Italian vase and delighted in telling this story!

When C. W. Snedden, the publisher of the *Fairbanks Daily News-Miner*, contacted Jo Anne and offered her a job editing the weekly women's section of the paper; she doubted that she could do the work.

Jo Anne credited her friend Kathleen "Mike" Dalton with encouraging her to take the job, showing her how to set the pages up journalistically and guiding her on story ideas. The *News-Miner* had a courier go to Jo Anne's home once a week to pick up her finished work, which would then be published the following week. It was a very popular section of the paper. Jo Anne was always grateful to Mike for helping her succeed at this job.

When our daughter Julie turned eight in 1963, Jo Anne was 25. She gave Julie a little birthday party with a fancy cake. Julie loved Jo Anne! She started spending some Saturdays helping her. Many tasks centered on Jo Anne's writing, such as putting paper in the typewriter, but she also did light housekeeping. The cozy cabin on First Avenue had simple furnishings with some exceptions. A Waterford crystal lamp was atop the claw-footed table in the front room. Julie was in awe of both and dusted them carefully, though she was scared of the claw feet that held onto glass balls.

Occasionally, Jo Anne would call Julie away from her dusting to ask her to erase a typo. Jo Anne typed her stories in duplicate or even triplicate. This involved using the round typewriter eraser to erase several copies carefully. Jo Anne would guide Julie to move the platen back to exactly where it was to continue typing. Amazingly, Jo Anne made very few typing mistakes. (Later on, Jo Anne would get a copying machine at home and be done with carbon paper!)

In addition to writing for the *News-Miner*, Jo Anne wrote and submitted stories for magazines and hoped to get a book published. Julie helped put the manuscripts into envelopes to mail to editors in hopes of publication. Sometimes, Jo Anne would send a query letter describing a story asking if they had any interest.

Jo Anne looked forward to the mailman's arrival. Julie would open the envelopes and lay the letters flat. Many of the letters were related to Jo Anne's writing. Jo Anne would read through them, pushing them aside with her *stick*. Some of these letters were negative responses, but every so often, they were positive, and an article would be published in a magazine with her byline!

In 1971, Jo Anne self-published *Fairbanks: The $200 Million Gold Rush Town - Historical Sketches* under Wold Press. As a softbound booklet, it was popular in Alaska gift shops, for residents and tourists alike.

Jo Anne was grateful to many people who helped her, especially in those years when she was trying to set up her home office for her writing. Her friend Rosamond Weller introduced her to a gentleman named Ed Parsons, who would change her life. Rosamond made him aware of Jo Anne's need for a unique phone system.

Parsons was well-known throughout Alaska and beyond as an electronics genius. He is best-known as one of the people credited with the invention of cable television in the 1940s! Among other things, he also worked with the Wien brothers to install the first radios for Wien Airlines.

Parsons generously volunteered his time to help Jo Anne by building a telephone system for her which included a speaker phone, the only one in Alaska at the time! Parsons sourced elements for the system, making it possible for Jo Anne to answer the phone by toggling a large switch with her *stick*. It was one of the first touch tone phones in the area. Once toggled on, she'd hear the dial tone and could switch to her typing pencil tool to actually dial a number to make a call. This ingenious phone system was a game-changer that made Jo Anne's day-to-day life more independent. She was deeply grateful to Ed Parsons.

Jo Anne lived her faith every day of her life. Many of us were inspired by her example of treating everyone with love, kindness, and respect. As Julie grew older and continued to work with Jo Anne, she was amazed at how organized and determined Jo Anne was in everything she did, including getting her first book published.

Gold City Girl is the story of a little girl's last summer in an Alaskan mining town before her family moves to Fairbanks. Jo Anne's dad had been a gold miner and she drew from her childhood experience.

Jo Anne had written *Gold City Girl* before the 1967 Fairbanks flood. She had submitted it to several publishers, but sadly, no one was interested. But Jo Anne didn't give up. She kept thinking that maybe the next time someone would like it.

When the devastating flood hit Fairbanks that summer, all of Jo Anne's papers were floating in the muddy waters that invaded their home on First Avenue near the overflowing Chena River. Jo Anne's stepfather, Glen, carefully scavenged through the contaminated water and miraculously found ALL of the pages of the *Gold City Girl* manuscript! He lovingly washed them all with a bleach solution and hung them up to dry.

After the pages had dried, Jo Anne retyped them once again, and sent *Gold City Girl* to another publisher, only to be turned down.

Then, when Jo Anne was about 30 years old, she met a lovely Fairbanks writer who had successfully published several children's books. Her name was Edythe Newell. Edythe liked Jo Anne's story and took a copy to her publisher, Albert Whitman & Company, on her next trip to Chicago.

Whitman liked it! *Gold City Girl* was published in 1972. She was on her way.

The Wold family's claw-footed antique table can be seen in the Wickersham House at Pioneer Park in Fairbanks.

CHAPTER 39

An Impromptu Meal, a Joyous Union, and More Book Deals

I continue to marvel at Jo Anne Wold's courage, faith, spirit, and determination. She was wise beyond her years. Many of us were inspired by how Jo Anne lived her faith. She had learned so much about love and kindness from her mother. Eleanor passed away in 1969, and Glen continued caring for Jo Anne in their new home on Third Avenue. Glen was a master baker and would leave for work at three each morning and return around noon to go to sleep. He arranged for friends to come throughout the day to help Jo Anne in the office and with cooking and cleaning.

When our daughter Shirley was in high school, she followed Julie's footsteps and started working with Jo Anne. The new house on Third Avenue had a lovely kitchen. Eleanor had been a fabulous cook and Jo Anne had a book of her mother's favorite recipes. Jo Anne had an amazing way of guiding people to help her. Shirley came home one day and exclaimed that Jo Anne had made the best barbecued ribs! Shirley didn't skip a beat in crediting Jo Anne with actually making the recipe.

After the success of *Gold City Girl*, Jo Anne's publisher, Albert Whitman & Company, published two children's books she had written: *Well, Why Didn't You Say So?* in 1975 and *Tell Them My Name Is Amanda in 1977.*

For over a year, every Thursday, a well-known Fairbanks pioneer, Clara Rust (1890-1978) would come to the house. Jo Anne was interviewing her for the next book she would publish. It was based on Clara's life as recorded in her journals and in the hundreds of hours of taped interviews Jo Anne pored over after their Thursday visits. In 1976, *This Old House: The Story of Clara Rust, Alaska Pioneer*, was published by Alaska Northwest Publishing Company. There was a well-attended book signing party honoring both Clara and Jo Anne. It was held at Harley Adamson and Paul Wagner's lovely Borealis Bookshop.

In 1981, the Tanana-Yukon Historical Society published *Wickersham: The Man at Home.* Judge Wickersham was an important personality in Alaska's early history.

Jo Anne was active in the community and was on the board of directors for the Fairbanks Concert Association. While Shirley was helping Jo Anne one cold November day, Jo Anne got a phone call from the president of the FCA frantically asking if Jo Anne knew of someone who could pick up members of the Chamber Music Society of Lincoln Center flying in from New York that afternoon. It was forty below zero outside, and the original volunteer had forgotten to plug in her car, and it wouldn't start.

The call was on Jo Anne's speakerphone system, which Ed Parsons had created. On overhearing the situation, Shirley started motioning to Jo Anne, pointing at herself and smiling. Having recently gotten her license, she had the family car that day and would be happy to go. Jo Anne passed this on, and the problem was solved. Shirley got assigned to pick up bassoonist Loren Glickman and his darling wife, Dobbie.

Shirley tried to give them the scenic if circuitous route from the airport to the Travelers Inn. She pointed out Alaskaland, now Pioneer Park. Then she headed to Cushman Street to be sure they saw the Fejes family's pretty log Alaska House Gallery and Judy Robertson Divinyi's Arctic Traveler's Gift Shop. At one point, Mr. Glickman asked, "When will we get to town?" To which she replied, "We've been through it three times!"

Mr. Glickman also asked if Shirley could suggest a rehearsal space for that evening. Shirley knew I wouldn't mind and she invited the group to our home to rehearse. Of course, I was happy to have them! The pianist especially enjoyed playing our 1892 Mason & Hamlin. I had been preparing a prime rib that day and a batch of my homemade dinner rolls and I invited them to stay for dinner. Everyone enjoyed a delightful time together, and the Glickmans became dear lifelong friends. All of this transpired because of Jo Anne.

Jo Anne enriched people's lives through her civic involvement and writing, which did not go unnoticed. Jo Anne received an honorary Doctorate from the University of Alaska Fairbanks in the spring of 1979. We all joined in celebrating that exciting occasion.

Not long after, Jo Anne started dating and fell in love with a kind and handsome man named Lee Schroer. One of the first gifts Lee gave Jo Anne was a word processor. This was a miraculous advancement for her writing, and especially editing. Lee would take Jo Anne on drives to the country and bring a picnic basket and a generator. Jo Anne could plug in the word processor and write in the fresh air under trees by a lake after sharing the meal Lee had made. Lee was one in a million!

Undoubtedly, one of the happiest days in Jo Anne's life was their wedding day on August 18th, 1979. Dick and I hosted the rehearsal dinner in our home the evening before the wedding. I got to see Jo Anne's sister, Bonnie, for the first time since the mid-fifties when I had taught her to take over recording Jo Anne's radio show. She and her husband lived in Florida.

The community was happy for Lee and Jo Anne. They enjoyed their life together, traveling and doing thoughtful things for others. They had a tradition of delivering their van full of gifts to friends on Christmas Eve.

Sadly, in October 1985, Jo Anne's fragile lungs could no longer function. Friends across Alaska joined Lee in mourning the loss of this amazing woman. She had lived a full life while reaching out with love to everyone she met. Jo Anne believed God's promise that we will all meet again. She was a treasured friend; I still miss her and think of her often.

Before she passed, Jo Anne was planning to publish a compilation of her stories that had been in her *Fairbanks Daily News-Miner* columns. She had written many thought-provoking and informative stories about Alaska pioneers who had made Fairbanks such an interesting place.

Dedicated friends of Jo Anne's finished gathering the *News-Miner* stories into a manuscript. In 1988, Northwest Publishing Company published *The Way It Was: Of People, Places, and Things in Pioneer Interior Alaska* posthumously.

Jo Anne was a great storyteller. People across the country continue to read and enjoy her books today!

A link to all of Jo Anne's books can be found in this chapter's Bonus Material.

The Wold family's First Avenue cabin and Judge Wickersham's frame home are now a permanent part of Pioneer Park's charming Gold Rush Town, which welcomes thousands of visitors a year. The cabin is now home to the delightful Frosty Paws Ice Cream shop.

CHAPTER 40

TRAILBLAZERS, SETTLERS, AND VISIONARIES

When I arrived in August 1953, Fairbanks was a small town. Fewer than 10,000 people lived within a 30-mile radius. Incorporated as a city in November 1903, it was only 50 years old. There were many trailblazers who had come before me. Here is a brief history of just a few of them.

LES AND MILDRED NERLAND

Les and Mildred were recognized as community leaders. Les's father had made the treacherous trip over the Chilkoot Pass, along with many who were looking to get rich by finding gold. But he wasn't interested in finding gold. He was interested in starting a business selling things to the miners who found it. That was the beginning of the Nerland's store.

Les and Mildred were married in 1926 and moved to Fairbanks in 1930. They were to manage the small home furnishings store for just a year while Les's parents traveled to Norway, but they liked Fairbanks so much that they wanted to make it their home and stayed.

Les gave time to help the state of Alaska. He was a delegate to the Alaska Constitutional Convention held on the UAF camps in the 1950s and served on the University Board of Regents. He was active in starting the Rotary Club of Fairbanks and devoted considerable time to the various Rotary projects over the years.

I met Mildred in the early 1960s through the P.E.O. Sisterhood, a philanthropic and educational organization that promotes education opportunities for women. I went to a meeting in the Nerland's beautiful home. Mildred, who was several years older, became my mentor. She was a gracious hostess with a caring personality. I learned so much from her.

DR. JAMES C. RYAN

Dr. Ryan was the school superintendent who had urged me to choose Fairbanks when I had offers to teach throughout Alaska. He had been a longtime educator there. He and his wife, Irice, became like family, and he even walked me down the aisle on my wedding day. Dr. Ryan retired from the Fairbanks School District in 1961, and I was sad when they moved away. In 1969, I was happy to have them return for a joyful dedication ceremony naming Ryan Junior High School in his honor.

Dr. Ernest N. Patty

Dr. Patty became the third president of the University of Alaska in 1953, but he was no stranger to Alaska and the University.

He was one of the first faculty members of Alaska Agricultural College and School of Mines in 1922. He taught geology and mining. The college's name was changed to the University of Alaska in 1935.

Dr. Patty did considerable work to develop the campus's growth over the seven years he served as president. The Patty Gym on the UAF campus is named in his honor.

Art and Dorothy Loftus

Art and Dorothy matriculated to the brand-new Alaska Agricultural College and School of Mines in 1922, when the school's only building, Old Main, was completed. There were six students and seven faculty members. Art and Dorothy left Fairbanks after graduation but often returned to visit in the summer. They had made many friends in Fairbanks and were active in the community.

Dorothy was a longtime member of my Fairbanks Chapter of P.E.O.

Lydia Fohn-Hansen

Lydia was teaching Home Economics in Iowa in the summer of 1925. She saw a notice on the school's bulletin board saying that Dr. Charles Bunnell, president of the new College in Fairbanks, Alaska, would be interviewing at her school, hoping to find a Home Economics teacher who would like to teach in Alaska.

Lydia interviewed and was hired! In 1925, she set off to this new college. Part of her job description was to teach classes along the Alaska Railroad. She also set up 4-H clubs and became a Home Demonstration Agent. Many of her interesting stories are documented online.

LOLA CREMEANS TILLY

Lola came from Illinois to the new college in Fairbanks in 1929 to work with Lydia to set up the Home Economics department. All was going well with their work until 1937 when Lola became engaged to marry Gray Tilly. She was told that she would have to resign from her University job. What might surprise my younger readers is that, in those days, married women were not allowed to teach in public schools!

This rule remained in effect until 1942 when there was a shortage of teachers due to World War II. At that time, Lola was allowed to return to her teaching position.

C. RUSTY HEURLIN

Rusty was born in Sweden and first came to Alaska in 1916. He left to travel the world and returned to Alaska in 1935. He made a life with his wife Ann in their charming log home in Ester, a small mining community 10 miles from Fairbanks. He had a studio on the property where he painted, which was large enough to accommodate his immense canvasses.

In 1950, Rusty taught painting at the University of Alaska in Fairbanks. Several local artists, including Arlene Darling and Bonnie Reem, studied with him.

Rusty's *Big Stampede* presentation is an amazing 45-minute show in the museum at Pioneer Park that continues today. It showcases many of his strikingly large paintings depicting the Alaska gold rush and the grueling trip over the Chilkoot Pass. The seating is on a rotating platform. The first enormous canvas is illuminated while the story narration begins. Then, the entire seating platform slowly circles on to the next painting, and the story continues.

Pioneer Park, then called A-67, was underwater during the 1967 flood. Miraculously, the flood waters didn't reach the height of the bottom of Rusty's paintings, and they were completely unharmed. On my last trip to Fairbanks, I took visitors to see the show. It was the first time I'd seen it in decades and it was as thrilling as ever!

PAUL AND MARGE HAGGLAND

In August 1939, Dr. Haggland, his wife Marge, and their young twin sons left their home in Seattle and moved to Fairbanks, where the Fairbanks Clinic had hired him for a one-year contract. The Haggland family liked Fairbanks, so they stayed and made it their home. Dr. Haggland became everyone's family doctor.

I became acquainted with Marge through P.E.O. At one of our meetings in the early 1960s, Marge shared stories about the interesting Russian pilots in the 1940s who had stopovers in Fairbanks on their way back to Russia. It was part of the Land Lease Program established in 1941, where the planes would stop to refuel in Fairbanks. I wish we had taped her stories!

JEWELL BOSWELL

Jewell moved to Fairbanks in 1940 when she was 27. Her husband, John, had worked for the Fairbanks Exploration Company for decades.

Jewell was a classically trained violinist. In the 1940s and 1950s, she and violinist Joe Fejes worked hard to gather enough musicians to create a chamber orchestra.

Finally, in 1969, the UAF hired conductor Gordon Wright to work in the growing Music Department. Gordon established the Fairbanks Symphony Orchestra and the

Arctic Chamber Orchestra, a touring arm of the Symphony. Jewell and Joe played in both of these through the 1970s.

JOE AND CLAIRE FEJES

Joe and Claire were married in New York City in 1942 and moved to Fairbanks in 1946. Joe was out of the service and decided to take up gold mining in the Fairbanks area.

Claire had grown up in New York City during the Great Depression. She studied at the famous Art Students League on West 57th Street. She was a sculptor at the time. After they moved to Fairbanks, Claire started painting Alaska Natives. She went to several villages to get a feeling of their lives for her art and for the books she wrote. Claire and Joe opened a beautiful art gallery, The Alaska House, in a lovely log building on Cushman Street. Her painting *Drummers of Point Hope* was featured on a Fairbanks Summer Arts Festival poster.

The documentary film *Alaskan Artist, Claire Fejes* was created for public television in 2002. It was first aired on PBS KUAC and is still available to view online. It traces Claire's remarkable life and her extended visits to Alaska's remote Native villages.

The link to view this historic film can be found in this chapter's Bonus Media.

NEVILLE ABBOTT JACOBS

Neville is a lifelong Alaskan artist and author known for her world travels. She and Claire Fejes often went on road trips, stopping to paint when something just right came into view.

Her painting *Northern Lights* was featured on a Fairbanks Summer Arts Festival poster. Neville's most recent book,

The Master of the Mountain, includes memories of her studies in Tibet.

JOHN AND EDITH HOLM

John and Edith left Minnesota and came to Fairbanks to homestead in the 1940s. I met them through their young son, Jim, my fourth grade music student in 1954. Jim surprised me on the first day of class when he sang. What a thrill to find a child with such a beautiful singing voice!

I'd already heard about his parents' musical talents. Edith had a lovely singing voice, and John was a talented accompanist. I asked if they would give a mini concert for the Denali students. Wow! They knew just the right songs to perform! The children loved them. (I still remember the song about a dragon!) Their mini concert was a huge success.

They established one of the first greenhouses in town on College Road in the 1960s. It was about a mile from our place, and I loved going there to shop and get Alaska-specific gardening advice.

Jim continued to please crowds with his voice and acting, performing with many theatre groups as he got older. John and Edith brought music and gardening joy to all of Fairbanks.

EDNA GARBERG

Eddie first came from Wisconsin to Palmer, Alaska, to visit the Matanuska Valley Colony, established during the 1935 New Deal. Wisconsin farmers had relocated here, and she took a year's sabbatical from her Wisconsin teaching job to find out how the project was going and report back to Wisconsin.

She stayed in Alaska for a year, returned to Wisconsin to make her report, and then, as soon as she could, came back to Alaska to pursue her teaching career in Palmer, Kodiak Island, and finally, Fairbanks.

She was a dedicated teacher, and the students loved her. Eddie was an active member of P.E.O. She became a part of our family. Our children called her Aunt Eddie.

SHIRLEY CALNAN SWANGER

Shirley came to Fairbanks to teach in 1950. She was a cute little redhead with a sparkling personality and was one of the first people I met in Fairbanks. Besides directing church choirs, Shirley was Fairbanks' sole instrumental music teacher, walking to the different schools daily. She introduced Dick to me and was my maid of honor. We named our daughter Shirley after her.

She left Fairbanks in the 1970s to teach in Germany. There, she met her husband Gene, and they had a darling little girl they named Kim. Julie and I toured Europe in 1974 and enjoyed seeing Shirley's family in Wiesbaden. She was a wonderful friend, and our children called her Aunt Shirley.

These are just a few of so many movers and shakers who did so much for Fairbanks in the years before I arrived. Later in the book, you will hear about more innovators who impacted Fairbanks after I arrived.

CHAPTER 41

A GROWING FAMILY, A NEW OPPORTUNITY AND A MUSICAL NURSERY SCHOOL

In November 1957, Alaska was still a Territory, Sputnik was circling the earth, and Dick and I were celebrating the birth of our son, Bryan.

Though Dick enjoyed his work at the Alaska Territorial Employment Agency, there weren't any opportunities for advancement. An interesting opportunity came in the summer of 1958. Our auto and home insurance agent, Ken Murray, Sr., came by to see us.

Aetna Life Insurance Company, out of Hartford, Connecticut, had contacted him to see if he knew any intelligent young men or women in Fairbanks who would be interested in training for life insurance sales. Ken recognized Dick's potential, and he said he thought that this might be a good opportunity. The company would fly Dick to the Hartford and Seattle offices for training, and Dick would have office space with Ken.

Dick and I talked about this opportunity, and we were pleased that Ken believed in Dick. He gave his notice to the employment agency and began studying for the courses he would be taking for Aetna Life.

After the training trips to Seattle and Hartford, Dick passed all the required tests and set up his office at Ken's agency in the Nerland Building on Second Avenue.

We have always been grateful to Ken for all he did to help Dick get started in the insurance business. Dick found his place in life by helping his clients provide for their families and their futures.

Along with his new job, Dick continued working with me to make our house a home. Though we were on a tight budget, Dick and I agreed that I would stay home with our children and give piano lessons there on Saturdays for extra earnings. I arranged to have my 5' Wurlitzer grand piano shipped up from my parent's home in South Dakota.

Dick and I had worked steadily to have all our bedrooms completed in the lower level of our home, so our former bedroom on the main level of the cabin became the new piano room! We put down carpeting, and I painted and made some lovely curtains.

I loved teaching piano lessons, and soon, I had a full schedule of students coming to our home each Saturday.

Bryan and Julie enjoyed their new bedroom/playroom Dick had finished for them on our lower level. They had many children's records, a record player, books, and toys.

There was a charming little picnic table for schoolwork and snacks. They were excited on Saturdays because they loved their babysitter, our neighbor Renee Farsdahl, who would come while I was teaching piano. She did lots of singing, storytelling, and artwork with Julie and Bryan, and they had fun.

When Shirley was born in St. Joseph's Hospital, new mothers and their babies stayed as inpatients for at least a week. That week, Julie and Bryan went to stay with Rob and Suzy Hall and their children, Jenny, Sarah, John, Felicity, and Louie. They lived in a charming log home on Illinois Street, which was not far from the hospital. The Halls had become our family's dear friends. Suzy was so good with the children; they all had a good time together that week.

We were active in the University Community Presbyterian Church (UCPC). I directed the church choir, and Dick was in my baritone section. I also compiled the church's monthly newsletter and taught Sunday School.

In the fall of 1962, I was offered a position in the school system, but Dick and I again agreed that I would stay home with our children instead of accepting. I dreamed of starting a musical nursery school to continue teaching and still be with my younger children when they were little. Julie was already in school, but I liked the idea because Bryan and Shirley could attend.

UCPC had just built their beautiful new Christian Education Building, and because I was giving so much time to the church's work, the Session permitted me to use one of the rooms in the beautiful new building for my new preschool.

I had been teaching in public schools for several years, so I knew many families, and my classes filled up quickly.

I called it Jo Scott's Musical Nursery School. I started it in 1962, seven years before *Sesame Street* began.

It was not a daycare! I played lots of reading readiness games with the children because I knew they could learn through these without pressure. I created interesting, colorful surroundings of books and pictures to stimulate the interests of my little students. I had the kids around me on the floor and used an autoharp for our singing circle. I had a lovely teacher, Jean Gordon, come in for an hour a day to teach art and French.

I had interesting people come in as guests; many were my students' parents, some originally from other countries. They would share their cultural traditions with the children.

Parents of two different students happened to be from Mexico and brought in all the materials needed to make piñatas and did so right before their eyes! I was very appreciative to Mrs. Cross and Mrs. Dickerson; we were all fascinated with the process. One looked like a big slice of watermelon when they finished, and the other a carrot! They brought wrapped candies to fill it and a decorated stick for the children to take turns trying to break it open. We attached the finished piñata to another longer stick, and held it up high in the middle of the room. (It was pretty heavy!) They sang the traditional piñata song as each child put on a blindfold and to take their turn:

> *See the gay piñata*
> *Hanging high above you*
> *Swing until you find it*
> *Swing and break it open!*

I had taught them how to count in Spanish, so at the song's end, they counted their swings: *Uno! Dos! Tres!* When it broke, the children scrambled to pick up the fallen candies. It was fun for them to learn about this Mexican tradition.

I operated the school through May 1968. I passed it on to a dear friend, Ruth Van Veldhuizen, who kept it going. It was a fun and fulfilling endeavor.

My in-home piano students in 1964 were: The Mitchell twins, Judy and Jan, Nancy Wellman, Bonnie Lundell, Lee and Barbara DeSpain, Laurel Baggen, Jill Baggen, Nancy Linck, Peggy Plowman, Phyllis Cashen, Jane Haycraft, and Kristi Ana Byrd.

My Musical Nursery School students in 1964 were: he Hessin twins Lynn and Lori, Cully and Erika Benson, Terry and Ann DeVries, Peter and Thomas VanFlein, Scott and Linda Redman, Bobbi Doner, Eric and Sonja Krejci, Tracy and Abbie Johnson, Crystal Bovee, Arun Sharma, Elizabeth Dugdale Alexander, Marilyn Childers, Colleen Murphy, Sonja Rosenberg, Peggy Klein, Jennifer Brice and some other Brice children, ` Sarah Peyton, Michael Romick, Kim and Leslie Wien, Lori and John Nerland, and Marilee Binkley.

Jo Ryman Scott

CHAPTER 42

A RENAULT, A GREASE GUN, AND AN INTREPID ROAD TRIP

It all happened during the summer of 1964. Some of my friends were making plans to drive to the lower 48 to visit their families and friends.

That sounded like a good idea to me. My parents lived in Aberdeen, South Dakota and my sisters, Jean and Alice, lived on farms nearby. That was about 3,000 miles from our home in Fairbanks, Alaska. Flying there with our three children would be costly.

So, I talked to Dick about driving one of our small Renaults to South Dakota. Unfortunately, Dick couldn't make the trip because he couldn't take the time off from work. We had both driven the Alaska and Canadian Highways before, so it didn't seem like it would be difficult for me to do by myself.

At this point we brought the children into the discussion. We got the maps needed for traveling from Fairbanks to Aberdeen. Julie, Bryan, and Shirley looked at the maps, too, and they were excited about the trip. Bryan looked forward to riding tractors on Uncle Vernon and Uncle Harley's farms, while Julie and Shirley looked forward to seeing their cousins, Anne, Beth, Evelyn, and Karen.

Dick and I each had 4CV rear-wheel-drive Renault Dauphines. Dick got mine all tuned up for the trip. He taught me how to change a tire, check the oil, and use a grease gun to lubricate the bearings every day.

We got our suitcases packed and Dick took our picture. Then we piled into the car and waved good-by as we went on our way.

(Now that I think about it, that was a bold thing for me to do with three little kids. But at the time, it was just an adventurous thing to do. Many friends were doing it, so I should be able to make this long trip, too.)

The kids were great travelers. I drove at least five hundred miles a day, and we stayed in motels along the way. Every morning before we set off again, I would check the oil and use the grease gun to lubricate the bearings.

I loved maps. Dick had equipped us with the maps I needed to make my way to South Dakota. So, every morning after doing the maintenance, we got out the maps and marked out our route for the day. The kids liked doing that with me.

The Alaska Highway #2 was paved part of the way. We drove on well-maintained Trans Canada Highway #16. We enjoyed the beautiful countryside.

We crossed the Alaska border into the Yukon Territory. The kids got a kick out of the name of the town Whitehorse, where we stopped for lunch.

We continued southeast on various Canadian highways through the provinces of British Columbia, Alberta, and Saskatchewan, which was another name the kids found funny.

After passing through Regina, Saskatchewan, I calculated that we had less than eleven hours left to go to reach Aberdeen. I was averaging about fifty miles an hour. The kids had fun playing silly games like I spy.

Finally, we crossed the US border into North Dakota and, a few hours later we entered South Dakota.

The only time I got a little bit lost was when we approached Aberdeen. They had built a new highway system since the last time I was there. After driving around a little, I got a sense of where I was and I finally found my parent's home on South State Street.

When I drove up the drive, they were there sitting on their front porch waiting for us. It was a happy reunion and of course they had been worrying about my making this long trip in such a little car, but we'd had a safe, fun trip.

We had a great time there. Bryan got to ride the tractors and help with some farm chores. Julie and Shirley had many hours of fun playing with dolls and playing dress-up with their cousins.

As for me, I enjoyed attending several gatherings where I saw friends and relatives I hadn't seen in years.

We enjoyed the six weeks we spent there, but it was time to get back home. We said our good-byes and got in our little Renault for the 3,000-mile trip back to Fairbanks. We followed on our maps, taking the same routes back that we'd taken to get to South Dakota. I kept up with the morning maintenance chores.

After driving for a few days, Bryan started asking when we'd get to "pink elephant." I couldn't figure out what he was talking about. When we approached Whitehorse, Bryan was excited and explained that's what he had meant! In his honor, we stopped there for lunch.

We found Whitehorse on our map. We still had about 600 miles to go before reaching Fairbanks. After one more overnight, we were on the homestretch of our journey home. Dick was waiting for us when we arrived, and we had a wonderful time sharing our adventures with him.

I never had to use my new skill of changing a tire. We had made it back to Fairbanks without a single flat tire or mechanical challenge – not even a fender-bender. In those days, gas was about 30 cents a gallon. We had spent less than $50 on gas for the entire trip.

We were happy to be home again. It was just in time to get ready for one of our family's favorite activities of the summer: The Tanana Valley State Fair!

CHAPTER 43

FAIR FUN, A NEW STOVE, AND GOLDEN DAYS

Our family enjoyed many local traditions over the years. Here are some favorites.

THE TANANA VALLEY STATE FAIR

Established in June 1924, the Tanana Valley State Fair is the oldest community fair in Alaska. In its early years, it was held in various places in downtown Fairbanks, such as the Moose Lodge and the Masonic Temple.

In 1952, the Fair secured a lease from the University of Alaska for forty acres of land on College Road, and it has expanded there over the years. The Fairgrounds are between downtown Fairbanks and the University.

The energetic Janet Baird became the Fair's manager in 1965 and held that position for almost 20 years. Under her leadership, the Fair got bigger and better each year. It attracted everyone from homesteaders to college professors, who entered everything from the largest cabbages to flower arranging.

The Fair has a small paid summer staff. Many volunteers are needed, so the manager has to know how to recruit enthusiastic volunteers to head the various divisions of the Fair.

Volunteers are also important because they encourage people to enter items in their divisions, which range from livestock to quilting to flowers and vegetables. They select quality judges to evaluate each entry, and cash prizes are awarded to the top ribbon winners in the division categories and to the Grand Champion division winners.

Our kids had fun preparing their entries for the divisions of hobbies, flowers, and vegetables. One year, Shirley was excited when she saw a ribbon on a six-pound turnip she had entered. She had started it from seed from a Penny Seed Packets for kids. (Dick said it was a fun way for Burpee to dispose of all the seeds they swept off the floor!)

In 1964, our family entered a new division called "Farm and Home Display." We had a booth about six feet square and called it "Family Fun for Everyone." We decorated the shelves and displayed items we had made or grown, such as bread, flowers, vegetables, clothing, and crafts. We had fun preparing the booth.

In 1971, I entered my frosted braids using my sweet dough bread recipe. I won the Grand prize, an electric stove given by the Golden Valley Electric Company. After winning the stove, I volunteered to be the Culinary Division's superintendent for several years. I had wonderful volunteers, and we decorated the booth so it would be an inviting place for the Fair crowds to visit. I was at that booth with volunteers all day and night during the Fair. It was fun talking to the folks who stopped by, and I encouraged them to enter the Fair the following year.

The Fair was and still is a family event. Children still have fun exploring the Fairgrounds, riding the rides, tasting all the foods and checking to see if they got any ribbons.

THE TANANA VALLEY STATE FAIR BAKE-OFF

The Tanana Valley State Fair Bake-Off was started in 1961 by a community-minded, ambitious young couple, Buck and Barbara Hazen. It was a new Division of the Fair.

My first entry was a plate of Orange Delight Cookies. My sister's mother-in-law, Pauline Angerhofer, had given me the recipe for "Mrs. Angerhofer's Orange Delight Cookies."

Make a batch of chocolate chip cookies, BUT delete the chocolate chips, and mix 2 tbsp. finely ground orange rind into the batter.

Here is the secret to what makes these cookies so delicious: Dissolve two cups of granulated sugar into 2/3 cup of fresh orange juice and 2 tsp. finely grated orange peel. As the cookies come out of the oven, immediately dip each one into the mixture, scraping the excess off the bottom of the cookie. Let the dipped cookies dry on waxed paper for 24 hours. You will see for yourself how delightful they are!

I was excited when I was awarded $10 for being the winner of the first Bake-Off! After all these years, the Fair and Bake-Off remain fun Fairbanks traditions. They're held in early August. Get a Fair catalog. There are opportunities for adults and children to enter items in the Fair.

GOLDEN DAYS

Celebrating Golden Days is another wonderful Fairbanks tradition. It was created by the Pioneers of Alaska Fairbanks in 1952 to commemorate the 50th anniversary of the discovery of gold. Italian miner Felice Pedroni, aka Felix Pedro, hit gold in a creek northeast of what is now Fairbanks.

Families have fun dressing up in costumes of those early days. I made costumes for the children, too.

A King and Queen Regent are selected each year by the Pioneers of Alaska Fairbanks. They preside over the week's events, which include the Golden Days Parade, the Kiddie Parade, a Tea with Pioneers, and a rededication of the monument near the Fort Knox Mine on the Steese Highway, where Felix Pedro discovered gold.

The gold rush of the early 1900s and the discovery of oil on the North Slope in the 1960s were boom times in Fairbanks.

The Golden Days celebration continues to be held each July. Thanks to its many dedicated volunteers, the Fairbanks Chamber of Commerce, and the Pioneers of Alaska Fairbanks, it continues to create a festive week of fun activities.

CHAPTER 44

SEWARD'S FOLLY, A GOLD RUSH, AND PREPARING FOR THE CENTENNIAL

There were many historical events that led to the 1867 purchase of Alaska from Russia.

After George Washington died in 1799, our nation's young leaders were interested in adding more land to our new country. They encouraged adventuresome pioneers to go west.

The Louisiana Purchase was a land deal made in 1803 between the United States and France. For 15 million dollars, the U.S. acquired 827,000 square miles of land west of the Mississippi River.

Between 1847 and 1860, more than 60,000 Mormon pioneers journeyed to the Great Salt Lake Valley in Utah by wagons and hand carts. Thousands of others arrived by ship to California and then traveled to Utah by wagons. Many Utah Mormons provided labor to complete the Transcontinental Railroad at Promontory Summit, Utah, in May of 1869.

The 1848 California gold rush brought more than 300,000 gold seekers to that region. Just two years after the discovery, California became a state.

About 14 years after the beginning of the California gold rush in 1862, Congress tried something different to entice adventurous settlers to go West to claim land. That year, President Abraham Lincoln signed the Homestead Act.

The Homestead Act gave land to settlers who proved up on their claims, meaning they cleared their claimed land, planted and harvested crops, and built a home, even if only made of sod. All this had to be accomplished within a prescribed number of years.

My ancestors on both sides of my family were poor but ambitious farmers in their native countries. My mother's family was from Norway, and my father's was from Switzerland. In the early 1860s, when they heard about getting land by simply working hard and proving up on the claim, they left their home countries and headed to America, both ultimately ending up in the Dakota Territory.

Almost fifteen years before Alaska would become a Territory, our Canadian neighbors built the transcontinental Canadian Pacific Railway between 1881 and 1885. It was initially used for freight. However, beginning in the early 1890s, they recognized what their railroad could do for Canadian tourism.

They were visionaries to consider tourism that long ago! To entice travelers, the Canadian Pacific Railroad built luxurious railroad cars and gorgeous hotels in lovely locations. These include the Banff Springs Hotel in the breathtaking Canadian Rockies in 1888, Chateau Lake Louise in 1890, also in the Canadian Rockies, and the Empress Hotel in Victoria, BC, in 1904. They continued to the East Coast and built the elegant Chateau Frontenac on a promontory in Old Quebec City, Quebec. I'm fortunate to have visited each of these beautiful hotels, which are still operating today.

In 1867 the United States purchased Alaska from Russia for $7.2 million. For even more historical reference, this was two years after the Civil War ended. Secretary of State William H. Seward was criticized for promoting the purchase of this land of ice and snow, and it became known as "Seward's Folly." Very few potential settlers ventured into this new Territory of Alaska.

However, thirty years later, in 1897, gold was discovered in the Klondike region of the Yukon Territory. Word about this discovery spread throughout the world. Shortly after that gold rush, prospectors heard about the 1899 discovery of gold in Nome, Alaska. Thousands of prospectors rushed to Nome, hoping to get rich quickly.

There was a national mania for gold, and no one called the Alaska purchase "Seward's Folly" anymore.

In 1902, news spread quickly that an enterprising young Italian gold miner, Felix Pedro, had discovered gold on a creek near Fairbanks. The rush to find gold in Interior Alaska was on! Fairbanks became a vibrant community with several exciting years of boom and bust as a result.

In the early 1960s, several Fairbanks visionaries joined with other Alaskans to start planning for a centennial to celebrate the 100th anniversary of its 1867 purchase.

In 1963, they established a nonprofit called the A-67 Exposition. In 1964, Fairbanks was selected as the central location for the statewide Centennial Exposition. The site for the Exposition was a 44-acre lot on Airport Way and Peger Road. Opening day was scheduled for Memorial Day weekend, 1967.

Building the A-67 Exposition took considerable planning and cooperation among several groups of creative people in Fairbanks. The Fairbanks architectural firm of Gray, Rogers, and Cotting, now Design Alaska, was chosen to design the A-67 Park. Les Rogers, a partner in the firm, oversaw the layout. Les is recognized as the quiet leader in getting the site established. Les was a creative thinker and began working on the design in late 1964.

Les worked in cooperation with the young, talented Exposition manager, Dennis "Skip" Cook, who shared his ideas with the board.

Urban renewal had been taking place in Fairbanks. Many dilapidated buildings had been torn down or burned. Instead of destroying more, Les contacted potential contractors in Fairbanks about moving twenty-nine of the remaining old buildings, including the little white church and a hotel, to the A-67 site to preserve their history.

It was a wonderful idea, but A-67 needed more money to move the buildings. Les had heard about a house-moving contractor in Anchorage who was interested in the project, and they were able to work out a deal. They *moved* those 29 buildings, the little white church, and the two-story log hotel to the site!

The buildings were historic frame homes and fragile little log cabins. After they were so skillfully moved, they were renovated and turned into charming little shops with wooden boardwalks connecting them. Over the next two years, many dedicated Fairbanksans created Gold Rush Town on the Exposition site. It was a massive project!

The dedicated team of organizers were determined to have the A-67 Centennial Exposition Park ready for visitors on Memorial Day weekend in 1967 as planned. It was a tremendous amount of work that needed to be accomplished in just two years.

Memorial Day arrived, and not only was it ready, but it looked absolutely phenomenal when they opened the gates!

Fairbanks Daily News-Miner, Friday, June 9, 1967—

CHAPTER 45

AN EXPOSITION, HARD WORK, AND A FIRSTHAND ACCOUNT

This chapter has a guest author, Dennis "Skip" Cook. He was the manager of the A-67 project from 1965 to 1967. He was kind enough to write this and has allowed me to publish it here. Enjoy this firsthand account from Skip on making A-67 a reality!

It was my honor and privilege to participate in this exciting Exposition. Here is my recollection in a nutshell:

When I joined the Alaska 67 Centennial Exposition staff in February 1965, Chuck Wenger, the Manager of the Chamber of Commerce, was heading up the staff effort.

The Chamber had been instrumental in having Fairbanks designated as the commemoration site.

Separate A-67 staffing had not yet occurred. Nor had offices separate from the Chamber been initiated.

When Chuck left Fairbanks suddenly in late 1965, I became the General Manager. We moved headquarters to the Exposition's site once facilities were available there.

The Executive Committee of the Board of Directors—my bosses—were a fine lot: Don Vogwill of the Golden Valley Electric Association (GVEA) was president. Curt Boone of Safeway oversaw site development.

Al Fleetwood of Alaska State Bank, Ron Nerland of Nerland's Home Furnishing, and CPA Frank Danner closely watched finances and contracts.

Captain Jim Binkley knew about tourism and tourists and oversaw public relations matters.

Mary Jane Fate championed the inclusion of Native Alaska heritage. And Wally Burnett oversaw the Park's concessions.

Geneva Emmal and her new arts board had founded the local Alaska Association for the Arts. She carried her arts expertise into the performing arts element of the Exposition.

At that time, the 44-acre site on Airport Way and Peger Road was virgin land. Nothing had been cleared, and nothing had been constructed.

The local Pioneer Igloo #4 was headed by Frank Young and Harrie Hughes. With the help of attorney Grace Schaible, they negotiated an agreement that allowed the use of the property for the Exposition with provisions that included the construction of a permanent Pioneer Museum.

The Pioneers viewed the Exposition as an opportunity to accomplish much they did not have funding to do.

The design layout and construction were under the direction of the architectural firm Gray, Rogers & Cotting.

Les Rogers was designated as the "on-the-ground" representative. Les and I worked very closely together to get the 29 structures moved to the A-67 site—Gold Rush Town!

Les guided all of us through the many challenges of creating a complex Exposition site on the raw ground—in less than two years!

This included extending utilities to the site, clearing, earthmoving, awarding of contracts, and overseeing contractors.

Building each major area was a challenge: the Central Plaza, the Civic Center, the Mining Valley, the Native Village, the Gold Rush Town, the Steamer SS Nenana, the Zoo, and the Railroad. They were all complicated to build.

Barry Jackson was the A-67 attorney. He had lots to do as we entered into construction contracts, acquired the SS Nenana. and moved the 29 buildings that constituted Gold Rush Town.

Barry also contracted for Federal and State exhibits. He hired staff and granted concessionaire permits.

My immediate staff included Pat Hill, my executive secretary—and assistants including Wally Baer, Dave Jones and Larry Carpenter. The staff grew exponentially as opening day approached. Hundreds of people worked at the Exposition site either for A-67 or for contractors and concessionaires.

Among cherished memories was the creation of "The Big Stampede," the display in which audiences sat on a revolving platform to view 15 huge murals painted by artist C. "Rusty" Heurlin while listening to the narration by the incomparable voice of Reuben Gaines. I enjoyed getting away from the busy office to drive out to Rusty's Ester home and studio to view the progress of the murals.

An un-cherished memory is of the night when I finally convinced my parents to attend a Showboat performance, the Exposition's key stage production.

On that particular night, the actors went on strike over pay issues, and we had to send the audience home.

However, the issues were resolved, and the show went on successfully for the rest of the season.

When the two-story log Chena Hotel in downtown Fairbanks was about to be demolished, we rescued it!

However, we had a challenge moving such a large two-story log structure to A-67's Gold Rush Town.

Many said this could not be done and the building would collapse.

However, skilled house movers did the job.

When the Palfy Plumbing Shop from 1st Avenue had been moved to the site and renovated into a saloon, it caught fire and burned shortly before opening day. It was replaced in record time.

The rainy summer of 1967 caused a chaotic time for the Exposition, both physically and financially.

Attendance was well below projections due to the weather, resulting in a financial deficit.

Hard as we sandbagged, the staff and volunteers could not keep the Chena River from invading the site. That mid-August 1967 flood caused considerable damage to the Park. It was a heartbreaking time.

But the people in Fairbanks rose to the occasion, and the A-67 Park re-opened the next May.

Pioneer Park is a treasured gem for Fairbanks. We are so proud of this beautiful, unique place.

– Dennis "Skip" Cook

CHAPTER 46

A GLACIER RESCUE, A GOLD RUSH TOWN, AND A LITTLE WHITE CHURCH

Of the many buildings in Gold Rush Town in Pioneer Park, the little white church is particularly interesting.

Presbyterian missionary S. Hall Young was born in Pennsylvania just a year before the California gold rush. He was sent to do missionary work in several western states in his youth. He was also sent to the Klondike and then to the Territory of Alaska to continue his work.

Young was interested in Alaska's wilderness. Few adventuresome people had visited the Alaska Territory since it was purchased from Russia in 1867. He became friends with the famous naturalist John Muir, who was about nine years older than Young. They traveled around southern Alaska in 1879 and again in 1880 when Muir discovered Glacier Bay.

There is a story of how Muir saved Young's life while mountain climbing above glaciers in southeast Alaska. Muir held Young's collar between clenched teeth to keep him from falling down a precipice. Young's 1915 book, *Alaska Days with John Muir*, recounts the terrifying story in detail.

In 1904, the 57-year-old Young was sent to Fairbanks to establish a church. This was just two years after Felix Pedro discovered gold nearby.

The little white church was built at the intersection of Cushman Street and Seventh Avenue. At the time, it seemed far away from downtown Fairbanks!

In 1931, a new church was built, and the little white church was connected to it with a breezeway. The steeple was removed from the little white church, and it became the Young Memorial Hall. Sunday School classes, church suppers, and other gatherings were held there for nearly three decades.

So, how did that little white church end up at Pioneer Park?

In 1957, they tore down the 1931 church and built a beautiful new church in its place. The original little white church, Young Memorial Hall, remained on the property until 1965 when the church needed the space to build a new Christian Education building. Session members of the First Presbyterian Church wondered what could be done with the historic Young Memorial Hall.

Charles "Chuck" Gray of Fairbanks has been a member of the First Presbyterian Church for many years and has written many stories about that church and its history. According to

Chuck, Session members were happy when they heard that the A-67 board was interested in obtaining the historic church.

The Session gifted Young Memorial Hall to A-67, who moved it to its current location next to the Wickersham House in Gold Rush Town at Pioneer Park.

This is the same little church where Dick was the sexton before we were married and lived in the tiny room up the little stairs to the left of the altar. On Sunday mornings, he would be awakened early when the pastor's wife, Virginia Alfson, loudly practiced the prelude for that morning's service. He never needed an alarm clock!

His little room is now the bride's dressing room when weddings are held there. The little white church is a treasure.

CHAPTER 47

A-67, ALASKALAND, OR PIONEER PARK?

What *is* in a name? Many locals can explain their emotional attachment to any one of these three names. Here is a little history.

In 1964, a parcel of land was being considered as a location for the Alaska '67 Centennial Exposition, A-67 for short. A-67 would celebrate one hundred years since Alaska was purchased from Russia.

The 44 acres belonged to Igloo No. 4, Pioneers of Alaska Fairbanks. It was called Pioneer Park. The land had never been cleared, and nothing had ever been built on it. They had owned the property for quite some time and hoped to build a permanent Pioneer Museum there, but they never had the funding.

Members of Igloo No. 4 were grateful when the A-67 board told them they were interested in the property. They worked with attorney Grace Schaible to negotiate an agreement to transfer ownership from Igloo No. 4 to A-67.

The Agreement included one crucial provision: The A-67 board had to promise to build a permanent Pioneer Museum on the lot as a part of the Centennial Exposition. A-67 complied, and the new permanent Pioneer Museum was completed by opening day, Memorial Day weekend, 1967.

After the Centennial celebration ended, the Park was turned over to the City of Fairbanks. At that point, the name was changed from A-67 to Alaskaland.

In 2001, the City of Fairbanks turned Alaskaland over to the Fairbanks North Star Borough to be part of the Parks and Recreation Department. Considerable discussion centered around that choice for the name. Some people felt it implied that it would be a theme park like Disneyland, and it wasn't that kind of a park.

Borough members reviewed the history of the parcel of land. They took into account Igloo No. 4, Pioneers of Alaska's original name for it: Pioneer Park. In November 2001, the Borough members agreed that the name of the Park should officially return to its original name.

Some readers may be sorry that the A-67 Centennial Exposition's name changed from Alaskaland to Pioneer Park. Considering this timeline of history, I hope that the spirit of honoring the pioneers' original name is better understood.

CHAPTER 48

ATTRACTIONS, STRUCTURES, AND AN UPDATE FROM SKIP

I asked Dennis "Skip" Cook to write an update chapter on Pioneer Park's many changes. Skip graciously went to the Park in 2024 and shared the following thoughts and an update on all of its attractions.

When my Fairbanks High School Class of 1958 went to Pioneer Park for our 65th Class Reunion picnic in July 2023, we had to dodge a deep ditch excavation that ran through the Park. This looked to be related to utility work. The remnant was still there in the summer of 2024 when we went to dinner at the Salmon Bake followed by a walk through the Park.

In my visit with Park superintendent Lee Williams, in preparation for this report, I learned the purpose of the ditch. A new 8" water line loop was installed to service existing and future Park facilities. Also, rotting wood stave sewer pipes were replaced. Several Gold Rush Town log cabins were unable to function as concessions due to substandard utilities. COVID-19 funds were used for this work. Next year, new electrical transformers and the replacement of worn buried electrical lines will upgrade the electrical system.

Throughout this report, references will be made to the difficulty in maintaining Park elements that were quickly installed in 1965-1966 in preparation for the Alaska 67 Centennial Exposition, especially when the August 1967 Fairbanks flood impacted those facilities.

I inquired of Park Superintendent Lee Williams about the various Park elements. I found him to be passionate about maintaining the historical accuracy of the Gold Rush Town, Pioneer Museum, S.S. Nenana, Harding Car areas despite modernization of other elements. I will briefly mention each of the Park's features.

EXHIBITION HALL

This iconic major building with its decorative Alaska Native masks, sometimes called The Pickle Barrel, was closed for a time due to deterioration of the underground portions of vertical exterior beams. However, these have been repaired sufficiently so that its activities, including the Bear Gallery, are again fully active. The master plan calls for replacement of this structure, largely due to ADA concerns such as having no elevator near the main entrance. Lee would love to have the building upgraded, but expense is a big factor.

THE HARDING CAR

This historic railroad car was the passenger car used by President Warren G. Harding during a visit to Alaska in 1923 to formally complete the Alaska Railroad which goes north from Seward on to Fairbanks. It is now protected from the elements by a roof over the top.

S.S. NENANA

This sternwheeler, which carried passengers and cargo on the Tanana and Yukon rivers from 1933 to 1954, is on the site. At 230 feet (70 meters), it is the second-largest wooden-hulled ship still in existence. Friends of the S.S. Nenana are now working to establish funding to make needed repairs and maintenance. Restoration proceeds under the efforts of the non-profit organization Friends of S.S. Nenana pursuant to a lease agreement. The steamer's cargo deck was closed to the public for several years due to structural problems. Repair of underpinnings has allowed that deck to be reopened. However, further major repairs that will cost untold dollars are necessary to upgrade and prevent further deterioration. ADA requirements will prevent open public use of all but the cargo deck due to narrow staircases and passageways. The first phase of major exterior waterproofing is underway. Major public and private grant funding is sought.

GOLD RUSH TOWN

This is a collection of over 30 restored historic buildings from early Fairbanks, including the first church in Fairbanks and a home owned by Judge James Wickersham. Roofs have been replaced on Wickersham House, cabins 7 and 19 and the little white church, which also had bulging walls repaired. One small cabin is considered beyond repair. Others have foundations, or lack thereof, that should be replaced. Yet concessions fill all available spaces. Lee fights with Borough Maintenance staff over keeping historic cabins versus teardown replacement costs. Steve Mitchell continues to be the chief docent at Wickersham House where he dresses as Judge Wickersham for his presentation.

DANCE HALL

This facility was added well after the exposition. It continues to be well used under lease to a local dance group.

PIONEER AIR MUSEUM

Containing aviation memorabilia and 14 historic aircraft, this was assembled through the efforts of aviation historian Randy Acord. This is operated under lease by aircraft enthusiasts. However, the Gold Dome is leaking and the operators are having difficulty meeting rent and utility costs. Several planes and a helicopter have recently been sold. There is talk of the entire museum operation being melded into the Antique Auto Museum when it relocates to larger quarters in the former Kmart building. If the museum moves, the dome would likely become the Park maintenance center.

TANANA VALLEY RAILROAD MUSEUM

This features the 3' (914 mm) narrow gauge 1899 TVRR Engine No. 1 restored by Dan Gullickson and a host of friends and businesses. The historic Tanana Valley R.R. Engine #1 is down for repairs being done by its faithful friends, but will soon be back on track for its periodic appearances.

CROOKED CREEK AND WHISKEY ISLAND RAILROAD

This operating 3' (914 mm) narrow gauge railroad circumnavigates the perimeter of the Park on raised ground.

Operated by the Fairbanks North Star Borough, this is the engine that takes visitors on the ride around the Park. The engine of the 1967 train had to be sent out for repair, but is now operational. Cars are undergoing restoration with one finished and two to follow.

MINING VALLEY

This area of the Park features a working replica of a Gold Rush-era sluice gate and some historic mining equipment. A dray wagon was recently added, and the stamp mill is undergoing restoration.

Alaska Salmon Bake

This culinary favorite is still going strong adjacent to the mining displays of Mining Valley.

PIONEER MUSEUM

This wonderful collection features a selection of Gold Rush memorabilia. This is operated by Pioneers of Alaska Igloo #4 under a lease agreement. Lee reports that these folks do a great job. New items have been added such as a bust of Felix Pedro cast in his homeland of Italy.

THE BIG STAMPEDE

Located in Pioneer Hall with The Pioneer Museum, The Big Stampede is a documentary show open from Memorial Day through Labor Day, with some showings during the winter. It features 15 large paintings by the famous Alaskan artist C. "Rusty" Heurlin, with a recorded documentary by Rueben Gaines. It is a stunning show. Viewers sit on a moving platform, designed by Roger Cotting, as the story moves from painting to painting. Pioneers of Alaska Igloo #4 also operates this under a lease agreement, and Lee reports what a great job they do.

KITTY HENSLEY HOUSE

Visitors to the Park can enjoy seeing the charming, modest early days in this home. Volunteers in costume host visitors to see all of the house and the "modern" conveniences of the early 1900s.

NATIVE VILLAGE

This element of the Park is history. The remaining kashims will be dismantled. The museum building is now used as a homeschool workshop by a local Folk School. Construction of the Morris Thompson Center near downtown Fairbanks now contains superior presentations of Alaska Native culture and history.

PALACE THEATRE

This authentic venue presents popular evening musical shows featuring talented local actors in costume performing entertaining early Fairbanks history.

PLAYGROUND

The Park has a large children's playground which is open to the public at no charge. The Folk School Fairbanks offers year-round classes and programs for all ages in crafts, woodworking, outdoor skills, and hands-on arts and sciences. A proposed plan for a major change in this popular area proved to be far too expensive. However, Phase 1 of playground equipment replacement is underway, with the kiddie playground already finished. Paving, an ice rink element, and pickleball courts are in the offing.

FAIRBANKS ARTS ASSOCIATION

This vibrant non-profit organization was incorporated in 1966 to promote contemporary and traditional arts in Interior Alaska. The original corporate name was "The Alaska Association for the Arts." With offices in the Exhibition Hall, the staff organizes a gift shop and art gallery shows throughout the year.

PARKING

The front parking lot that faces Airport Way has been repaved and is in good shape. However, it is not sufficient to service needs at the river portion of the Park. In accord with the master plan, new parking will be developed soon along Peger Road.

MASTER PLAN

This plan has proven to be largely out of reach financially. The time of the anticipated implementation is already past. However, it is still a guideline for ongoing change. Lee does not foresee the major elements occurring in the near future. In summary, Pioneer Park has become the center of history and recreation envisioned by the Pioneers of Alaska when they entered into the agreement for the development of their 44 acres via the Alaska 67 Centennial Exposition. The Park is now a vital part of the Fairbanks North Star Borough's park system, which gives security and an avenue for continued maintenance and development.

– Dennis "Skip" Cook

CHAPTER 49

MORE TRAILBLAZERS, SETTLERS, AND VISIONARIES

In a previous chapter, I acknowledged some movers and shakers who had been active in Fairbanks before I arrived. Here are highlights of more wonderful people who influenced my life and gave so much of their own to make Fairbanks a better place after I got there!

DR. WILLIAM R. AND DOROTHY JANE WOOD

Dr. Wood became the University of Alaska's fourth president in 1960, one year after Alaska became the 49th state. During the thirteen years Dr. Wood served as president, many new buildings and departments were added. Active in campus life, he and his wife Dorothy Jane established a lovely holiday ball, which became an annual black tie event with students helping to host. He rarely missed a Nanooks game, and Dorothy Jane played violin in the Fairbanks Symphony Orchestra.

He retired in 1973 and five years later was elected Mayor of Fairbanks. He completed many creative ideas due to his gift of generating enthusiasm for his projects and recruiting interested volunteers. Along with Harry "Red" Porter and Jeff Cook, he sought funding to build the new Fairbanks Memorial Hospital after the 1967 flood destroyed St. Joseph's Hospital.

He founded the nonprofit Festival Fairbanks, which obtained funding for the Golden Heart Plaza, which was dedicated in 1986. Over a thousand people watched the unveiling of Malcolm Alexander's bronze statue The Unknown First Family. Later, with Dr. Wood's leadership, members of the Rotary Club of Fairbanks contributed a beautiful clock tower and carillon for the Plaza.

Dr. Wood was a true trailblazer. The William Ransom Wood Pedestrian Bridge connecting the Golden Heart Plaza to the north side of the Chena River was constructed in his memory after his passing.

LEE AND LESLEY SALISBURY

Lee and Lesley arrived in Fairbanks in the summer of 1955. Lee had been hired to teach in the University's new Speech and Drama Department.

Since there was no theatre building on campus or in the community, Lee made a theatre out of anywhere he could find space. He staged performances in the old museum on campus, which is now Signers' Hall. (The old museum was in the Eielson Building.) He also used the Schaible lecture hall in the Bunnell Building. It's very apt that the new theatre in UAF's Fine Arts Complex is named in his honor. Finally he had a real theatre!

Lee was a fantastic talent. His enthusiasm drew crowds to the plays he produced. His wife, Lesley, taught private string lessons and played a big part in the creation of the Fairbanks Symphony and the Chamber Orchestra.

RON AND LOU DAVIS

Ron and Lou came to Alaska in 1953, leaving their Minnesota home and settling in Palmer. They lived there for five years until Ron accepted a job offer from the Northern Commercial Company in 1959 and they moved to Fairbanks. They immediately became involved in the arts in Fairbanks.

Lou was a substitute teacher during the years their children were in school. In 1964, Ron went to work with Nerland's Home Furnishings.

Ron had a beautiful baritone voice and sang in the community chorus. He was often the handsome star of Fairbanks Light Opera Theatre (FLOT) shows. These included *South Pacific*, *Showboat*, and *Guys and Dolls*. He reprised his role in *Guys and Dolls* at the UAF Salisbury Theatre. He was eager to work with the gifted director Lee Salisbury. Ron and Lou both enjoyed performing with FLOT, and Lou chuckles as she tells me that Ron always had the romantic leads while she would get a minor role.

They enjoyed being active in everything from Golden Days to the Chamber of Commerce.

BILL AND BONNIE BRODY

Bill came to UAF in 1967 to teach printmaking, drawing, and painting. Born in New York City, he was raised in Tucson and was fresh out of graduate school at Claremont University in Southern California.

He describes his unique painting style as deriving "from a visceral feeling of what it is like to be in some particular place, be it on a hillside in the wilderness, or inside my own private introspection." His Alaska wilderness paintings are well known, and he still comes to Alaska every year to paint large, immersive works.

He and his wife Bonnie, another New York transplant, met in Fairbanks. Their children attended my Junior High Fine Arts Camp in the early 80s! Bill's oil painting *Fairbanks Summer* was featured on a Fairbanks Summer Arts Festival poster.

ANN DOLNEY

Ann was a war bride from Germany who came to Fairbanks with her husband, Ed, in the late 1950s. They established Ann's Greenhouse on Sheep Creek Road in 1965, starting with one and adding many more over the years. She prepared many gorgeous planters and hanging baskets that brightened the whole town.

She became my dear friend. I had fun working for her in the greenhouses in the summer of 1974. I learned so much about gardening in Alaska and marveled at Ann's knowledge about the *thousands* of plants she had for sale.

JOHANNA FLUEGEL

Johanna, who our family lovingly called Fluegel, was our dear across-the-street neighbor on Caribou Way.

She had left Germany in the early 1930s with her young son, Walter. When they arrived in New York, she found housework jobs from new friends she made.

She heard about opportunities in Alaska! She and Walter went to Fairbanks, where she met new people and quickly found housekeeping jobs. Walter began studies at the University.

When we had just moved our dry cabin to our lot, I came home one day and she had left a gorgeous tomato plant for me as a welcome! She was an avid gardener and always generously shared vegetables and herbs, along with helpful tips for my own gardening.

We had a family tradition that Fluegel would come over on Christmas mornings, and she always brought her signature round lemon cake drizzled with lemon juice and sugar glaze. Yummy!

MARDY HOECKLE

Mardy had come from North Dakota to teach in Fairbanks in the early 1950s. I met her at a teacher's meeting shortly after I arrived in 1953. We immediately became friends as we were both from the Dakotas. She taught elementary grades at Barnette, and the kids loved her!

She became an honorary aunt to our children. Aunt Mardy did many creative activities with them, and they liked visiting her collie dog and cats. She would join Fluegel every year for Christmas morning family brunch. Aunt Mardy had an old-fashioned home in downtown Fairbanks, complete with a big old Monarch cook stove like Mother's. She used it to bake our family Thanksgiving dinners!

V.G. AND FRANCIS BAKER

Francis and V.G. lived in a beautiful log home on Westwood Way, a couple blocks from our place. They had a big yard full of flowers, and Francis was known for having a large patch of beautiful purple crocus that came up through the melting snow each spring. Artist Pat Babcock captured these in her beautiful watercolor *Pasque Flowers From Francis' Garden*, which was featured on a Fairbanks Summer Arts Festival poster.

Francis was a beautiful lady and operated the popular Jade Shop on College Road for many years. It wasn't just jade! She supported local artists and had Alaskan-made art, gold nugget jewelry, soapstone carvings, and, yes, beautiful jade pieces, too. She had lived in Fairbanks since the 1940s and knew Fairbanks' history. She was a fascinating storyteller, and a visit to her store meant you would find not just Alaskan art but a story about the artist and some Alaskan history as well.

I admired these people and the many others I met early on who were doing great things to make Fairbanks a vibrant community.

CHAPTER 50

A New Professor, Musical Theatre, and a Concert Hall

A lot was happening in the arts in Fairbanks during the sixties!

The Fairbanks Concert Association presented concerts with many visiting musicians. In the spring of 1965, we all enjoyed the Chicago Symphony Orchestra. Ruth Forbes was the gracious president of the association and literally rolled out a red carpet at the airport for all arriving performers. She always brought her silver tea set for the lovely receptions after the concerts in the lobby, adding an elegant flair.

The Concert Association welcomed a new board member when the energetic Charles W. "Charlie" Davis joined the University of Alaska Music Department in 1963. His students called him Professor Davis, but those in the community lovingly called him "Charlie." He and his wife Beverly, an accomplished pianist, became a vibrant part of the arts community.

Charlie began planning to found a summer music camp for high school students at the University of Alaska Fairbanks campus in the summer of 1964. Plans were going well, but on March 27th, the Good Friday Earthquake occurred. The quake was powerful in Fairbanks, but extensive damage occurred in the Anchorage and Valdez communities. It was felt throughout Alaska's southeast coastline and beyond.

When it happened, Shirley, Julie and I were shopping at the newly-opened Woolworths store. We were at the check-out stand waiting to pay for our purchases. When I first felt it I thought I was fainting. The kids remember me saying, "I think I'm losing my cookies!"

Things started falling off the shelves in the store. We left our items at the cash register and raced outside with everyone else. The sidewalk was rolling in slow waves. It was very eerie to see.

I went to a payphone on the street to call Bryan, who was home alone. He said calmly, "Oh, I'm fine. But Muffy was scared!" Muffy was our evidently "scaredy" cat.

Fairbanks didn't suffer extensive physical damage, but some people doubted that the inaugural Music Camp could be held that summer. Charlie had faith that the earthquake couldn't stop his plans, and he was right.

The 1964 Camp was a huge success. It added dance and theatre with time and became the UAF's Summer Fine Arts Camp. It continued to create positive life-changing opportunities for hundreds of high school students for many years.

Charlie also founded creative learning opportunities for anyone in the community who loved music. He established a community chorus, which attracted many singers. He made everyone feel needed.

As a general music teacher in the school system at the time, I recognized how Charlie could help music educators like myself. We were grateful when Charlie offered exciting music classes at the University in the spring of 1968.

I took an Opera Workshop class that Charlie offered in 1969. He shared interesting aspects of producing an opera, like costuming, staging, and promotion. J. Brian Matthews was in that class as well. He was inspired to call a meeting of people who shared the enthusiasm for establishing a musical theatre organization.

Theresa Reed, Henry Cole, and Henry Nolden joined Charlie and Brian at that momentous meeting. They outlined what they wanted to create, and the Fairbanks Light Opera Theatre was born. There's a humorous story that when brainstorming for a name, Fairbanks Light Opera Players was suggested, but they all agreed that FLOT was a better acronym!

The University of Alaska Fairbanks Music Department cooperated with FLOT to present Charlie's production of Gian Carlo Menotti's *Amahl and the Night Visitors*.

Auditions were held, costumes were designed, and rehearsals were scheduled. It all came together in December 1969 when *Amahl and the Night Visitors* opened to a packed house, with Charlie conducting the pit orchestra.

The beautiful new Civic Center at Alaskaland housed a theatre, a gallery, exhibition areas, and office space. In the fall of 1970, FLOT presented its first performance there: *H.M.S. Pinafore*, with Charlie conducting. Charlie became very important to FLOT because of his experience directing musical theatre.

The Fairbanks community benefited from all that Charlie did in those early years. The University's Music Department grew under his leadership. When they built a beautiful new Fine Arts Complex at the University, they named the Charles W. Davis Concert Hall in his honor.

Cast members for Amahl and the Night Visitors were: Theresa Reed (the mother), Henry Cole (Melchior), Henry Nolden (Kasper), and Jessie Arrington (Balthazar). Many other Fairbanksans participated as shepherds.

Cast members for H.M.S. Pinafore were: Ron Anderson (Ralph), Jim Fritts (Captain), John Turner (Sir Joseph), Dick Brown (Dick Deadeye), Theresa Reed (Josephine), and Karen Parr (Buttercup).

CHAPTER 51

TWO MIKES: ONE A GREAT BROTHER AND ONE A GREAT UNCLE

I am writing this story on what would have been my brother Mike Ryman's ninety-fourth birthday. Mike and I had so many adventures together, especially while living on our old farm near Scatterwood Lake.

Our nearest neighbors, the Eske family, were about a mile east of us. We saw the Eske children every day during the school year. Mike and I would walk or ride our pony Jimmy the mile to their farm, and they would walk the remaining mile to our one-room country schoolhouse with us.

But we didn't see our neighbors often during the summer months. We all had chores to do and we never went to each other's houses just to play.

In the 1930s, during the Great Depression, my brother Mike and I had fun making up our own games to play in our large farmyard or our big old farmhouse. Mike was my best friend during those years. We never fought or got angry with one another. I had all sorts of creative ideas for adventures, and Mike just did whatever I suggested we do for fun.

My brother Mike was named after our Great Uncle Mike on my father's side.

The only information I have about my mother's ancestry is that it dates back to the Tollefson family leaving their farm near Oslo, Norway, to go to the United States in the early 1860s to homestead in Iowa.

However, for my father's family history, I got some interesting background stories from my Ryman cousins.

My dad's family came to America in 1863. Melchior Reimann, his wife Magdalena Bosley Reimann, and their one-year-old son, Melchior, left their modest farm in the foothills of the Swiss Alps to go to America. They boarded a small ship, joining their Swiss friends and relatives for the three-month trip across the Atlantic Ocean to America. How I wish they had kept a journal of that challenging trip!

Many Swiss people had heard about the 1862 Homestead Act, passed by the U.S. Congress which provided opportunities for hard-working immigrants to acquire virgin farmland, especially in the Dakota Territory, Wisconsin, and Iowa.

After arriving in the United States in June 1863, the boatload of Swiss families went on to Jeffersonville, New York where other Swiss families had relocated.

There were several generations of "Melchiors" in the Reimann family. Many new Americans changed the spelling of their family names, and our family was no different. The name "Melchior" was changed to "Mike" and the last name "Reimann" was changed to "Ryman."

My grandfather, John Casper Ryman, was born in Jeffersonville on December 1, 1863. It's interesting to consider that this was just two weeks after Lincoln gave the Gettysburg Address and our country was experiencing a terrible Civil War. I wonder if our ancestors and other Europeans who came to the United States during this time were aware of America's challenges with slavery and the war with terrible battles going on between 1861 and 1865.

Did they realize many communities in both the North and the South had been destroyed? And did they realize all the reconstruction work that had to be done after the War? Perhaps that was why they stayed put in Jeffersonville for twenty years or more before trying to realize their original dream of homesteading in the Dakotas.

The toddler on the ship in 1863 was also renamed Mike of course, and was our Great Uncle Mike. He went with his younger brother, my grandfather John, to the Dakota Territory in 1880 to see about homesteading there. His brothers Will and Cap and his sisters Mattie and Ann, followed. They went on to homestead land as well, in Brown County near the small community of Mansfield and in the area around Aberdeen.

In the early 1900s Great Uncle Mike decided to leave his siblings and move to Anaheim in Southern California, where he was a neighbor of the Knott family, on land that would become Knott's Berry Farm.

Mike was very clever and invented many things. He was credited with inventing the converter belt on threshing machines, even securing a patent on it. He never completed renewal rights when it came time however, so he lost any further royalty payments. He didn't have a family and he never returned to visit his siblings who stayed in Brown County. Mother was fascinated with the stories about my dad's Uncle Mike and when my brother was born in 1930, they named him Mike.

Great Uncle Mike lived a more adventurous life than his siblings. I'd like to have met Great Uncle Mike! He passed away in Anaheim in 1933 when I was just four. I felt like I knew him from Mother's fascinating retelling of his tales.

I was always proud of my dear brother Mike Ryman. He was one of the first few Warner High School graduates who went on to finish college. Mike was a farm boy, and many weren't encouraged to pursue a four-year degree, as they were expected to stay on the farm. Mike graduated with a degree in geology from the South Dakota School of Mines in Rapid City. He was smart and a good thinker, just like the man he was named for. He also relocated to Southern California.

My brother Mike passed away suddenly in January 1980 from a heart attack while jogging near his home. He would have been 50 years old that summer. I'm writing this story especially for his children and grandchildren. I am happy to be in touch with them and I hope this story inspires them to research even more of our family's history, especially my Great Uncle Mike that their dad/grandfather was named after!

CHAPTER 52

Arts in Letters: AAA, FAA, NEA, and ASCA

I always enjoyed meeting the parents of my little Nursery School students. In 1965, one of the parents I met was Geneva Emmal.

I had read *Fairbanks Daily News-Miner* articles about the work being done to establish the Alaska Centennial Exposition, and Geneva was an active A-67 board member. She was a big part of organizing the musical theatre productions held in the Civic Center during that summer's celebration.

Geneva was also busy working on founding a local arts association, and she encouraged me to join her new board. I was interested in everything she planned, so I agreed.

Her husband Bill was an attorney, and completed the necessary paperwork to create this new 501(c)(3) non-profit corporation. The board named it the Alaska Association for the Arts (AAA).

I learned so much working with Geneva. She was an excellent leader and a creative thinker. She appreciated her board members and chose them based on what each of us could give to the organization.

The National Endowment for the Arts (NEA) was established by Congress and signed into law by President Lyndon B. Johnson in 1965. Geneva went to Washington, DC, in 1966 to meet with the NEA staff.

She informed the AAA board of what Congress was planning for the arts. She learned that every state was encouraged to form its own State Arts Council as quickly as possible. NEA later told us that Alaska was one of the first states to establish its state arts council.

She also learned that the governor of each state would appoint the Executive Director of their council. The governors would also name council members from various communities in their state for representation.

Geneva had been working closely with Alaska's Governor Bill Egan, and she kept him updated about establishing Alaska's Arts Council. Governor Egan appointed Geneva the first Executive Director of the new Alaska State Council on the Arts (ASCA) in 1966. He recognized that Geneva was the leader in Alaska who had worked to establish ASCA.

With Geneva's guidance, AAA had a busy board. We needed her guidance because most of us were new to all the planning and work involved in bringing artists to town.

In the spring of 1966, our AAA board brought the cast from the Anchorage Lyric Opera to present *The Sound of Music* at Hering Auditorium. The entire board worked on details of guest transportation, honoraria, housing, publicity, and finances. It was an outstanding production, well attended, and we met our budget.

I was in charge of AAA's first fundraising efforts. There was no party or concert, just plain old phone calls asking for support.

In the meantime, the A-67 board hired Bob Banks, a professional performing arts producer, for the centennial celebration. He organized a 30-member resident stock company of professional actors, singers, tech, and sound people. Geneva, who had musical theatre training, was a member of the company.

Several musicals were planned to be on stage that summer. Dick and I enjoyed seeing Jerome Kern's *Showboat*, which starred Bob, and Geneva as well. It was a phenomenal performance.

In the summer of 1968, our AAA board received word that the Canadian Opera Company from Toronto would be touring the West Coast and Alaska with a production of *The Barber of Seville*, complete with a small chamber orchestra. The Canadian government highly subsidized the arts which helped make the cost of the production much less than it would have been without their help.

I was excited to hear this news, and at an Arts Association board meeting, I expressed my interest in bringing *The Barber of Seville* to Fairbanks in December. They thought this was ambitious thinking on my part, but I thought we could do it. Geneva agreed, and since I was the most enthused about the idea, she asked me to head the committee to bring the production to Fairbanks.

That September I carefully selected the heads of my committees. These included welcoming details, guest housing and transportation, public relations and publicity, scheduling for Hering Auditorium, ticket sales, programs, outreach to teachers in the schools and UAF Music Department, and the post-performance reception.

Music teachers throughout the local schools familiarized students with the comic opera's music and libretto. Many children and university students attended the opera, and had a more enriching experience thanks to these efforts.

At first, we were concerned that ticket sales were going slowly, but thanks to a rush of last-minute sales, we sold out two days before the one-night performance. *The Barber of Seville* played to a packed house at Hering Auditorium. The lobby reception after the opera was delightful. I credit its success to everyone who helped in so many ways. The experience of bringing the Canadian Opera Company to Fairbanks helped me in my future arts endeavors.

Several years later, the Alaska Association for the Arts changed its name to the Fairbanks Arts Association (FAA). Board member Mardee Roth was instrumental in making this happen. Executive Director June Rogers guided the FAA's important work for years.

I am the last surviving member of the original AAA board from 1966. I created its Historian's Scrapbook, which is still in their Pioneer Park office. FAA continues to be a vibrant organization today. As of this printing, Executive Director Jess Peña is doing an excellent job continuing its mission.

Fairbanks has a rich history of arts organizations, which I would like to recognize here. These organizations were all started by volunteers, and volunteers continue to be their heartbeat:

- *Music Trails, later named Fairbanks Concert Association FCA – 1946*

- *Fairbanks Drama Association and Children's Theatre FDA – 1963*
- *Alaska Association for the Arts AAA,*
- *later named Fairbanks Arts Association FAA – 1966*
- *Fairbanks Light Opera Theatre FLOT – 1969*
- *Fairbanks Symphony Orchestra FSO – 1969*
- *Fairbanks Summer Arts Festival FSAF – 1980*
- *Fairbanks Shakespeare Theatre FST – 1993*

CHAPTER 53

ADRENALIN, 100 SHEETS OF SHEETROCK, AND A 100-YEAR FLOOD

In August 1967, Fairbanks, Alaska experienced the greatest flood in its history. It began raining on August 8th and did not stop until August 15th. All of Fairbanks was flooded, some places with up to five feet of water. More than 12,000 people were evacuated. Fairbanks and Nenana were declared national disaster areas. Six deaths were reported, along with damage exceeding $170 million.

Everyone who was in Fairbanks in 1967 has a flood story to tell. Here is mine:

The summer started beautifully enough. On Memorial Day weekend, our family visited the Alaska 67 Centennial Exposition that had just opened. But following that glorious weekend, it rained almost every day that summer. The rainy weather kept the crowds from attending, and it rained especially hard during the first two weeks of August.

People joked and asked friends if they were building their arks, never dreaming how devastating the ensuing flood would be.

On a treacherous rainy August day, the A-67 staff and many volunteers spent hours on the banks of the Chena River, filling sandbags and trying to keep the swollen river from flooding the beautiful new Park.

Their efforts were in vain, and the raging water went over the sandbags. More than a foot of water flooded the entire Park.

Back home, Dick and I thought our place wouldn't have any problems because our property was several miles from the river. We were remodeling the entire lower level of our home, turning the old furnace room into a bedroom for Bryan, expanding the bathroom into what Dick liked to call an English bath, making a place for a washer/dryer, and creating a large office space for Dick to be able to work from home. (He was ahead of his time!) He had just brought all the file boxes from his former office at Ken Murray's agency, and a new copying machine had been delivered earlier in the summer. He had installed an office phone line, so he was already using his new office even while under construction.

Julie had been busy helping keep our home tidy during the project, which affected the main floor as well. She had picked up our large collection of classical LP records from piles on the floor and carefully placed them on top of the baby grand piano to clear floor space.

One hundred sheets of sheetrock were delivered on August 14th. They had been carefully passed through the coal bin opening and were lined up in the lower level, ready to be installed the next day. It was exciting to see the progress and the bedrooms taking shape!

That night, we were prayerful for the families in Island Homes, a subdivision directly on the Chena River. We heard on the radio that flood waters had risen, and people were on their rooftops waiting to be rescued. Our faithful sheetrock installer was one of those people.

When Dick and I heard that, we decided to take a more cautious approach to the situation. After the children were in bed, we moved Dick's important client files from his new office on the lower level up to our main floor and stacked them on chairs.

Dick noted that my adrenaline had kicked in. Without hesitation, I grabbed the newly delivered copying machine, carried it up the stairs, put it on a chair, and headed back to the office for another load.

The following morning, we kept our eyes on the swell of water that had started to slowly approach the south edge of our property, only 40 feet from the house.

Suddenly, the children came running to find us exclaiming that water was sweeping across Caribou Way onto our front lawn like a tidal wave. The sleepy little Noyes Slough that runs along College Road had overflowed!

It was time to leave immediately. We didn't try to save anything from the house, but as we put the kids in the car, we grabbed packs of meat from the garage freezer and threw it into the trunk.

I ran to the corral to get Tom Thumb, our pony we had rented from our friend Frank Stowman for the summer. Tom Thumb always had his halter on, and I quickly tied a rope to it and got him over to the car. I got in the front passenger seat, rolled down the window, and wrapped Tom Thumb's rope around my fingers. The kids were in the back seat, and we made our way up the driveway to College Road.

Several inches of water already covered the road and sidewalk and it was like driving through a shallow lake. People were driving towards us on this lake, and we all gauged where the curb might be on the side of the road to stay in our lanes. We were driving slowly when Tom Thumb got spooked about something and tugged violently on the rope. Since I had the rope laced around my hand and fingers, one of my fingers was seriously wounded when he lurched. Dick found a cloth to absorb the blood and we rewrapped the rope around my whole hand and forged on.

Dick and I agreed that we would drive to the home of our dear friends, Carl and Ruth Benson. They lived on Farmer's Loop, up in the nearby hills, safe from the flood waters.

They were remodeling their home, too. It was a long slow journey, but we arrived unannounced at their front door and they graciously welcomed us. Their children, Sonja, Erika, and Cully, were good friends of our children and they all thought this was an incredible adventure.

I was fortunate because Ruth was a nurse and used her skills to take care of my seriously wounded finger. I still have a scar reminding me of that day.

The children slept in a Jamesway in the Bensons' backyard. This was a military surplus canvas version of a Quonset hut that would be used for temporary housing.

The Bensons welcomed not only our family but also our pony Tom Thumb. Erika had a horse, too, and there was room in the corral. Mr. Stowman came the next day with his trailer and we said goodbye as he picked up Tom Thumb. We would not see him again until the next summer.

After we realized we wouldn't be able to return to our home for some time, we decided we should relax and enjoy this time with our friends.

The older children found a makeshift army camp in the woods behind the Benson's home. They called it the "Three Bear's House." They found intact C-ration boxes, complete with tiny foldable can openers, pilot bread, and miniature cans of spaghetti. They were probably twenty or thirty years old, but the kids opened them up, ate them, and survived!

Free groceries were distributed at the KFAR tower two miles away. This was food from local grocery stores that otherwise would have spoiled. Ruth and I prepared meals, and the children helped as much as possible.

Our children enjoyed doing dishes at the Bensons' because there was a dishwasher! That's when Dick and I decided that we needed to get a dishwasher when we got back home again. We had always thought it was good work for the children to do dishes. But by having a dishwasher, we could create other helpful work they could do instead.

Three days after we left our flooded home, Dick and Carl drove to the base of University Hill. Then, they took a boat to our house a mile away.

They discovered that the lower level was completely full of water, and had overflowed a foot into the main floor. Everything above that foot-high waterline on the main floor was safe. The LPs on top of the piano were perfect, thanks to Julie's unrelated cleaning project weeks earlier! The water didn't reach chair level, so the crucial files from the office were high and dry. The copier was safe and sound. Sadly, what didn't have the same fate was my set of cherished music books that Aunt Mary had sent me in 1939 when I broke my arm. They were in a box on the garage floor, under the sewing machine table we'd set up for Julie. That box and others, along with everything in the lower level, ended up underwater. The hundred sheets of carefully stacked sheetrock were no exception.

But we were all safe and we were fortunate to be with the wonderful Benson family. There was a lot of work ahead to rebuild after what would later be referred to as "Fairbanks' 100-Year Flood."

Special thanks to the Alaska Film Archives at the University of Alaska for the extraordinary flood footage included in this chapter's Bonus Media.

CHAPTER 54

AFTERMATH, RESILIENCE, AND THE POWER OF TIDE

After the flood waters receded, Dick and I made many trips back to our home to assess the situation and clean up the mess.

The damage wasn't limited to the house itself. A logging company's sawmill was located just a block away, and oodles of massive logs floated along Caribou Way and into our yard. Not only that, several of their 50-gallon oil drums floated in as well, spilling rivers of crude oil onto our front lawn, exactly where the children had seen the "tidal wave" rushing in the morning we evacuated.

I had read somewhere that detergent could break down oil spills, so I purchased several boxes of Tide laundry soap.

Ruth Benson helped me spread the Tide powder all over the oily water and we hoped for the best.

We had been at Carl and Ruth's for two weeks when UAF Professor Pat Kinney let Carl know that his young family had gone out of state due to the flood. He told Carl we were welcome to live in their UAF housing. We gratefully accepted the kind offer and were there until the last week of October. We returned to the house and camped out for the rest of the winter while we continued clean-up and reconstruction. It continued to be a big adventure for the children!

Miraculously, Fairbanks was unseasonably warm and sunny that fall, and the snow came late. Everyone living in the floodplain appreciated the extra time to close up their homes before winter set in, replace windows and doors, and get heating systems back up and running.

After the flood, some friends decided to buy property in the subdivisions developed in the hills around Fairbanks, not far from where we took refuge. We also considered doing this and even looked at a place. But we liked our home on College Road, with its location close to both the university and downtown Fairbanks. We would rebuild.

Some Fairbanks visionary arranged for ten retired bankers and financial planners to come to town. They gave their time to help families in need. Anyone affected by the flood could sign up to have one of these knowledgeable professionals work with them to plan for their financial needs.

Burt McKay, a retired banker from a little town in South Dakota, was assigned to help us. He was a kind and knowledgeable man. He became a family friend, and our children called him Grandpa Burt.

Burt gave us the financial guidance we needed. First, he had us list all of our losses. Then, he helped us apply for the Small Business Administration (SBA) 2% loans that were made available, well below the 5.5% prime rate. We had been building out-of-pocket since we were married in 1954. With this financial help, we hired professionals immediately to rebuild our home and make it livable again. We completed the work by mid-January, much sooner than we could have dreamed. Dick gradually got his office in the lower-level functioning, and I returned to teaching at my Musical Nursery School. The icing on the cake was the final appliance we installed: A dishwasher!

Fairbanks was full of resilient people who all worked long hours to get our homes and offices back in shape. Many tradespeople came from out-of-state to work because so many families needed electricians, carpenters, and plumbers. As it turned out, the flood became a boon for Fairbanks. Thanks to the SBA loans, the local economy was stimulated by the money everyone spent on repairs and new construction. Stores bustled as people replaced items that were destroyed in the flood.

In the spring of 1968, lush grass covered our whole front lawn. I don't know if sprinkling Tide made the difference, but it went from tidal wave to Tide soap to a tidy green lawn in ten months!

For years to come, time periods were described as "before the flood" or "after the flood," and if we couldn't find something, our favorite response would be, "It probably got lost in the flood."

The 1967 Fairbanks flood was categorized as a 100-year flood. Many people erroneously believe that if they experienced a 100-year flood in a particular year, they would not see another one like it for 99 years. This is not the case. The true definition simply states that it is one so severe it has only a 1% chance of hitting in **any** given year. In 1968, it was feared that Fairbanks would beat the odds and be in that 1% for a second year in a row, but that didn't happen.

As a result of the 1967 flood, stream and precipitation gauges were installed in the Chena River basin to monitor water levels and help prevent further disasters. The U.S. Congress subsequently approved the Flood Control Act of 1968, authorizing the building of the Chena River Lakes Flood Control Project, which includes the Moose Creek Dam, the Tanana River Levee, and various drainage channels.

CHAPTER 55

A Bestie, an Auntie, and a Secret Story

The year was 1965. It was a beautiful, warm September afternoon in Fairbanks, Alaska. The first day of school had just ended. Many parents were waiting in their cars for their children to run out of University Park Elementary, about four miles from downtown Fairbanks. I spotted our sixth-grade daughter, Julie, running toward the car. She had someone with her. She exclaimed that she wanted me to meet her new friend, Beckie Hood.

The Hood family had moved to Fairbanks that summer. Beckie's dad, Dr. Donald Hood, had been hired as the new director of the Institute of Marine Science at the University of Alaska. Beckie had two younger sisters: Barbie, who was about our son Bryan's age, and Susie, who was about our daughter Shirley's age. Their mother's name was Betty. I told Beckie that I was happy to meet her and looked forward to meeting her mother, too. Beckie and Julie soon made plans for our families to get together.

The Hoods had driven up the Alcan Highway in their Volkswagen van from Bryan, Texas, where they had lived while Don was a professor at Texas A&M University. The previous year, they had lived in England, where Don was on sabbatical at the University of Nottingham. The family was happily settling into the UA campus in a charming old log home that had once housed the UA's first president, Dr. Charles Bunnell.

When we met, I immediately liked Betty Hood. She was about seven years older than I was. She was a talented homemaker and entertainer. Don would frequently call in the afternoon to let her know that he had a group of visiting scientists on campus who would all be coming to their home for dinner that evening. I always admired how she could put together a lovely dinner party on a minute's notice. Her meals were creatively presented, and they were delicious.

Born in 1922, Betty was the youngest of five children. She grew up on a farm near Adair, Oklahoma, where she loved riding her horse, Beauty. She was always a good student, but in those days, girls in her small town were not encouraged to go to college. After she graduated from high school in 1939, Betty clerked in a five-and-dime store.

Then came World War II. In 1942, the United States War Department established an ordnance plant, Oklahoma Ordnance Works, near Adair to produce smoke-free powder and TNT for the war effort. Betty was hired as a lab technician and received on-the-job training. It so happened that Don

Hood also worked there for a short time as a chemist, and they met there.

Soon, the War Department embarked on a secret mission to build an atomic bomb, which it named the Manhattan Project. The department realized it needed to set up operations quickly in a remote location. An area was chosen in south-central Washington state, on the Columbia River near the small farming community of Hanford. In 1943, the War Department approved the acquisition of 40,000 acres of land in the area and relocated about 1,500 displaced people to new locations.

In the autumn of 1943, ground was broken at this new site, which came to be known as Hanford Engineering Works. Betty was among the first wave of workers to accept jobs there. At the age of 21, she left home for the first time, traveling to Washington by bus. She enjoyed seeing the beautiful Rocky Mountains along the way and discovered that traveling was fun! (Eventually, when she and her friends had time off work, they would take a bus and ferry from Washington State to Victoria, BC, and stay at the historic Empress Hotel.)

Betty's first job with Hanford Engineering was as a bookkeeper and hospitality greeter. One of the men she greeted that fall of 1943 was J. Robert Oppenheimer. She didn't realize it at the time, but he was one of the "fathers" of the atomic bomb. Soon, she was promoted to work in the labs. The pay was better, but the working conditions were more dangerous. She didn't know the details, but she knew that the materials she moved around with tongs behind thick glass panels were hazardous. She also knew that she was working on something important and secret. She was told not to talk about her work with anyone.

In 1944, Don Hood joined the project at Hanford as a chemist. Betty and Don became acquainted again and began dating. Then, in August of 1945, the big news came: All the employees at Hanford Engineering were told that uranium, produced at another secret site, was used in the world's first atomic bomb, which was released over Hiroshima, Japan, on August 6, 1945. The plutonium in the atomic bomb that was dropped on Nagasaki, Japan, three days later had been manufactured at Hanford Engineering. Shortly after the bombs were dropped, the war was over.

In November of 1945, Betty and Don were married in a little church in Richland, Washington. Shortly afterward, they moved to Texas so Don could continue his post-graduate studies at Texas A&M University. Betty worked outside the home as a lab technician to help put Don through school. They wanted to start a family, but for many years, Betty had miscarriages. She quietly wondered if working in that lab was the problem.

Finally, in 1954, Betty gave birth to a healthy baby girl. They named her Rebecca. A short time later, Barbara was born, and four years later, Susan joined the family. This was the family I met in Fairbanks in the fall of 1965 when our long and close friendship began. Soon, Betty and Don were "Aunt Betty" and "Uncle Don" to our children, and we were "Aunty Jo" and "Uncle Dick" to theirs. Susie and Shirley started telling their school friends and teachers that they were cousins, and the Hoods and Scotts became related by affection. Our surnames evolved into the Hoodsies and the Scottsies. For many years, we spent lots of time together, including most holidays. Betty worked for Dick in his financial planning office for a few years in the early 1970s.

In August 1976, Beckie and Scott Davis were married in our home, which led to one of our family's favorite memories.

Their wedding rehearsal was the night before the wedding. It was a beautiful summer evening, and Beckie and Scott and the rest of the wedding party were rehearsing their vows in our gardens. Suddenly, our quarter horse Morgan came running wildly by the wedding party and onto the lawn. He slowed down to munch on the delicious grass. He had escaped from the corral! I had to act quickly to catch Morgan. I yanked a bunch of carrots from my nearby vegetable garden, and I slowly approached the halter-less Morgan with my outstretched hands, holding the carrots, which he loved. I coaxed him back to the corral, where his pony buddy Tom Thumb remained. Tom Thumb had missed his chance to get out of the corral. Happily, the outdoor rehearsal resumed. It happened to rain the next day - their wedding day – but we were flexible and moved the ceremony and celebration indoors. It was a lovely event.

Shortly after the wedding, Don and Betty left Fairbanks. Don had retired from the university, and they bought property in Friday Harbor, Washington, where they built a home and planted a huge garden and orchard. The Hoods returned to Fairbanks to visit many times over the years, and Betty and I remained close friends. Don and Betty would stay in the guest house next to our pool, and we enjoyed wonderful times together with our families. In the winter of 1985, they returned to Fairbanks for Barbie's wedding to Dirk Sisson, and in August of 1987, they returned for Susie's wedding to Blaine Sisson, which took place in our yard. It was a beautiful day, and we had no interruptions from our barnyard friends, Tom Thumb and Morgan. Beckie stayed in Alaska for many years, and Barbie and Susie remain there, so there were still Hoodsies in our lives.

Betty and Don's involvement in the Manhattan Project was rarely discussed in the family. But late in Betty's life, when her daughter Barbie was helping her sort her jewelry, Barbie found a tiny pin with the inscription "A" in the middle and "Bomb" across the base. The mother-daughter conversation that followed illuminated a chapter in Betty's life that even her daughters had known little about. Before Barbie wrote a story about it years later, it was a chapter I had never known about either.

Don died in 2002 at the age of 83, shortly after the family had gathered to celebrate Betty's 80th birthday. Five years later, in January of 2007, Betty celebrated her 85th birthday in Friday Harbor. Her long-time friend Nancy from their Hanford Engineering days came to her birthday party and spent the afternoon with Betty. They enjoyed recalling their younger years working together. At one point, Nancy asked Betty if she had applied for her settlement from Hanford Engineering Works. Betty hadn't known about a settlement. It turns out that Congress had passed a law compensating workers who had suffered illnesses that could be traced back to their exposure to dangerous substances during their service to the Manhattan Project.

Betty quickly obtained the claim forms and discovered that both she and Don had suffered illnesses that qualified. As Don's widow, she could apply for both of them. Just after she turned 86 in 2008, she received two settlement checks from the federal government: one for herself and one for Don. She shared with her daughter Barbie that she didn't accept the checks because of the qualifying illnesses, as difficult and disruptive as they had been, but because of "… all the trouble I had having babies."

I hadn't seen Betty for many years when she passed away in the summer of 2010 in Orem, Utah. She was 88 years old. At age 85, she had moved to Utah to be closer to Beckie and her family. Because traveling became difficult, she hadn't been able to make a trip to Fairbanks for some time.

For all the years that Betty and I were such close friends and talked about many details of our lives, Betty never shared her story of working on the Manhattan Project at Hanford Engineering. Her silence tells a lot about her integrity. She kept her experiences at Hanford a secret until her last days, honoring her duties to the war effort long after the war was over. I am sharing them here with the blessing of Barbie and her sisters. Betty was a powerful woman whose wisdom showed up in everything she did. Over all the years of our friendship, I learned so much from her.

After Dick passed away in 2020, I became the only one left of the "Aunt Betty, Uncle Don, Uncle Dick and Auntie Jo" couples. I happily receive visits from the Hoodsie girls. Together, we share memories of the years since 1965 that the Hoodies and Scottsies have been "related by affection." We are creating new memories with every visit!

Jo Ryman Scott

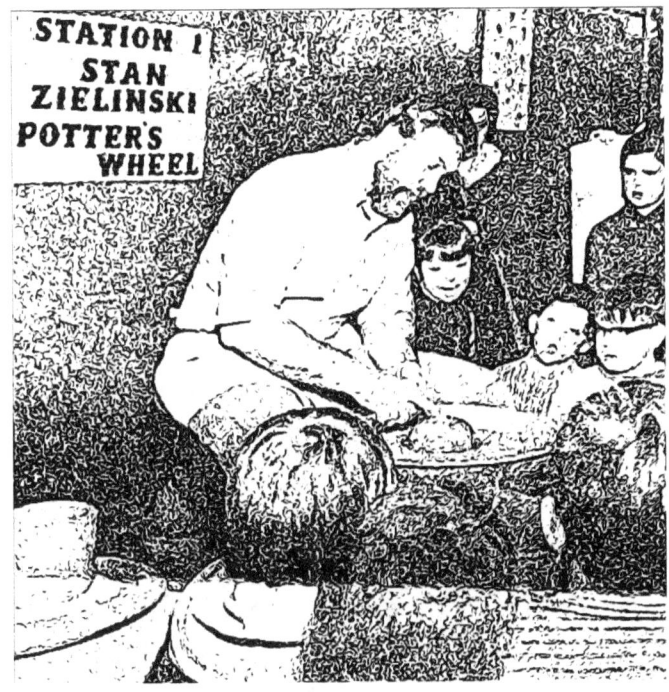

CHAPTER 56

SPINNING WOOL, BLOWING GLASS, AND THROWING CLAY: *ART IN ACTION*

After years of teaching in my Nursery School, I returned to teaching general music part-time at University Park Elementary. I was ready to pursue some other ideas I had.

I continued volunteering with Geneva Emmal and the Alaska Association for the Arts (AAA). I particularly enjoyed working on its Education Committee. For some time, I had dreamed about establishing an arts program to introduce elementary-age children to the many talented visual artists in the Fairbanks community.

Since I only taught part-time in the fall of 1968, I had time to organize my thoughts and plan for this new arts program. I appreciated University Park's vice principal, H.O. "Red" Williams.

He was a dedicated educator and was always available to hear my ideas. He listened intently when I explained the concept of an ART IN ACTION event at University Park.

I proposed inviting four well-known local artists to set up art stations in the school's large, bright gym. I would have four classrooms at a time cycle through the stations, starting their art journey at one and watching the artists do their work for about six minutes.

Then, I would ring a bell, and each class would move on to the next station, where they would observe that artist. After visiting all four art stations, those four classes would return to their rooms, and another four classes would come to the gym for their turn. At the end of the event, every class at U. Park would have visited the four artists' stations.

I told Mr. Williams that I would provide each teacher with information and pictures of each guest artist before the event so that the teachers could prepare their students for what they would experience.

Mr. Williams liked the idea, and I immediately started planning. I contacted these artists who generously volunteered their time to participate:

- Stan Zielinski: Potter's wheel
- Margaret Boyd: Oil painting
- Bill Berry: Pen and ink sketching
- Marsha Romick: Silversmithing

With Mr. Williams' help, the first of many ART IN ACTION events came to be in the spring of 1969. A school board member happened to do a school visit at the time that

ART IN ACTION was in full swing. She couldn't get over the exciting things she saw in the gym!

Mr. Williams and I were happy that many teachers appreciated all the information given to them before the children went to observe the artists. Seeing the amazement on the kids' faces was rewarding as they saw artists in action up close for the first time. This is what Mr. Williams and I had hoped would happen.

A few years later, I was teaching kindergarten at Denali Elementary. Our principal, Patty Haggard, asked me to organize a second ART IN ACTION there. I happily agreed and made it a much larger event this time, doubling the number of artists to eight. It was held at the Denali gym in February 1972.

The following artists volunteered their time to share their talents:

- Stan Zielinski: Potter's wheel
- Arlene Darling: Oil painting
- John Bradbury and Wolfgang Hebel: Glass-blowing
- Turid Senungutuk: Printmaking
- Mary Eubank: Wood carving
- Helmut VanFlein: Clay sculpting
- Gina Brown: Pen and ink sketching
- Marsha Romick: Silversmithing

Eight classrooms came at a time, and we did the same six-minute rotation that had worked so well at University Park. Once again, I prepared advance information about each artist and what they would do for the teachers to share before the event.

The Fairbanks Daily News-Miner published a nice article that included pictures of some of our artists. Over 700+ students got to see artists in action that day!

Some teachers from other schools asked me to help them organize an ART IN ACTION in their schools. I was happy to do this, and the event became popular in the community.

Later that year, I organized FIBER ARTS IN ACTION for one of the schools. Penny Wakefield Alt demonstrated weaving fabrics, and she wore a beautiful outfit she had made with yardage she had woven. The children loved visiting Penny's station. Another guest that day brought her spinning wheel, and everyone, including me, was intrigued to see how it worked.

After this, my long-time friend Mary Jane Fate helped me organize NATIVE ARTS IN ACTION at Denali. Mary Jane helped me invite well-known local native artists who demonstrated beadwork, sewing leather mukluks, making parkas, and sketching on ivory walrus tusks.

One dear Alaska Native fifth grader was very proud that his aging grandmother was one of the guest artists that day. This made me happy! She was making caribou leather moccasins. Native children were not only learning to be proud of their heritage, some were inspired to learn how to create their Native arts and crafts.

Later on, I organized CAREERS IN ACTION at Denali, and combined it with WHAT MAKES IT WORK? I invited various business people to share what they did for a living. We had everyone from a watchmaker to a telecommunication specialist. It was especially fascinating when the watchmaker took a watch apart and showed the children how it worked, and the telecommunication specialist did the same thing with a phone!

All of these programs had exponential outreach, and as recently as this year, I got a touching note that made me realize this. I heard from the son of the dear little fifth grader whose grandmother was making the caribou moccasins. He said his father had told him how much it meant for him to see his grandmother and his Native arts included in an event that *all* of the children were excited to attend!

CHAPTER 57

AN OLD-FASHIONED
DEPOT, AN OLD ENGINE,
AND A NEW VISION

As I've said before, it was Dr. James C. Ryan who encouraged me to choose Fairbanks over any other teaching offers I had in Alaska when I graduated college. I was happy to finally meet him in person, though we had spoken on the phone once and exchanged several letters. When I arrived in Fairbanks in August 1953, Dr. and Mrs. Ryan met me at the old-fashioned, turn-of-the-century Alaska Railroad depot. They had offered to have me stay in their home until I could establish my housing.

It was a lovely evening when I arrived. I had my first glimpse of Fairbanks as we left the train depot, and I felt certain that I was going to like Fairbanks. As we were leaving, I noticed a big rusty train engine draped with heavy-duty chains, probably indicating that no one was supposed to climb on it.

I was intrigued by this old engine and Dr. Ryan told me it was the Tanana Valley Railroad Engine No. 1. It looked like an interesting historic relic. I was surprised that it wasn't protected from the weather. I had lots of questions about it, but we arrived at the Ryan's home, and any questions were forgotten as my Alaska adventure had begun!

It was several years before I learned more about that engine. It was built in 1899 in the Yukon Territory and was the first steam locomotive there. In 1905, the engine was moved to Fairbanks, where it became the first steam locomotive in the Territory of Alaska.

Decades later, it would have another first. Fairbanks local Dan Gullickson saw Engine No.1 for the first time. It was on display at the Friends of the Tanana Valley Railroad Museum (FTVRR) in Alaskaland, now Pioneer Park. He also thought it was an interesting historic relic! He expressed an interest to the people at the museum in restoring it. They liked Dan's engaging personality and felt he seemed to have some knowledge about how to do the restoration. No one else had ever offered to restore it! Dan was granted permission to give it a try.

He encouraged others in the FTVRR to work with him on the project. They worked together to figure out parts that were needed. The engine was more than one hundred years old by this time. Some parts had to be manufactured because they were no longer available. It was tedious and laborious work.

How long do you think it took to complete the job? Two years? Five years? Seven years?

It took ten years of dedicated work!

Dan was the visionary leader of the all-volunteer crew who saw the project to completion. Finally, in the year 2000, one hundred and one years after it was built, Engine No. 1 was completely restored.

It continues to operate with volunteers from the FTVRR Museum Station on special occasions. When not in use, it's proudly displayed in the museum, sheltered from the weather.

It's become one of Fairbanks' historic treasures and a favorite highlight of a trip to Pioneer Park. We are grateful to Dan for being a visionary thinker and assuming this monumental undertaking.

CHAPTER 58

A Farm Dream, a Beach Dream, and a Lunar Landing

By the spring of 1968, the year after the flood, we had finished remodeling our home and started to rebuild the grounds. The front lawn had survived, perhaps from my Tide experiment, after several barrels of crude oil had spilled over it. And by that summer, our vegetable garden flourished again.

After renting Tom Thumb for a few summers, we decided to buy this amiable pony and keep him year-round. Bryan contributed some of his own money to the purchase.

We decided that if we were going to have Tom Thumb year-round, he needed to have a barn. Dick and our carpenter,

A.C. Lindemann, built Tom Thumb's beautiful barn that fall. The following year, Dick bought our beautiful horse Morgan so Tom Thumb would have a buddy. My dream of having horses was finally realized!

Dick was always thinking about accomplishing important work as easily as possible. He constructed a slanted drainable pipeline to the horses' water tank in the corral so we didn't have to carry water to the horses each day. We turned a valve from the comfort of the house every morning, counted to thirty, and turned it off. The horses were watered! We had to remember to drain the line during winter by opening a different valve each time we gave them water. A frozen pipeline would be a serious problem.

Dick also installed an electrical outlet on the corral fence post near the horses' water barrel. He put a submersible water heater in the barrel during the winter months. It kept the water from freezing even at sixty below.

We purchased bales of fresh-cut hay from the fields of Henry Gettinger and Vince Howard. They were good friends who had farms on Chena Hot Springs Road. They always helped us unload the bales and get them into the back of the barn.

June 1969 was unseasonably hot in Fairbanks. Our children dreamed of a swimming pool to cool off. They found a $299 above-ground pool in the Sears catalog. They made plans to combine their savings to buy it. I remember when they showed this pool picture to their dad. Being from California, Dick had long been dreaming of putting a pool in our yard. But he wasn't impressed with the quality of the Sears pool the children could afford.

Always trying to improve on an idea, Dick suggested that if they would chip in their money to purchase a heavy-duty liner, he would pay for the installation. His thought was to hire a front-end loader to dig a shallow hole so the pool could be partially below ground, and he could already envision how he could put a deck around it!

The liner was ordered, and the hole was dug.

Dick used 2' x 12' cedar boards to build a 24' diameter bottomless barrel held together with steel cables. This made a circular cedar wall that looked like an old-fashioned whiskey barrel. With lots of help, he positioned it in the hole.

Dick and the children stapled sheets of Styrofoam insulation all around the inside. It became quite a game for the kids to find and remove every pebble in the soil at the bottom of the hole. They smoothed it out and placed sheets of insulation there, too. Then, the vinyl pool liner was installed.

The children had planned to fill that pool with water and then jump in. But Dick had to add the plumbing. He installed a water pump filtration system and plumbing for filling and draining the pool. The children were anxiously waiting for the day they could fill the pool. It was finally finished after working all of June and half of July.

But Dick decided that for safety reasons, the pool deck and fence he had envisioned needed to be built before filling the pool. Another setback for the kids' dream of the day they would fill the pool! Dick hired our friend A. C. Lindemann to help build the fence and the pool deck. They finished in only three days!

NOW, it was finally time to fill the pool! We used our well water, which came out of the ground at about 50 degrees. Every drop of water needed to go through the softener so the pool water wouldn't rust. Filling the pool with 13,000 gallons of soft water took several days.

On July 20, we had our opening pool party, inviting A. C.'s wife and children to join us. The children joyfully put on their swimsuits and came to the pool's edge, ready to jump in. They cautiously dipped their toes in the water and then jumped back. While the water had warmed up a little, it was still 58 degrees.

A. C. saw the children's hesitation about jumping into that cool pool, so he reached into his pocket and suddenly threw in a handful of coins. Wow! Those kids jumped right in, forgot about the frigid temperature, and started diving for the coins. Shirley claimed that if you just let your fingers go numb and kept moving you would get used to the chilly water.

Our family remembers July 20, 1969, as the day the Scott and Lindemann kids landed in the new cool pool.

But it has a more significant meaning in our country's history: That was the day the Apollo 11 astronauts landed on the moon!

CHAPTER 59

A Captain, A Sailor, and Babies Switched at Birth

I have many wonderful teacher stories, and this one is about how I came to produce Gilbert and Sullivan's *H.M.S. Pinafore* four times in twenty years.

I think theatre experiences help students develop an appreciation of music and how to work cooperatively with each other to produce a good show.

As a general music teacher, I became acquainted with a very creative seventh grade teacher, Mrs. Pestano, as I would roll my piano into her classroom to teach twice a week. Before moving to Fairbanks, she had produced an excellent abridged version of Gilbert and Sullivan's *H.M.S. Pinafore* with seventh graders. We thought it would be fun to produce it at Denali with the sixth and seventh grade students. I was delighted to have so many students with good singing voices and was confident they could handle the parts.

We ordered a copy of the dialogue and reviewed it together and in March of 1955, Mrs. Pestano and I moved forward with plans to produce it in May. I began introducing my sixth and seventh graders to the story and music of that delightful comic operetta. They loved the story and the music and were excited about performing it.

Mrs. Pestano worked with me to hold auditions for the leads. It was an excellent operetta for their age group, and we could use all the students who wanted to be in the show. The boys who didn't get a lead were sailors, and the girls who didn't get leads could play the parts of Sir Joseph Porter's "sisters and his cousins and aunts." Mrs. Pestano, trained in theatre, was the drama coach, and I was the vocal coach and pianist.

Since I taught music to all grade levels, I began introducing the play's story and music in each class I taught. Every child at Denali was familiar with the operetta's music, and the story of babies switched at birth was so funny to them. By May, all our leads knew their parts, and the chorus was ready for our show date! The entire school enjoyed seeing the dress rehearsal the afternoon of the performance. They thoroughly enjoyed the show since they knew the story and the music.

A huge crowd of parents and friends attended the evening performance in the large Denali cafeteria. The show was a big success, and our students performed like professionals.

Mrs. Pestano was an excellent drama coach. I was sorry when she and her husband left Fairbanks in the fall of 1955. I learned so much working with Mrs. Pestano. *H.M.S. Pinafore* is a great way to introduce children to the theatre and fun music and I went on to produce it three more times!

Miraculously, more than sixty-five years later, Jere "Skip" Haley found me on Facebook. He was one of our sailors in that 1955 show. We enjoyed spending time on the phone, and between the two of us, we were able to recall most of the leads:

- Rusty Grossman: Captain Corcoran, of *H.M.S Pinafore*
- Norman Lee: Sir Joseph Porter
- Leila Jo Bowman: Josephine, the Captain's daughter
- Mia Brundin: Buttercup
- Phil Pope: Bos'n

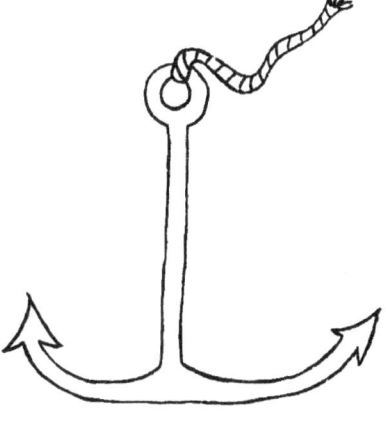

H. M. S. P I N A F O R E
by Gilbert and Sullivan

Produced through special arrangements with the
Willis Music Company

Presented by the Sixth Grade Classes, University
Park School, Fairbanks, Alaska

Monday, May 3, 1971   8:00 p.m.

Program cover by Larry Woolf

Director - Mrs. Richard (Jo) Scott, Vocal Music
                                          Teacher

CHAPTER 60

MORE SISTERS AND COUSINS AND AUNTS

I was called to teach vocal music at University Park in 1961. Many teachers knew about the fun students and teachers had at our Denali *H.M.S. Pinafore* performance in 1955, so they asked me to produce it there, too, and I happily agreed. We all loved this musical because anyone who didn't get a lead could be a sailor, a sister, a cousin, or an aunt.

As a general music teacher for all grade levels, I told the operetta's story and taught the songs to all of University Park's students, just as I had in 1955. I had many sixth graders with good singing voices. All the leads were sixth graders except for Jane Haycraft, who was only in fifth grade. She was a talented and pretty child.

Eric Rice was a musical child and got the lead part as the Captain. However, his classroom teacher told me he could not be in the show. Though a bright child, he had not been doing his classwork.

The Captain's role in the show was a principal lead, and I knew Eric would do an impressive job. I had a little talk with Eric and told him what his teacher had said. Eric acknowledged that he hadn't been doing his classwork and couldn't think of any good reason for not doing it. So, I encouraged Eric to think about this situation. He loved music and wanted to be in the show.

Finally, Eric agreed to talk to his teacher and promised to do his classwork promptly from then on. He kept his promise to do all his classwork on time and was permitted to be in the show. He was a fabulous Captain! (Years later, Eric told me that he had become a better student due to the lesson he had learned.)

We again invited the whole school to attend the afternoon dress rehearsal as we had at Denali. Familiar with it, the children were excited to see the play performed and could follow the story and songs.

Another student who did a great job was Mark Nielsen. He sang and acted the part of the fiendish Dick Deadeye particularly well. The adult audience booed and hissed at him! He didn't understand that he played Dick Deadeye so convincingly that the audience was reacting to his believable performance. I was so sorry I hadn't prepared him for this possibility. I shared this with him after the show and when he understood, he was proud of so much booing. Years later, I was touched when Mark told me what an important part of his life that show was.

A huge crowd of parents and friends enjoyed the evening performance, held in the University Park multi-purpose room in May 1961. It was a great show and another fun success.

I have kept in touch with Jane Haycraft, and we recalled the following leads:

- Eric Rice: Captain Corcoran, of *H.M.S Pinafore*
- Michael Davidson: Sir Joseph Porter
- Jane Haycraft: Josephine, the Captain's daughter
- Sherry Cook: Buttercup
- Mark Nielsen: Dick Deadeye
- Art Bergh: Lowly sailor

Ten years later, I was again teaching vocal music at University Park, and was able to follow the same plan to introduce the whole school to the show's songs and story. We presented our third *H.M.S. Pinafore* in May 1971.

This University Park production featured these talented leads:

- Steve Feder: Captain Corcoran, of *H.M.S Pinafore*
- Debbie Tampke: Josephine, the Captain's daughter
- Jeff Schierenbeck: Ralph Rackstraw, a sailor
- Bill Hawkins: Sir Joseph Porter
- Kristin McDonald: Buttercup
- Randy Foster: Dick Deadeye
- Karen Campbell: Hebe, Sir Joseph's cousin
- Clayton Swanson: Bos'n

This was the first production I had done with a pit orchestra:

- Conductor: Mrs. Christa Bruce:
- Ensemble: Jim Papp, Porcia Fenton, Karen Campbell, Stacey Shallock, Randy Bradbury, Leonard Neidhold, Joan Heidel, Stephanie Morehouse, and Vickie Rauk.

Three years after that, I was back at Denali. Though I was teaching kindergarten full-time and not vocal music in 1974, the sixth-grade teachers and I wanted to produce *H.M.S. Pinafore* just once more before I retired from teaching that spring.

I held rehearsals with the sixth-grade students at noon hours, after school, and even on Saturday mornings. I baked cinnamon rolls for the dedicated students who came on a Saturday morning!

With the beautiful new Denali School multi-purpose room completed, we did just one afternoon show and invited our students, parents, and friends. There was lots of room for the big audience that turned out. It was a terrific show, and it was special for me to be able to produce it one last time.

One of the sailors, Tom Mackin, had attended my Musical Nursery School eight years earlier. I knew his lovely mother, Jean, and she brought a huge box of raised donuts for our little cast party after the show.

All four Pinafore performances over those two decades ignited the students' love of music. It is fun to hear former students tell me how much they treasure those memories.

As for me, I smiled while writing these chapters!

THE 1970S

CHAPTER 61

A POTTERY WHEEL, A
VERY LONG COUCH, AND A
CONCERT GRAND

I retired from teaching in the Fairbanks School District in May 1974. I had thoroughly enjoyed my 21 years of teaching, but now I had other things I wanted to explore.

Dick had his office in our home, so I enjoyed being at home with him and with our three children. Our family kept working on our building projects, and there was always some construction going on!

I had been impressed watching Stan Zielinski use his potter's wheel at our ART IN ACTION events. I decided to enroll in his pottery class at UAF's Art Department. I learned how to use the potter's wheel and glaze my creations. I gained even more appreciation for ceramic artists! I enjoyed it so much that I went back for the second semester.

Dick and I made a short trip to Seattle that fall. We stopped at the Sherman & Clay Music Store near our downtown hotel. Their showroom had a beautiful 1892 Mason & Hamlin nine-foot concert grand piano.

It had come from an estate sale. Its beautifully carved large legs reminded me of a picture of Brahms performing on a piano resembling this one. I loved it! Dick was planning on buying me a car that fall, but I told him I'd much rather have this piano!

When we returned home, he measured the living room extension we had just added. The nine-foot piano would fit perfectly on one wall of the new addition. We purchased the piano, and it was air-freighted to the Fairbanks airport. From there, our faithful H & S Warehouse friends arranged for its careful delivery to the house. It fit perfectly along the far wall of the new addition as planned!

Dick was designing built-in seating for the addition that would seat about twenty-five. He had built the framework around the two remaining walls. We knew we wanted the seat portion to be covered in black Naugahyde, and we wanted to choose an appealing fabric for the back that might bring out the deep blue of the new carpeting.

We happened to go to UAF's new Pub, and they had banquette seating similar to what Dick had in mind. It had a beautiful patterned velvet fabric on the back. We asked our favorite upholstery experts, Lil and Austin, if they could find it for us. They found the fabric featured in a book on mid-century modern design and were able to order it for us.

It looked stunning and provided lots of seating, perfect for the gatherings we would host with guest artists performing on our "new" antique piano. The idea of having concerts in our home became a reality!

We knew the piano needed to be rebuilt. Sherman & Clay connected us with Ed McMorrow, a young, skilled piano restoration professional. Ed knew that piano. He had seen it in the showroom and knew exactly what needed to be done to restore it properly. When Sherman & Clay reached out to introduce us, he was happy the piano had been purchased by someone who wanted to restore it.

But first, he needed some help from Dick. Indeed, this old piano was unique! Instead of pegs for tuning, it had what were called screw stringers. Four of these screw stringers had broken over the years, and parts were no longer available.

Ed spent considerable time on the phone, carefully explaining to Dick how to take measurements on the old piano's tuning section. Dick followed his instructions carefully, and Ed had those four new screw stringers manufactured in Seattle. Once they were finished in February 1975, we flew Ed to Fairbanks. He stayed at our home while working on the piano.

The rebuilding project was no small task. Dick was interested in being able to help Ed when needed, and he enjoyed watching Ed's progress. It took over a month, but oh, my! The results were amazing! The piano had a magnificent sound.

Dick and I hosted a concert in March, 1975, and Ed was an honored guest. It featured UAF's new Professor of Music, the brilliant pianist Dr. James Johnson. Over 40 guests enjoyed Johnson's thrilling concert, followed by a reception with refreshments and conversation. Guests enjoyed visiting with Ed and Dr. Johnson.

That fall, I started taking piano lessons with Dr. Johnson. It was an inspirational and exciting time for me. The last time I seriously studied piano was in 1946 when I was a junior in high school, before my piano teacher, Miss Remde, moved to California.

I thoroughly enjoyed my lessons with Dr. Johnson. I practiced for more than four hours a day, learning several Chopin Etudes and works by Schumann and Debussy. It was a wonderful time in my life. I was no longer working outside the home, and our children were busy pursuing their own interests.

With our construction projects finished, Dick and I were wondering how we could share our home and grounds with others.

CHAPTER 62

A POOL HOUSE, A DOME, AND A CAMP IN OUR YARD

In the spring of 1976, Dick was at it again with new construction projects. He built a sauna by the pool, for summer and winter use. The whole family worked with him on these projects, and our children developed plumbing, electrical, and carpentry skills. Dick worked with our good friend Dar Seim to build an adjacent pool house. It turned out to be a charming little clubhouse with dressing rooms for boys and girls.

As our children started venturing out on their own, I dreamed of having a day camp for kids in our yard. The new pool house would be a great home base!

My long-time friend Michelle Bartlett was on the Tanana Valley Community College (TVCC) staff during the 1970s. One of her jobs was to create a variety of educational summer activities for youth. She had asked me to teach some of these classes, but I didn't want to leave my yard and garden in the summer.

However, I had an idea! I called Michelle and asked if she would be interested in having TVCC offer an educational day camp for kids at our home and grounds. I would organize the camp and hire the staff. The camp could include swimming, horseback riding, and art classes. Michelle liked my idea!

Dick and I would sponsor the two-week camp in cooperation with TVCC, who would handle the registration and payroll. The camp was held on our grounds from Monday through Thursday, between 8:45 am and 4:00 pm. The instructors were paid through TVCC, and Dick and I contributed our time and the camp facilities. We enjoyed being able to share our place. At first, it was known as Jo Scott's Summer Day Camp, and TVCC advertised it as open to "the first forty 4th through 7th graders who signed up."

I had never attended a camp as a kid, so I needed ideas and guidance about organizing one. My friend Patti Shechter had considerable experience working in camps for kids. I had become acquainted with Patti while we were both teaching at Denali. I was impressed with her work with children. I asked her to be the director of our new camp, and she accepted! One of her many good ideas was the tradition of opening and closing the camp day with a flag ceremony.

I hired dedicated teachers. Diane Egley taught horsemanship and P.E. activities. Terry Tomczak taught swimming. She and our camp nurse, Sandra Connelly, remained in the pool area throughout the day for safety reasons. Melinda and Joel Mattson team taught music and drama and used our living room and piano for their classroom and performances. Penny Alt volunteered to be on hand for physical therapy, and when not helping Dick with the finishing touches on the pool house, Dar taught carpentry and nature studies. Dar's wife, Kathy, was a faithful volunteer during the camp years. The Seim children had fun attending camp, so it was great for the family to be together.

Our teachers made our first summer a big success. Word of the camp spread, and it filled up quickly the following year. We wanted it to be affordable, so, over the years, Dick and I waived or reduced the registration fees for children whose parents could not afford the cost.

The original 1976 camp was for ages 9-13. I started with younger children and established the camp well with that age group, but my goal was to eventually have the camp for junior high students. That was the age group I wanted to reach. Finally, in the summer of 1978, it was renamed Jo Scott's Junior High Fine Arts Camp and was open only to grades seven through nine.

Talented teenagers Erika Benson and Jann Laiti taught horsemanship using their horses along with ours, Tom Thumb and Morgan. All four horses had kind dispositions, and the class was very popular. When registration grew to 56, we needed more horses and more teachers. The excellent young horsemanship teachers Karen Babcock, Lisa Montano, Judy Swartz, Nancy Schikora, and Druska Salisbury joined the staff in various years. One creative camper that I'm still in touch with, Kate Sample, went on to teach at camp!

I was never one of the teachers. I had fun visiting classes and doing extra activities with the campers, such as churning butter and baking bread. The rest of the time, I enjoyed mowing the lawn and taking care of my flowers while exciting classes were happening all around me.

Dick was always there to maintain the pool, hot tub, and sauna, and he was continually working on solar panels to help heat the pool.

Around this time, Dick had been reading about the work that Buckminster Fuller was doing with geodesic domes. Dick met two young carpenters who were also interested. Dick bought a kit of the fittings needed for connecting beams to build a dome. The two carpenters worked with Dick and Bryan to construct a 30' diameter dome that summer! It ended up being an important camp classroom. Later he would build an even more elaborate two-story dome as his workshop, complete with a Toyo heater and a winch to lift things to the upper level.

One of our campers was Vivica Genaux, who came when she was in the seventh grade. I could see her potential even then. She went on to go to UAF's Fine Arts Music Camp, and would soon attend Festival classes. She went on to study at Indiana University Bloomington. She has become an internationally well-known mezzo-soprano, concertizing all over the world. Dick and I were able to visit her and her lovely husband, Massimo, in their charming home in Venice, Italy. Fairbanks is very proud of her.

I loved *all* of our campers! They were well-behaved, smart, kind kids. I recognized that not one of them had special needs. In those days, students with special needs weren't integrated into regular classes. Many of my campers had never been around anyone their age with a disability.

I reached out to a special ed teacher friend and asked her to recommend a junior high student who might enjoy our camp. I wanted to waive the registration fee to facilitate their participation. My friend recommended a boy with mobility issues who would need help getting to the various classes. His sister was just a couple years older but had become a great aide to him, so I waived her registration and welcomed them both to camp. She was a wonderful helper to her brother throughout the day, especially in horsemanship and swimming classes. They both enjoyed participating in all that we offered.

This was one of the most exciting things I had ever done. My campers were so kind and helpful to them both, and they were touched in a meaningful way.

The camp was a positive experience for our campers and staff for seven years and was a perfect way to share our home and grounds. We were grateful to Michelle and TVCC for their years of exceptional support; we could never have succeeded without it.

Life was good!

But I was always thinking of what we could do next...

CHAPTER 63

A PIANO COMPETITION AND THE SEED OF AN IDEA

Dick and I attended a lovely holiday gathering at Duane and Joan Mikow's in 1977. There, I met Jack Distad, a math professor at UAF. Like we were, Jack was a dedicated supporter of UAF's Music Department. He told us about his idea of establishing the University of Alaska Fairbanks Biennial Competition for Students of Piano, Voice, and Strings.

Jack recalled my work bringing the Canadian Opera to Fairbanks nine years earlier. He asked if I could help him organize this competition. It sounded interesting, so I agreed.

One of the first things Jack asked me to do was contact the community to request contributions to the Music

Department. We needed this financial support to provide prize money for the competition winners. People were very responsive, and I obtained the necessary funding based on the budget Jack had prepared.

Jack also had the idea of commissioning a composer to write a piece that each entrant would perform. He asked me to select that composer. I asked Edward J. "Eddie" Madden, a popular visiting professor at UAF's Summer Fine Arts Camp from Boston. He was well-known as a gifted musician and composer and graciously accepted.

Jack selected outstanding nationally-known judges:

- Ozan Marsh: Piano, University of Arizona, Tucson
- Kathryn Harvey: Voice, San Francisco State
- Raphael Hillyer: Strings, Founder of the Julliard String Quartet

Kathryn suggested inviting the talented pianist Robert "Bob" McCoy as competition accompanist for vocalists and instrumentalists.

Jack was pleased with the two-day statewide competition held at UAF's Charles W. Davis Concert Hall in May 1978.

At the "after-the-competition" meeting with Jack, Eddie, Bob, and the three judges, an enthusiastic discussion emerged. I shared my interest in establishing a study/ performance festival in cooperation with the University's Music Department.

Ozan suggested that he, Kathryn, and Raphael be my Honorary Board Members. I was happy to accept his suggestion.

I had been thinking about how to establish a festival. Although I had heard about many festivals, I had never attended one. When these noted musicians supported my idea, I became more serious about making it happen. I spent considerable time thinking about what my first move should be.

I had successfully established funding to organize many events over the years and believed I could be the producing director. I needed to find a well-known, talented musician with just the right personality who would be the new festival's artistic director. That person would need to know master teachers and performers to invite.

Raphael was impressed with Eddie's talents as a composer, teacher, and performer, saying, "his virtuosity is in his versatility." We realized that Eddie would be the perfect choice. Eddie accepted the offer to be the artistic director of the proposed festival. He suggested that our first one should concentrate on jazz.

Eddie and I went to UAF music faculty member Dr. Theodore "Ted" DeCorso to see about collaborating with the university to make this happen. After discussing the idea with other music department faculty, Ted reported that they agreed that Fairbanks would be receptive to a festival and that the UAF Music Department would partner. Jazz Festival '80 was ready to plant.

THE 1980S

CHAPTER 64

THE SEED GERMINATES
AND STARTS TO GROW

The Festival didn't just *happen*. Once the UAF Music Department came on board and the seed idea of Jazz Festival '80 was planted, many people helped as we took the next steps.

For starters, I felt it was essential to keep a well-documented history of the organization. I asked my friend Kathy Seim to be the Festival Historian, and she gave her time to help in this way. Kathy sought guidance from the University of Alaska Fairbanks' Rasmuson Library Archives staff to learn how to prepare the Festival's historic materials properly. Years later, she showed the process to my dedicated friend, Linda Witt, who continued as Festival Historian.

The main hurdle, of course, was financing. My dear friend Jean Mackin, a former member of the Alaska State Council on the Arts, let me know that the National Endowment for the Arts (NEA) was offering grants to first-time jazz festival applicants. She obtained the necessary forms for me to apply. In the summer of 1979, Ted DeCorso, Jean Mackin, and I wrote a proposal to the NEA on behalf of the UAF Music Department asking for $10,000 to help produce Jazz Festival '80 in April 1980. In January 1980, the NEA awarded us a grant of $7,000. It wasn't what we had requested, but it was very encouraging.

This grant was possible because we submitted the proposal through the University, which is a nonprofit. To widen my own scope of donors, I would need to establish a 501(c)(3) nonprofit status for the proposed festival myself. My friend Linda Hulbert was a huge help in starting the necessary IRS paperwork to apply for this.

Two IRS employees from the Seattle office became my phone friends. I called them when I needed help completing the forms to ensure I was doing everything right. Since I had not yet produced a festival, they guided me to name my new corporation "Jo Scott's Center For Cultural Developments, Inc." which I could later legally change to "The Fairbanks Summer Arts Festival, Inc."

I had carefully prepared a budget of $30,000 for the festival. Because we received only $7,000 from NEA, I had to ask the community for more funding to meet our budget. While awaiting my nonprofit status, UAF could accept donations on behalf of the festival. I came up with the idea of Guarantors, whose pledge, or part thereof, would only be used if needed. I went to friends who had expressed interest in helping raise the additional $3,000 and asked them for a financial pledge. I ended up receiving fifteen $1,000 pledges! The Kiwanis Club of Fairbanks generously opted to contribute $1,000 outright. I felt confident that with this safety net we would have more than enough to cover all projected expenses.

We bought plane tickets for Eddie, the six Boston-based guest artists he selected, and for our Spotlight Guest, Clark Terry. They were excited to be coming to Alaska and we were off and running.

One week before the Festival's first day, I received a letter from the IRS. When I opened it, I was delighted to read that my nonprofit status had been approved. The Festival was coming into bloom!

Many of the Festival's archived documents are included in the Bonus Media QR files at the end of each chapter of this book. To make an appointment to visit the Archives in person, call 907-474-2791.

.

CHAPTER 65

JAZZ FESTIVAL '80
SPROUTS AND BLOOMS

Jazz Festival '80 would run from April 21-26, 1980. The six Boston jazz musicians that Eddie invited to join him as guest artists were all dedicated teachers and master performers:

- Greg Hopkins: Trumpet, Berklee College of Music
- Fred Buda: Trap set drummer - Boston Pops, percussionist - Boston Symphony
- Jack Dryden: Bass, Berklee College of Music
- John LaPorta: Clarinet, Berklee College of Music
- Paul Schmelling: Piano, Berklee College of Music
- Karen Cameron: Cabaret vocalist, Boston

- Eddie Madden: Trombone, jazz pianist, arranger, composer, conductor

They all arrived together the Friday prior. Dick and I hosted the fun group in our home the next day. We worked on plans for the coming week, and they rehearsed together.

Paul enjoyed playing our recently rebuilt 1892 Mason & Hamlin 9' grand piano. Eddie accompanied the delightful jazz singer Karen Cameron, who rehearsed songs she would sing the following week. I especially enjoyed hearing her sing *You Must Believe in Spring,* a new song by French composer Michel Legrand.

Dick and I took the group to dinner at the Pump House on Chena Pump Road that night, and we enjoyed introducing them to friends who were dining there.

We made reservations at the Chatanika Gold Camp on the Steese Highway for a fabulous Sunday brunch the following day. That morning, I sat next to Fred Buda, who shared the news that the Boston Pops had just hired John Williams as its new conductor, taking over after the popular Arthur Fiedler retired.

Our guest artists from Boston had a great time meeting so many local people. Because school was in session during those April days, Festival class times were limited to after school and evenings. Registrants Jay Lewis, a Fairbanks radio personality, and Mark Neidhold, a talented high school student at the time, still tell about enjoying the life-changing private drum lessons with Fred Buda.

I wanted the community to meet the guest artists that week, so I arranged for them to give cameo performances around town. Eddie was the enthusiastic presenter for these. Some Fairbanks students and parents had previously met Eddie as he had been a favorite visiting jazz professor at UAF's amazing Jr. High Fine Arts Camp.

The guest artists visited 7th-12th graders' big band classes in all the schools that week! The students enjoyed meeting the artists, who graciously encouraged them to keep up their music studies.

Eddie and the guest musicians worked evenings with the registrants in the Festival Jazz Band. The band comprised high school musicians, UAF students, and adults from the community. It was a talented group of eager registrants. They were ecstatic when Eddie arranged for our Spotlight Guest, Clark Terry, to fly in early and rehearse with the Jazz Band on Thursday and Friday nights.

It was fun to watch them rehearse the pieces they would be performing at the final concert on Saturday night. The band members were excited to be playing with jazz legend Clark Terry! He was a remarkable teacher and gifted performer. He inspired the registrants to rise musically above what they dreamed they could do. Our Festival Jazz Band ended up sounding quite pro!

Eddie had the right personality to excite a large audience about this new Festival. He was a terrific master of ceremonies, and the audience loved him. Held at UAF's Davis Concert Hall, Eddie welcomed the audience to the fantastic Thursday night jazz concert featuring all the visiting guest musicians, including himself on trombone. It was well received by a full house, closing with a standing ovation.

We had another full house at Hering Auditorium for the final concert. Eddie was the popular emcee again and made the audience feel proud of this new Festival. Clark Terry and the Boston artists closed the concert. It was an amazing way to finish our first Festival.

We hosted a reception in our home after the concert, honoring the guest artists, our Guarantors, and friends from UAF and the community. At that reception, one of my local friends, who happened not to be a jazz fan, asked me rather brusquely, "Jo, why did you organize this Festival for jazz music? Why didn't you include classical?"

This is what I had hoped would happen! I planned to include classical music someday. This request would have to come from classical music lovers in the community. I graciously thanked my friend for her positive suggestion and started planning to include classical music in the next Festival.

After the guest musicians left Fairbanks, Eddie wrote a letter to the editor of the *Fairbanks Daily News-Miner* thanking the community for their support of the Festival. He expressed how happy he and all the Boston artists were to perform in Fairbanks and how much they enjoyed the warm hospitality they received. He again shared that the Fairbanks community could be proud of this new Festival.

Ed and Alene Christiansen, two of our Guarantors, also wrote a letter praising the Jazz Festival '80's Saturday evening concert. They expressed their pride in having this new Festival in the Fairbanks community.

I was grateful to C.W. Snedden, the publisher of the *Fairbanks Daily News-Miner*, for his encouragement and financial support of the Festival and to the News-Miner itself for the excellent coverage of the Festival's activities that week.

All these things were helpful as I started thinking about organizing next year's Festival. We had brought in more revenue from registration fees, concerts, and other contributions than we had expected. After Jazz Festival '80 closed and all the costs were tallied, we lacked just $600 to cover all expenses.

Each Guarantor was asked to pay only $40 of their $1000 pledge!

They were pleased to hear this good news, but instead of giving just their $40 portion, they all opted to give the full pledge to support the Festival's continued growth. The Kiwanis Club of Fairbanks, which had opted to contribute $1,000 outright, continued that generous yearly donation for the next 29 years.

A week later, I met with the UAF Music Department faculty. They had voted to continue the University's support and encouraged me to continue with plans for the following year's Festival. This support was critical to the Festival's success. I shared the feedback that people wanted a longer session and also the requests from the classical musicians. We decided the 1981 Festival would have a two week session, and we would rename it Jazz to Classics.

What an exciting time for me. The festival idea that had been planted not only bloomed, but it flourished!

CHAPTER 66

1981 JAZZ TO CLASSICS

I was grateful that the Music Department gave me the green light to prepare for the following year's Festival, Jazz to Classics.

At the same time, I was busy preparing for the sixth season of Jo Scott's Junior High Fine Arts Camp. I was grateful to continue working with Michelle Bartlett and the UAF's Tanana Valley Community College (TVCC). I had good teachers, and the 56-camper limit filled up quickly.

I spent considerable time fundraising for the Festival and listening to what classical musicians wanted. I went to Boston to meet with Eddie to begin preparing our registration form and catalog. He figured out what classes to add for classical musicians. As plans for Jazz to Classics materialized, I sent contracts out in March 1981.

After Boston Pops percussionist Fred Buda received his contract, he called to share how impressed he had been with Jazz Festival '80 and gave me an assignment. He urged me to go to Boston as soon as possible to meet with William "Bill" Moyer, the Personnel Manager for the Boston Pops and the Boston Symphony (BSO).

Buda told me to share with Moyer my vision of what I thought the Festival could become. He would speak to him first and said that Moyer might have ideas about how the BSO could help our young Festival. I made a reservation to fly to Boston. I needed to meet with Eddie to finalize our catalog and registration form, so I planned to meet Bill Moyer as well.

This may surprise some of our readers, but in 1981, Northwest Orient Airlines operated daily non-stop flights from Fairbanks to Boston. Northwest had become a Festival supporter, and they provided my plane trip, saving the Festival $650. On my first evening there, I stayed up most of the night, putting my vision of what I thought the Festival could eventually become on paper.

The following day, I walked over to Symphony Hall, where Bill welcomed me to the home of the Boston Symphony Orchestra. He graciously listened to my vision for the Festival's future and thought my ideas were applicable not just to local Alaskans but also to people from around the states.

Moyer thought he and the BSO could help our new Festival in various ways. They would give us a 1/4-page ad in all of the Pops' concert booklets that summer. He would speak with John Williams regarding his availability to be our Festival's Spotlight Guest at our Jazz to Classics concert. He arranged for the BSO's Cambridge String Quartet to be excused from the last two weeks of concerts at Tanglewood so they could be guest artists at the coming summer's Jazz to Classics.

When I shared that I was looking for a classical pianist to work with UAF's pianist, Dr. James Johnson, Moyer suggested that I meet his son, Fred Moyer, a concert pianist. We did hire Fred, and he and James Johnson worked well together and became good friends.

I enjoyed the productive meeting. Bill was sincerely interested in our Festival, and I am grateful to Fred Buda for assigning me the task of contacting him. Bill Moyer joined Ozan Marsh and Kathryn Harvey to become an Honorary Board Member of the Festival!

Eddie and I then met to complete the catalog and registration form. We wanted people to be able to afford to register. With the grants and contributions we had received, we kept the registration fee under $100. We included the perk that Festival registrants would be able to attend all the concerts by showing their Festival ID. The two-week, Monday through Friday Festival would begin on August 10, 1981.

When I got back to Fairbanks, there was a lot of work to do. We wanted to get information out to potential registrants as soon as possible. The UAF Printshop did a great job printing our catalog, with the pull-out registration form conveniently stapled in the middle. I had volunteers lined up to help me mail the catalogs. In the days before computer mailing lists, we hand-addressed each one.

We had considerable in-kind publicity to help us spread the word. We appreciated the help from the *Anchorage Daily News,* the *Fairbanks Daily News-Miner*, and the Fairbanks radio and television stations.

Local media personality and Festival registrant Jay Lewis was excited to help the Festival. Jay helped write and design ads for flyers and for the newspaper, radio, and television ads, giving the Festival the professional look we were working to achieve.

Another talented volunteer, Diane Hansen, did design work at the UAF Print Shop. She created the Festival's first logo and the concert programs. She was a gifted artist, and we appreciated her help.

In a personal note from John Williams, he regretted not being our Spotlight Guest because of date conflicts with his Tanglewood schedule. Eddie invited Boston jazz clarinetist Dick Johnson to be the Festival's Spotlight Guest. We were happy to welcome back every guest artist from Jazz Festival '80 except for John LaPorta and Paul Schmellling, who had scheduling conflicts.

Our new jazz and classical artists were:

- Dick Johnson: Spotlight Guest, Boston
- Bob Winter: Boston Pops, Berklee College of Music
- Sheila Fiekowsky: BSO Cambridge String Quartet
- Bernard Kadinoff: BSO Cambridge String Quartet
- Jennie Shames: BSO Cambridge String Quartet
- Robert Ripley: BSO Cambridge String Quartet
- Fred Moyer: Piano, Boston Pops
- Gerald Webster: Trumpet, Washington State University
- Irv Gilman: Flute, University of Albany
- Byron McGilvray: Choral, San Francisco State

The Festival Jazz Band and Orchestra, both conducted by Eddie, and the Festival Chorus, conducted by Byron, became popular draws for registrants. These dynamic groups had evening rehearsals, making attendance easy for people with daytime jobs.

I felt some anxiety that summer of 1981 and started wondering if I had made a huge mistake in thinking that with just volunteer help, I could make the Festival work with its new August dates. Some people said that Fairbanksans would never give up two weeks in the summer to register for classes and attend concerts. I felt that the people who gave their time to the Fairbanks Light Opera Theatre would be happy to do just that for the opportunity to further develop their talents by studying with some of the best teachers in the country.

I was so busy running my Junior High Fine Arts Camp the months prior that I didn't have time to talk with many people about the Festival. However, two remarkable women, June Ulz and Ruth Storvick, whose daughters were enrolled in Camp, were my angels that summer. They believed in my efforts to establish this summer Festival and assured me that many community members were excited about it. They gave me the love, encouragement, and helpful ideas I desperately needed that summer and helped spread the word. They were registrants, and their enthusiasm and support continued during the Festival. I will never forget what June and Ruth did for me that summer.

Jazz to Classics was a resounding success, both financially and artistically. We had more than 200 registrants and full houses at all of the concerts.

Our three final evenings started with the Pops Concert, featuring our guest musicians in an evening of Jazz to Classics; the Classical Concert, our guest musicians in concert with the Festival Chorus and the Festival Chamber Orchestra; and the Finale Jazz Concert, featuring Spotlight Guest Dick Johnson with the Boston musicians and the Festival Jazz Band.

My vision for a summer Festival had materialized. Bill Moyer was right, and we had several out-of-state registrants, all ready to come back and bring friends. Best of all, many other local arts groups asked if the next Festival could include their areas of study. Again, precisely what I'd been hoping for!

Jo Ryman Scott

FAIRBANKS SUMMER ARTS FESTIVAL

JAZZ TO CLASSICS   DANCE   THEATRE   VISUAL ARTS

CHAPTER 67

NEW CLASSES, NEW ARTISTS, NEW NAME!

The Festival thrived and expanded beyond my initial hopes, largely thanks to numerous requests from local arts groups eager to have their areas of study included in future festivals.

The transformation began with the Festival's roots as Jazz Festival '80 and then evolved into Jazz to Classics 1981. In 1982, we were able to act on many of the community suggestions, and it would now be recognized as the Fairbanks Summer Arts Festival. This new name marked a pivotal moment in our journey, symbolizing a broader commitment to the arts in all its forms.

To ensure each area of study was effectively managed, we counted on dedicated local volunteer coordinators. These coordinators carefully selected the guest artists who would lead workshops and classes in their area. Additionally, they prepared detailed biographies and course descriptions for inclusion in the festival catalog and registration forms.

I felt truly fortunate when a group of local dance educators—Ruth Glenn, Darrel Balough, Nancy Molloy, Lisa Shoen, and Claire West—proposed adding dance workshops to our newly envisioned Festival. Their enthusiasm was contagious, and I was more than happy to give my approval.

Board member Jean Mackin was also eager to enrich our program by incorporating theatre classes. She teamed up with Walter Ensign and Hugh Hall, which led to the inclusion of Shakespeare workshops.

The visual arts segment of the Festival came into being thanks to the initiative of a young and talented Fairbanks artist, Jim Behlke, who generously volunteered to serve as its local coordinator. I was particularly excited when he extended invitations to two nationally recognized art educators with whom he had studied. Their involvement promised to elevate the level of instruction we could offer.

Moreover, Jim had the creative vision to suggest producing a high-quality, four-color printed Festival poster each year. He showed my board and me a striking painting he'd done of a single flower, and we were immediately taken with it. Jim designed the poster, beautifully incorporating the names of our guest artists for that summer's Festival along the bottom.

The energetic Theresa Reed and other local classical vocalists were interested in inviting Kathryn Harvey. Theresa volunteered to be the local coordinator, and we hired Kathryn as our classical music vocal guest.

Vocal studies were more accessible than instrumental studies because no instrument was needed, and vocal class registrations propelled the growth of the Festival in those early years. Byron McGilvray had been very popular, especially with people from the Fairbanks Light Opera Theatre (FLOT.) We invited him to return; he had another commitment but highly recommended Gary Unruh to take his place that year. As Byron had, Gary successfully attracted many singers to register for the Festival Chorus. It was open to anyone who loved to sing, with or without formal training.

We had Kathryn Harvey to thank for our opera and musical theatre vocal coach, Bob McCoy. He had come to Alaska as the accompanist for the piano competition in 1979 and would remain a dedicated Festival musical theatre guest artist for 20 years.

Thanks to another suggestion, Eddie worked with instrumental musicians to establish the new Festival Chamber Orchestra.

All of these new areas of study helped registrant enrollment top 300! These were truly exhilarating times for the newly branded *Fairbanks Summer Arts Festival*, marked by new beginnings and a vibrant celebration of creativity.

ALASKA
IS A
RAINBOW

Words and Music by.
Mike Monaghan

First Performed at the
Fairbanks Summer Arts Festival, 1986
(Limited Edition)

CHAPTER 68

1982 FAIRBANKS SUMMER ARTS FESTIVAL

We were excited to include all the new areas of study in our newly renamed Fairbanks Summer Arts Festival for the 1982 season.

We hired our only paid staff member to date: an office manager to be present in our Great Hall ticket booth/office at all times. The rest of us volunteered.

One of our registrants suggested we make a tee shirt, so we contacted Fairbanks' own Raven Screens to do just that. Our first signature Festival tee sold for $7, and our beautiful Jim Behlke Festival posters were available for $10. Our office manager took care of these sales, but I hoped one day we'd have an actual gift shop!

Besides our musical theatre, dance, and classical voice additions, Eddie added two outstanding instrumental jazz musicians to our lineup:

- Mike Monaghan: Saxophone, Boston Pops
- Mark Henry: String bass, Boston Pops

Additionally, Eddie invited a third musician, Chris Calloway, to join us in 1982. Chris, a gifted jazz singer, came highly recommended through various musical interactions Eddie had enjoyed in Boston while she was studying at Boston University. She is the daughter of the legendary Cab Calloway, known for his role as a bandleader and singer at the famous Harlem Cotton Club. Chris had performed alongside her father in the all-black cast of Pearl Bailey's *Hello Dolly*, a show in which Eddie had played in the pit orchestra. Their prior connections made her addition to the Festival particularly special.

Eddie and I completed the catalog with the registration form, and began the mailing adventure, announcing the dates for the 1982 Fairbanks Summer Arts Festival: July 26th through August 6th. Registrations started to pour in, and we had over 400 participants sign up. We were ready for them!

I vividly recall picking Chris up after her late-night flight from New York to Fairbanks. She arrived exhausted yet full of excitement. By the next day, Chris fully embraced the festival spirit, reveling in the warm community and vibrant atmosphere. Her cabaret workshop became an instant favorite among attendees, with students thoroughly enjoying her engaging teaching style.

Beyond offering daytime workshops on campus, Eddie wanted our jazz musicians to engage with the broader Fairbanks community. He arranged for Chris and the other performers to make cameo appearances around town, where the local audiences responded with overwhelming enthusiasm.

Eddie was busy all day and evening during the Festival and was essential to its artistic success. He maintained the tradition of connecting our guest musicians with local music educators. They conducted valuable workshops for students in grades 7-12 across Fairbanks and North Pole schools, offering these young musicians a unique opportunity to work closely with professional artists.

We finished the 1982 Festival with three well-attended evening concerts in the Davis Concert Hall:

Wednesday, August 4th: *An Evening of Classics* featured our guest artists, with the Festival Chamber Orchestra conducted by Eddie Madden and the Festival Chorus conducted by Gary Unruh.

Thursday, August 5th: *An Evening of Jazz* featured our special guest, jazz vocalist Chris Calloway, performing with our jazz guest artists and the Festival Jazz Band conducted by Eddie Madden.

Friday, August 6th: *An Evening of Pops* featured all the guest musicians in the Festival Pops Orchestra conducted by Eddie Madden, and the Festival Chorus conducted by Gary Unruh.

With donations, registration fees, and ticket sales, we were successful in balancing the 1982 Festival budget. We continued to have challenges but always listened to and acted on people's suggestions. These were exciting times for all of us who advocated for the arts in Fairbanks.

We organized a memorable concert in our home after the final concert for 50 significant donors who had made substantial contributions to the Festival. The evening was a success, with guests enjoying Chris and the jazz musicians' performances. Eddie helped coordinate this delightful gathering. As a token of appreciation, I gifted each donor the new Festival poster featuring Jim Behlke's painting *Columbine,* signed by all the guest artists.

I was humbled to receive the *Fairbanks Daily News-Miner*'s Community Service Award at the annual Chamber of Commerce awards dinner. C. W. Snedden, the *News-Miner*'s publisher, had supported the Festival since its inception. Snedden and his wife Helen were always interested in elevating projects that local people were doing to promote the positive growth of Fairbanks.

Along with Chris, both Monaghan and Henry also quickly became cherished long-term guest artists. Monaghan was so moved by his experience at the Festival and the breathtaking Alaskan landscape that, upon returning to Boston, he was inspired to compose *Alaska Is a Rainbow.* He performed it for us the following year, and his composition resonated deeply with everyone who heard it. *Alaska Is a Rainbow* became a staple at the Festival's opening concert for years to come.

A link to all of the Festival Posters can be found in this chapter's Bonus Media.

CHAPTER 69

A New Gift Shop, More New Classes, and a New Registrant

A lot of exciting developments took place in 1983! We launched "The Night Fairbanks Danced," a fantastic fundraiser featuring Festival musicians that was held at Westmark Hotel's beautiful ballroom. It attracted a large crowd and became a cherished Festival tradition for several years.

Festival workshops and private lessons gained popularity, and rehearsals for the Festival Orchestra and Chorus continued in the evenings to accommodate those who worked weekdays.

We had been selling our signature tee shirts and posters out of the Festival office. I envisioned establishing a Festival Gift Shop one day. In June 1983, my friend Suzi DiVargas expressed interest in helping to create one. We visited the Demientieff family at Raven Screens, who assisted us in ordering several quality items featuring the Festival's logo.

When the items were delivered, Suzi arranged them beautifully in the Great Hall, setting up a charming Festival Gift Shop that included all of the fun new items and the signature tee shirts and posters. Our little shop was ready for business on the first day of the Festival and became a huge success! We priced items to make a small profit to ensure they remained affordable for participants looking to purchase souvenirs. Suzi was perfect for leading this project, and I appreciated her wonderful initiative.

I was fortunate to have dedicated volunteers manage our Festival Gift Shop: Chris Duke, Terry Tomczak, Virginia Damron, Judy and Carl Divinyi, Dee Lashbrook, Suzanne McBride-Ruedy, and her two daughters, Victoria and Vanessa. It looked great each year, and thanks to these volunteer managers, we generated substantial profits that went directly back to the Festival.

Jim Behlke continued as the local coordinator for visual arts. After the success of the first Festival poster in 1982, he produced beautiful paintings for posters for the next four years. We then began to feature other local artists' work. I have always been grateful to Jim for his years of dedication. Tom and Nelda Nixon later took on the local coordinator role many years later.

Dick and I hosted art shows in our yard featuring artwork by our visual arts guests, attracting visitors from all over the country. Out-of-state attendees enjoyed purchasing original art while surrounded by beautiful flowers in an Alaskan garden.

Over the years, notable visual arts guests have included Bob Kapelis, Ruth Weisberg, Judi Betts, Rita Baragunda, Jean Flanagan-Carlo, Bill Brody, David Mollett, Jessie Hedden, Linde Kienle, Ray Pierotti, Joan Kimura, Rachel Clark, Ree Nancarrow, Karolyn Holman, Nikki Kinne, Vladimir Zhikhartsev, Mary Lee Guthrie, and Marcia Guthrie.

Both Byron McGilvray and Gary Unruh returned in 1983, with Byron conducting the Festival Chorus and Gary leading the newly added smaller Chamber Chorale.

Also in 1983, local classical voice coordinator Theresa Reed was eager to have guest artist Kathryn Harvey add Festival Opera Workshop classes. Musical theatre classes were combined with these, and that area of study became known as Opera and Musical Theatre (OMT). Kathryn agreed and suggested that our outstanding vocal coach, Bob McCoy, create opera and musical theatre workshops.

A new registrant that year was a voice student of Bob's at the University of Maryland School of Music, Nancy Peery Marriott. Nancy had asked Bob where he went every summer. After he told her about the Fairbanks Summer Arts Festival, she decided to follow him to Alaska! Nancy registered for OMT classes and enjoyed the workshops and performance opportunities. Having attended festivals worldwide, she noted that none compared to ours. Nancy went on to participate in more than 20 years of OMT and would make a significant impact on the Festival in the years to come.

CHAPTER 70

1984 Fairbanks Summer Arts Festival Cab Calloway

Chris Calloway had been a guest jazz vocalist with the Festival Big Band since 1982 and later created and taught the Festival's first cabaret workshops. We were thrilled when she said she might be able to coax her father, Cab Calloway, to be our Spotlight Guest for 1984!

Born in 1907, Cab Calloway was an American singer, songwriter, dancer, band leader, and conductor. He was also an actor who mixed jazz and vaudeville during his early years, performing at Harlem's famous Cotton Club. The audience loved him!

When Cab agreed to be the Festival's Spotlight Guest, I told him I would be happy to fly his wife, Nuffie, to Fairbanks, too.

My friend Cathy Schultz, the manager of the beautiful new Sophie Station Hotel, offered a reduced rate for the Festival's guest artists in the lovely Presidential Suite. It had a full kitchen, dining room, living room, large bedroom, and bathroom. Cab and Nuffie were the first of our guests to stay in that Suite. Festival fans stocked the kitchen with homemade Alaskan goodies prior to their arrival.

I was grateful to Alaska Airlines for providing Cab and Nuffie's airfare, and Chris, Dick, and the Festival fans joined me to meet them at the airport. It was really exciting for all of us!

Cab drove a Lincoln Town Car in New York, and he was happily surprised to see that Ralph Seekins provided him with the same car for his use in Fairbanks. My young, dependable neighbor Greg Bovee drove Cab and Nuffie around town to get acquainted with the community and the University. Greg recently told me he still remembers that fun assignment in 1984.

Eddie organized the unforgettable August 4th concert and served as the gracious emcee. Cab performed for a sold-out house at Hering Auditorium.

The Festival Jazz Band, made up of registrants and guest artists, backed up Cab in all of his arrangements. The registrants had a thrilling time playing that concert with the great Cab Calloway. When he performed his hallmarks, Minnie the Moocher and Hi-De-Ho, the crowd happily sang along.

Cab had lived through many challenges, including when black entertainers were not allowed to be housed in the very fancy hotels where they performed. In Fairbanks, Cab was treated like the star he was.

After his last Festival performance in 1985, I was backstage to thank him when he came off stage. I could still hear the crowd applauding wildly and continuing to sing Hi-De-Ho. I was truly touched when Cab came to me and quietly asked, "Jo, do you think they really liked me?" I assured him they most certainly did!

Cab was a great performer and a gracious gentleman. He and Nuffie had a wonderful time with Chris and all of us at the Festival that week. In fact, he had such a good time that he agreed to return the following year for Festival 1985.

Cab's performances at the Festival brought us national publicity. Thanks to Cab and all our guest artists, the Festival was growing artistically and succeeding financially

These were exhilarating times for the Festival!

CHAPTER 71

AN ENCORE,
A NEW TRADITION,
AND SHOES TO FILL

The return of Cab and Nuffie Calloway in 1985 was a joyous occasion for all of us. Their presence, not just in Chris's cabaret workshops but around the campus, gave the Festival extra excitement.

We had just added Barbershop Workshops, with Patty Gallagher and her husband leading the new chorus. I enjoyed seeing Cab sitting in the back row of the Davis Concert Hall, listening to them rehearse.

Guest artists and Festival registrants had many opportunities to perform. One of our out-of-state registrants,

Mary Jane Harris, had a creative idea. She invited people to perform informally in the late afternoons in the Davis Concert Hall. Those mini-performances became very popular. We formalized Mary Jane's idea, changing the time to the noon hour and the location to the Great Hall. We called it Lunch Bites. People were invited to enjoy their sack lunch or refreshments while they listened. Greg Hopkins and the Boston jazz guys kicked it off each day with a rousing number.

It was attracting big crowds, and people of all ages attended. I enjoyed seeing little children enjoy the music, and on Wednesdays, we featured special Lunch Bites performances for them. It was a fun and informal way to introduce children to sitting through a concert. The music filled the Great Hall, and when the hall's large glass doors were opened, the music could be heard around the campus. I thoroughly enjoyed introducing all of our Lunch Bites performers right up until I retired.

The demand for Cab Calloway was so high that we scheduled two back-to-back Davis Concert Hall shows as a double grand finale of the 1985 Festival. They both sold out. The energy in the hall was electrifying at each one, especially when Chris joined him on stage for a few numbers. It was a thrilling experience for everyone present.

After the successful 1985 Festival, Eddie Madden realized that, because of his busy year-round music schedule in Boston, he would not be able to continue as Artistic Director. It would be challenging to fill Eddie's shoes, as his dedicated work since Jazz Festival '80 had been invaluable. The people he brought on board would continue: Myron Romanul as Festival Orchestra conductor and Greg Hopkins leading the Festival Jazz Band. I felt good because they had both been hand-picked by Eddie and understood the Festival's mission. They were eager to help it continue to grow and succeed. I reached out to Fred Buda, our extraordinary Boston Pops percussionist guest since the beginning, and he agreed to be the Festival's new Artistic Director!

CHAPTER 72

FESTIVAL FUNDAMENTALS AND FROSTED BRAIDS

When I started the Festival as the Producing Director, with Eddie Madden as the Artistic Director, we each took on our roles. Eddie would take care of hiring the musicians on the artistic end, and I began selecting a small board for the production side. Each board member had specific talents that were important to the Festival's business growth and artistic success: Diane Egley for programming and tickets; attorney Randy Clapp for legal help; financial advisor Dick Scott for fiscal planning; CPA Dave Stephenson for tax help; and State Council for the Arts member Jean Mackin for arts consulting.

For the first 23 years, the Festival had no paid year-round office staff. My dear friend Judy Robertson Divinyi began working as our first paid year-round employee in 2003. She was a lifesaver for me, and her husband, Carl, became a popular Festival volunteer. Volunteers did important jobs for the Festival. I appreciated each of them and credited them for their dedicated work.

The Festival covered the cost of guest housing in either UAF student housing apartments or private homes. Many Fairbanks families graciously offered to host guest artists at no charge. Many guests returned to the same hosts year after year and became like part of the family!

Ralph Seekins of Seekins Ford, Lincoln, Mercury Dealership had been providing courtesy cars to Fairbanks arts groups that brought guest artists to the community for years. I reached out to Ralph when I started the Festival, and he was eager to provide cars for our guest artists for the duration of their stay. By our 20th year, Ralph provided 22 cars for the two weeks. That was a huge gift, but he saw we could use even more. He got in touch with other local dealerships and encouraged them to provide cars as well. From that time on, Festival guests also enjoyed cars from Tyler Cook, John Hill, John and Jim Immel, and Robby Giinther. They all became wonderful supporters of the Festival, and I appreciated them so much.

A tradition started in my kitchen in 1981. Each year after the Festival, I baked yeast bread braids and took four fresh-baked frosted braids to each dealership as a token of my sincere thanks for their generous support. Over the 30 years that I produced the Festival, I also delivered hundreds of these braids to large-gift supporters. Individuals, local businesses, oil companies, airlines, newspapers, print shops, and university offices were recipients of these frosted braids. It became known as Jo Scott Bread. More than once, funny enough, I was told that my baked goods helped secure ongoing Festival support.

As I went around trying to drum up donations from the likes of Alyeska Pipeline, British Petroleum, and Alaska Airlines, every time someone sent a check, I would follow up with a thank-you call and ask if I could drop off some sweet bread for their offices. (No one ever declined, as people weren't gluten-free in those days!) A little buzz went around town: "You don't say no to Jo!"

With this support and through grants and corporate gifts, we were able to hire talented guest artists. They came for less than what they would have gotten at other festivals, but several shared that our Festival stood out for the many courtesies offered to them. Besides food, housing, transportation, and honorarium, each guest received a full registration ID and could attend all concerts and take any class offered. With a wide variety of areas of study, many took advantage of this unique benefit. We had jazz instrumentalists taking jazz dance classes, classical musicians taking theatre, and visual artists taking creative writing. We enjoyed making their time memorable. Our artists often told other performers about their positive experiences at the Festival, and that led us to invite many new artists through these recommendations.

From the first Festival on, the guest musicians were paid $200 a day, while guest artists in the other areas of study were paid $150 a day. The musicians received more because they had extra duties besides their workshop classes, like rehearsals and concerts.

The conductors of the jazz band, orchestra, choruses, and opera received an extra $500 for the additional work they did, like selecting and ordering music prior to the Festival. Guest musicians who performed solos in concerts with choruses or orchestra received an extra $200. Every guest also received a $200 meal allowance.

When I started inviting Spotlight Guests, our location enticed many star performers. Many of our guests had never been to Alaska, and the thought of going intrigued them!

I paid each Spotlight Guest $2,500 for their concert performance, provided their airfare and a courtesy car, and hosted them at Sophie Station Hotel's Presidential Suite. Our Spotlight Guests may have gotten higher fees elsewhere, but many told us that the Festival had given them priceless memories they would treasure forever.

To add a personal touch, Dick and I started hosting a brunch in our home on the Sunday before Festival began. The brunch opened with the guests gathering in a large circle on our front lawn for a moment of meditation, reflecting on a successful and inspiring two weeks to come. Over the years, this opening brunch became a vital meeting time for guest artists, their local coordinators, and other volunteers. Of course I baked and frosted braids for the occasion, but we were grateful to master chef Barb Chalstrom, her daughter Andrea, and their dedicated staff at The Works Creative Catering, who prepared delicious main dishes for the outdoor brunches, providing china and silverware as well.

We had seating for everyone at tables around the pool deck, in the pool house, and in the living room, dining room, and sunroom. Some people enjoyed their brunch sitting on the lawn. It was an exciting time for returning artists to see each other again and for new guest artists to get acquainted with everyone.

The local coordinators were seated with their corresponding guest artists, who were given their class lists, classroom locations, and details on housing, cars, and campus parking.

At about 2:30, we would all head to UAF's Great Hall, where the guest artists met up with the registrants during a lovely reception. From there, everyone would go into Davis Concert Hall. Guest artists were formally introduced, announcements were made, and some guest musicians performed. It was always a great way to kick off the Festival.

At our last brunch, the year I retired in 2009, we served more than 150 guests. These included guest artists, the Festival board, local coordinators, volunteers, financial supporters, and friends of the Festival. More than 1,000 registrants signed up for Festival classes that year.

The Fairbanks community remained loyal to what we were working to accomplish in those early years. New traditions, returning artists, and repeat registrants kept the Festival momentum going!

Jo Ryman Scott

CHAPTER 73

1986 Fairbanks Summer Arts Festival Terry Gibbs and Buddy DeFranco

Our energetic new Artistic Director, Fred Buda from the Boston Pops, immediately got busy making plans for the 1986 Festival.

He invited vibraphonist Terry Gibbs and jazz clarinetist Buddy DeFranco to be our Spotlight Guests. When applicable, I always invited the spouses of our Spotlight Guests. Terry and Buddy's wives were delighted to be included.

392 Jo Ryman Scott

Spotlight Guests were generally in Fairbanks only briefly to perform at the Festival's closing concert. But Fred arranged for Terry and Buddy to be at the Festival the entire second week. They led jazz workshops and rehearsed with Greg Hopkins and the Festival Jazz Band, who would perform with them at the final concert. Terry and Buddy inspired the registrants to play at a higher performance level than they dreamed possible.

From 1986 to 1988, Chris Calloway's Cabaret Workshops attracted so many new registrants that we eventually offered three classes with fifteen students in each class. Chris encouraged me to bring up jazz pianist and vocal coach Dean Burris, and Dean recommended bassist Ernie Provencher. We had so many registrants that we were happy to be able to afford to fly in, house, and pay these added musicians and give the class professional backup players, complementing Chris's professional coaching.

The classes were not just for experienced singers. Anyone with a desire to learn about performing cabaret was encouraged to register.

For many years, singers Linda Knighten, Barb Harris, and Barbara Pitsenberger were the dedicated local coordinators. They lined up venues where the classes could perform. Chris had the unique talent of bringing the best out of every student, and they gave impressively polished performances all around town. What a great experience that was for the singers, and the audience loved them. Some of our Festival cabaret participants are still singing today.

Backed by the Festival Jazz Band, Terry Gibbs and Buddy DeFranco closed the 1986 Festival to a packed house in the Davis Concert Hall, where they received a standing ovation. It was an energizing concert. Fred had done a stellar job filling Eddie's shoes as Artistic Director, adding his own flair to boot. We were ready to start on plans for 1987!

CHAPTER 74

1987 Fairbanks
Summer Arts Festival
Sarah Vaughan

I started making plans for our 1987 Spotlight Guest in early spring. When booking spotlight artists, I often worked with a talent agency. The agent then contacted the artist's manager to work out the details, and a contract was written.

I became phone friends with Courtney at Triad Music Agency in Los Angeles. I had booked with Triad before, and Courtney faxed me a listing of available artists.

I was thrilled to see Sarah Vaughan's name on the list! I let Courtney know we would love to invite her with her trio to be our Spotlight Guests on the first Saturday evening of August 1987.

Courtney made all the contract arrangements through Sarah's manager and then reviewed them with me. I agreed with everything in the contract, and Sarah and I both signed it.

All was fine!

But Courtney called me a few days later to let me know that Sarah's manager had repeatedly called her to alert her that Sarah was certainly *not* going to go to Fairbanks. He realized that he himself had helped make the arrangements and that Sarah had signed it, but he insisted that Sarah wouldn't want to go!

Courtney kept calming him down while reassuring me that our contract was valid and that I didn't need to worry about anything he was saying. She just wanted to tell me what was happening in the manager's head. He was thinking, "Who wants to go to Fairbanks, Alaska?!"

Well, Sarah *did* come, and she *loved* Fairbanks, Alaska! Fairbanks, Alaska loved her too!

Dick had spent several hours printing an eight-foot banner on his new computer. The dot matrix bold lettering proclaimed ***WELCOME, SARAH VAUGHAN!***

In those days, you could meet passengers right at their gate! Dick and I, along with members of the Festival Jazz Band, were at the Fairbanks International Airport holding the banner and cheering as Sarah and her entourage came out of the jetway!

Her courtesy Lincoln Town car was waiting, and I took Sarah and her assistant to the Sophie Station Hotel. Dick brought the trio in our car, and her many fans followed.

Sarah and her assistant had the luxurious Presidential Suite, and the members of her trio each had nicely appointed rooms.

Sarah's fans had brought goodies for her and had stocked her suite with homemade bread, cookies, jams, and freshly smoked Alaska salmon. They joined Dick and me in showing her to the suite and offered refreshments. She was quite overwhelmed with all of this gracious attention.

I was sitting with her on the lovely couch in the suite. Sarah was looking at the large banner Dick had created just for her, and she quietly said, "Nobody has ever done this for me before!"

She was excited to shop for Alaskan items and asked if I could take her shopping. I told her I would be happy to, and I had fun driving Sarah and her assistant around town in that Lincoln Town Car. She was interested in buying gold, and I took her to a place specializing in Alaskan jewelry. She chose a sizable gold nugget to bring home. She had a marvelous shopping spree and happily pumped a lot of money into the Fairbanks economy that day. The arts are good for business!

Some Festival Jazz Band musicians took the trio fishing, and they all had a great time.

Sarah packed the house at Hering Auditorium the next night, and everyone loved her amazing concert.

The following day, several fans gathered at the airport to say farewell. Some jazz band members gave Sarah and her trio packages of frozen Alaska salmon to take back to Los Angeles. Jennifer Brice, a reporter for the *Fairbanks Daily News-Miner*, had written an excellent article about Sarah's concert that had just come out. She brought the paper to the airport for Sarah, who was thrilled to read it.

I was touched when Sarah so graciously thanked me for her wonderful time. We discussed her possibly returning for a June 21st Summer Solstice concert some year, and we agreed to stay in touch.

Again, in those days, you could see off a traveler right at the gate. They boarded the plane as the crowd cheered and waved goodbye. Their visit had enriched so many lives.

Courtney from Triad called me the week after the concert. She was eager to tell me that Sarah's manager came by after Sarah returned. Courtney shared that he plunked himself down on a chair by her desk and calmly and slowly said, "I still can't believe it. Sarah has never returned from a concert without complaints about everyone and everything."

He continued, "But this time, Sarah returned from Alaska raving about the wonderful time she had at the Festival in Fairbanks. She had NO complaints! She was amazed at how much fun her trio had, too."

This story shows the caring hospitality of the Fairbanks community. A little bit of love and kindness goes a long way. Sadly, Sarah became ill not long after this, and I never got to see her again. She touched my life, and I was so grateful to have met her.

CHAPTER 75

1988 FAIRBANKS SUMMER ARTS FESTIVAL ROSEMARY CLOONEY

In my late teens, Rosemary Clooney was one of my very favorite singers. She was just a year older than I and was already a big star. How I wished I could meet her. I was a farm girl in South Dakota so that didn't seem likely.

I listened to all her hits on the radio. My favorites included *Tenderly* and *Beautiful, Beautiful Brown Eyes*.

I was thrilled when, in 1944, my parents bought a lovely combination radio-record player console! It was the first time we had a record player at home. On our Saturday trips to

Aberdeen, I often went to Engel's Music Store. In those days, you could go into a booth and listen to a record, whether you bought it or not. When I saved enough money, I would pick the one I'd heard that I liked the best and take it home! I didn't have many, but I did buy records of my favorite stars: Bing Crosby, Margaret Whiting, and Rosemary Clooney.

I enjoyed following Rosemary's life and musical journey. In 1979, she wrote about her challenges in her memoirs. Her life story touched me. She had an unhappy childhood. When Rosemary was 15, her mother and her younger brother Nick (George Clooney's father) left their Kentucky home and moved to California.

Rosemary and her younger sister, Betty, were left behind to fend for themselves. Their father was an alcoholic who provided little support for his two daughters. Betty and Rosemary started singing at various places in their hometown to earn a little food money.

They won a local singing contest, which helped them start their careers as "The Clooney Sisters" until Betty decided she didn't want a singing career.

In 1951, at 23, Rosemary's solo *Come On-A-My House* recording became a number one hit. It brought in the money and acclaim that Rosemary needed to move on with her singing and acting career.

In early 1953, she and her dance teacher, Dante DiPaolo, fell madly in love. However, he needed to leave Los Angeles to work in another city.

Later that year, Rosemary had a whirlwind romance with an older movie star, José Ferrer, and they eloped. It was said that Dante was heartbroken when he heard the news.

Bing Crosby believed in Rosemary's potential and had her cast with him in the 1954 movie *White Christmas*, which remains popular today.

The mid-1950s were difficult times for many big stars because young people preferred the songs that Elvis Presley sang. They no longer wanted singers with big bands. Rock and roll became the new music.

Many stars weren't getting the performance opportunities they had previously enjoyed. Sadly, some of these former big names turned to drugs. This was a challenging time for Rosemary, too. She had five children with her unfaithful husband. She wanted to take care of them. She initially became addicted to sleeping pills, and her career was suffering.

She sought treatment, and she slowly recovered. She began accepting small singing jobs to get her career going again, and life became better for Rosemary from then on.

The story goes that in 1973, she was caught in a traffic jam in Los Angeles. Cars were lined up all around her in a dead stop. She found herself alongside a cute Thunderbird convertible, and when she glanced over and saw the driver, she realized it was her first love, Dante Paulo! She yelled through her car window, "Call me!" and yelled out her phone number.

Dante was so happy to see Rosemary! Twenty years had passed since they first met and fell in love. Of course, he called her! They were married, and Dante promised Rosemary that he would always be by her side to care for her from that moment on.

Rosemary's career was revived when her long-time friend Bing Crosby invited her to perform in a show celebrating his 50th year in show business: *Bing!*

On March 3, 1977, Rosemary, Bob Hope, Pearl Bailey, Bette Midler, and other stars performed on a Pasadena stage with Bing and his family. *Bing!* was broadcast on television.

In January 1988, I contacted my phone friend Courtney at Triad Music in Los Angeles and told her I was looking for a Spotlight guest for that summer.. She was who had been so helpful in booking Sarah Vaughn. So she sent me a listing of stars she had available.

Imagine my surprise and joy when I looked through Courtney's list and there was Rosemary Clooney's name! I called her immediately, and Courtney confirmed that Rosemary was available for our Festival date.

This was a dream come true. Forty years after being the farm girl from South Dakota wishing I could *meet* Rosemary Clooney, it turned out that I would get to do more than just meet her. I would actually *hire* her to perform in the closing concert in the Festival I had established. I was overjoyed.

I always let local fans know I welcomed them to help me meet and greet the Festival's spotlight guests. Todd and Doris Ray were big Rosemary Clooney fans and offered to help welcome her. Todd, Doris, and other fans joined Dick and me to meet Rosemary's plane at the Fairbanks International Airport. Everyone was excited, and it was a genuine thrill for me to meet my teenage idol.

Rosemary was happy to be in the beautiful Presidential Suite at the Sophie Station Hotel. Todd and Doris had done a lovely job stocking the room with Alaskan treats and abundant flowers. Generous Ralph Seekins, as always, provided a new Lincoln Town Car for Rosemary and her gentleman friend to use during their stay. Looking back, I feel certain that her gentleman friend was Dante, her first love!

When she arrived, Rosemary had the beginnings of a bad cold. Amid other gracious things Todd and Doris did for Rosemary, they later prepared a pot of homemade chicken soup and delivered it to her suite.

Rosemary recovered and sang beautifully at the Festival's final concert at Hering Auditorium on Saturday, August 6, 1988. The audience loved her and gave her a rousing standing ovation. After the show, Festival sponsors and fans attended a reception honoring Rosemary. It was a delightful evening with a large crowd at the Westmark Gold Room.

Rosemary was a kind and gracious lady. When I saw her off at the airport, she thanked me sincerely for all of the arrangements we had made, and said she'd had a great time.

Before she boarded the plane, she said casually, "I think Maggie would enjoy coming to this Festival as much as I have," and she slipped Margaret Whiting's phone number into my hand.

You can bet that I kept that number!

CHAPTER 76

1989 FAIRBANKS SUMMER ARTS FESTIVAL KARL HAAS AND MARY CLEERE HARAN

In 1989, Fred and I started the tradition of opening the Festival with the Spotlight Guest concert on the Friday before Festival classes began. This gave out-of-town people a chance to come in a few days early, enjoy the opening concert, which was included in their registration, and connect with others. They could do some sightseeing on Saturday, and Sunday morning, guest artists and coordinators had Brunch, and there was the meet-up for everyone at the Great Hall Sunday afternoon.

It was exciting making plans for the opening concert. I wanted to invite Karl Haas to open the Festival as our Spotlight Guest in this new time slot. He hosted what was once known as the "most listened to classical music radio show in the world," *Adventures in Good Music*. It was produced in Michigan and syndicated nationwide on National Public Radio. In Fairbanks, it aired on KUAC-FM from the UAF campus. Born in Germany in 1913, he emigrated to the US in 1936. Trained as a concert pianist, he also had a mellifluous speaking voice, and his radio shows were enthralling.

When I hired him, I received many promotional materials about him, but no headshots or pictures of any kind were included.

The Friday curtain time came, and the air was filled with anticipation. The Davis Concert Hall was packed and buzzing with excitement. When Karl Haas walked out on the stage, the audience paused for a beat before it erupted into warm applause.

He graciously bowed to acknowledge his welcome. After the applause ceased, Karl remained center stage. He quietly looked out at the audience, slowly gazing to his left and then to his right. He stood resolutely and calmly announced, "Well, I didn't know what *you* looked like, either!" His witty remark was met with an explosion of laughter and applause, a moment that truly set the tone for the rest of the evening.

The theme music for *Adventures in Good Music* was the second movement from Beethoven's *Pathétique Sonata No. 8 in C minor*, performed by Haas live for each program. He didn't disappoint, sitting down to play it for us. We settled in for our own evening of *Adventures in Good Music* live! Haas was a gifted pianist who enchanted his audience with his musical stories, told in his deep, rich voice.

His concert was a triumph. The audience, many of whom were his loyal radio listeners, were captivated by his performance and showed their appreciation with a standing ovation. What fun it was to finally put a face to the voice we all knew so well!

We were off and running for another Festival. On Monday morning, the Great Hall was buzzing, everyone was finding their classrooms, and our Festival office was a hub of activity. The set list for the first Lunch Bites of the season was filled, and everyone reconvened for that during the midday break between classes.

Chris Calloway and her father, Cab, had commitments in Europe that summer and regretted missing their trip to Alaska. Our cabaret pianist and vocal coach, Dean Burris, recommended the talented singer Mary Cleere Haran, who became our exciting new Cabaret Workshop coach.

Mary Cleere was from San Francisco and debuted in New York City in 1985. She was fiercely proud to call herself a cabaret artist. Her shows were big productions, and she played in the best cabaret rooms in New York, from the Algonquin's Oak Room to Rainbow and Stars.

Dean and Mary Cleere made a great coaching team, and their cabaret classes filled quickly. The singers were encouraged to create a quick patter to introduce their songs. From the first day, they were preparing for the various performances the coordinators had set up in venues around Fairbanks.

Mary Cleere was the Spotlight Guest for the final concert on Saturday, August 5th, 1989. Accompanied by Dean, she put on a great show. The crowd at the Hering Auditorium gave her a standing ovation.

The new opening date format worked beautifully, and we opted to keep it. After each Festival, we pored over all of the comments and suggestions submitted by our guests and registrants. They had great ideas! We appreciated all feedback and were always working towards providing the Festival experience people were looking for. Literally, the day after each year's final concert, we were already looking at improvements and additions for the following year.

THE 1990S

CHAPTER 77

Hal Holbrook in
Mark Twain Tonight!

Every year, I was excited to think about who our Spotlight Guest might be. To kick off the Festival in 1990, I had my hopes up to bring Hal Holbrook and his iconic one-person stage show, *Mark Twain Tonight*. This show, performed around the world, was a masterful portrayal of the legendary Mark Twain, brought to life by Holbrook's uncanny depiction of Twain's speech, mannerisms, and look, all performed in what seemed like his book-filled 1830s library.

In my first phone discussion with Holbrook's manager, Bennett Thomson, he stressed that before committing, they would need to be assured all the stage requirements would be strictly followed.

I read his detailed list, and I realized it would take considerable research and time to obtain all the props for the set. Books, furnishings, and even the rug had to be just so. I showed the list to our own theatre expert, Festival board member Jean Mackin. She carefully reviewed it and felt confident she could source everything on the list.

I signed the contract. As always, we offered for the Festival to pay for Holbrook's wife to join, and he appreciated this invitation. It was fun to welcome his wife, *Designing Women*'s Dixie Carter, to Fairbanks as well. Hal and Dixie enjoyed the warm reception at Sophie's Station Presidential Suite and had fun using the courtesy car to explore the sights.

Susie Hackett graciously agreed to come on board and began working with Jean to gather the necessary props to bring the stage alive. In a recent phone conversation, Susie recalled some of the challenges that she and Jean faced. She said that Bennett monitored every step of the production to ensure that the stage and backstage were set up properly. Susie and Jean had attended this one-person show in Anchorage years earlier, so they were familiar with the production.

But when it came to actually setting the stage, there were plenty of details to consider. Susie recalled their search for an acceptable "very large oriental carpet" that was required, pivotal to defining the stage playing area. Fairbanks did not have much of an oriental carpet supply, but Jean found one in a conference room at Key Bank! A bank executive kindly allowed the Festival to borrow it. After placing it on the Hering Auditorium stage, however, it was discovered that it needed to be deeper to fit Bennett's specifications. Local artist Melinda Mattson came to the rescue. She artistically created and installed an extension, making the carpet appear to be the correct depth and showcasing our community's resourcefulness.

Acquiring other specific props was also challenging. Bennett was a taskmaster for details but was willing to make concessions, given local availability. Fairbanks families with furnishings appropriate to the Twain era kindly loaned items such as a desk, bookcases, and, of course, many books. This community involvement was crucial in bringing the stage to life. Bennett had stage-managed this production worldwide and knew what was needed and what would work. Susie and Jean enjoyed working with him.

Hal's stage makeup was precise and time-consuming and made him look uncannily like Mark Twain. The set turned out beautifully and I'll always appreciate Jean and Susie's hard work. Four local theatre technicians, Hugh Hall, Tom Kjera, Bruce Hansen, and Greg Gustafson, donated their time to meet the technical needs of the shows. They did an excellent job, and Bennett approved.

The *Mark Twain Tonight!* show at Hering Auditorium sold out quickly. It was a crowd-pleasing success, and the audience gave Holbrook a rousing standing ovation. Few in the audience that night had any idea of all of the time and work Jean Mackin and Susie Hackett had spent creating the set. It was so professional-looking that many assumed it traveled with the show. This successful outcome was a testament to the hard work and dedication of everyone involved.

Holbrook was a gracious guest artist who'd done some homework on Alaska. He put an intriguing rider in his contract. He had read about Susan Butcher, the Fairbanks dog musher who had won the Iditarod that year for the fourth time. The rider required that the Festival give Susan two comp tickets to attend his performance and that, after the show, she be allowed backstage so they could meet. What an extraordinary contract requirement! We were more than happy to oblige. Susan graciously accepted, loved the show, and enjoyed meeting Holbrook, and Dixie, as well.

The 1990 Festival was off and running, and this was only the beginning!

CHAPTER 78

1990 AND 1991 FAIRBANKS SUMMER ARTS FESTIVALS MARGARET WHITING

Every Saturday night as a teenager in South Dakota, our family gathered around our old radio and tuned in to *The Hit Parade*, sponsored by Philip Morris cigarettes. We listened intently to see which song would be number one that week!

The number one song was often by one of my favorites, Margaret Whiting! I loved reading anything I could about her life.

Margaret Whiting had a happy childhood. She lived in Detroit before her family moved to Los Angeles in 1929 when she was five.

By moving to LA, her father, songwriter Richard Whiting, met many important musicians. The singer-lyricist Johnny Mercer collaborated with Richard on many songs, such as the theme song for *Tinseltown, Hooray for Hollywood*. Another movie song he wrote was Shirley Temple's *On The Good Ship Lollipop*.

Margaret was lucky to have grown up in a musical home! As a child, Margaret met Gus Kahn, Harry Warren, Leo Robin, and Jerome Kern, who often visited the Whiting home in LA. She was always around at these gatherings.

One evening, as a young girl, her mother asked Johnny Mercer and the other guests to listen to Margaret sing. The story goes that Margaret sang two songs in her nightgown and then went up to bed. Mercer and the others recognized this little girl's potential. Mercer was intrigued by Margaret's talent.

Mercer ended up being a mentor and father-like figure to Margaret when her own father passed away when she was just 13 years old.

Through his arrangements with Capital Records, which Mercer founded with Buddy DeSylva and Glenn Wallichs, Margaret's recording of *That Old Black Magic* became a national hit in 1942 when she was only 18. (I remember the Saturday night around our radio when that song made number one on *The Hit Parade!*)

Moonlight in Vermont followed this hit in 1943, with many more after that. Other well-known Whiting favorites include *It Might As Well Be Spring*, *Silver Bells*, and *Baby, It's Cold Outside*. Mercer sang this last one as a duet with Margaret. (I remember when all of these made *The Hit Parade*, too!)

Though Margaret was fortunate to have had the support of Mercer and others, it was also her own hard work over the years that made her one of America's favorites.

With a busy singing career spanning several decades, in the 1980s she added teaching to her repertoire, and gave much sought-after cabaret master classes.

I was thrilled to have confirmed *Mark Twain Tonight!* for the 1990 opening performance. I was looking for a special musical guest to kick off a new decade of the Festival, so I searched for the paper that Rosemary Clooney had given me with a wink when I had dropped her off at the airport two years earlier. It was a number for future use. She had said, "I think Maggie would enjoy coming to your Festival as much as I have!"

It was time to use that number. I dialed, and after two rings, Margaret Whiting answered. I started to say, "Hi, this is Jo Scott," but was immediately interrupted. "Oh, Jo, I was so hoping you would call. Rosie told me what a wonderful time she had at your Festival in Alaska!"

What a thrill. I told her that besides wanting to invite her to be our Spotlight Guest for that year's final concert, I was hoping to have her as a Guest Teacher-in-Residence for the Festival's cabaret classes during the two weeks of Festival as well. She loved both ideas!

I worked directly with Margaret to draw up her contract. In addition to teaching three cabaret classes daily, she would be the featured artist performing in the last concert with Greg Hopkins' Festival Jazz Band.

Margaret was a popular teacher, and her students realized what a gift it was to be able to study with her. She taught the students how to present themselves professionally when they were performing. She had so much to offer. Margaret ended up returning for a second year. All of the students loved her! The three cabaret classes filled to the limit of 15 in no time as soon as the catalog came out. They came from all over the country.

Jo Ryman Scott

New York's Dean Burris continued as pianist/vocal coach, and LA-based Ernie Provencher returned as bassist. It was a remarkable opportunity for the cabaret students to have these professional musicians backing them up.

Barbara Pitsenberger, one of our local cabaret coordinators, volunteered many hours to help organize the classes and arrange venues for the student performances. Besides the popular University Wood Center's Pub, she booked venues all across town where Margaret's students would perform. Margaret was the gracious emcee at these shows, introducing each singer with a personal note.

Barbara also acted as Margaret's personal assistant. She took her shopping, and made special visits to local Festival supporters like my dear mentor helenka Brice. Barbara did a remarkable job as the coordinator both summers.

Margaret's performance at the Festival's final concert brought the house down. She worked with Greg and the Festival Jazz Band to present a fantastic evening of *The Songs of Johnny Mercer and Richard Whiting.*

Margaret wove personal history into her delightful patter in the story behind each song. The packed crowd at Hering Auditorium gave her a standing ovation with many cheers, which earned them a wonderful encore.

What a special treat it had been to not only have Margaret as our Spotlight Guest for two years in a row, but to have her as Guest Teacher-in-Residence for the entire two weeks of the Festival for those two years.

Those were giddy times for me, and for the lucky Festival registrants who had the opportunity to study under her.

Wow! 1990 was a banner year for the Festival. We opened with Hal Holbrook in *Mark Twain Tonight!* and closed with Margaret Whiting. What a way to kick off a decade!

Years later, when Dick and I moved to New York City, we got to meet Margaret's lovely daughter, Debbi Bush Whiting. Much as Margaret had done to preserve Johnny Mercer's legacy after he passed, Debbi did the same for her mother. She devoted her time, talent, and resources to preserving the musical legacy of her mother, her grandfather, Richard Whiting, and her father, Lou Busch (composer of Hello Muddah, Hello Fadduh, the theme from What's My Line, and many others). Debbi has kept their music alive by producing tribute concerts, establishing The Margaret Whiting Award, and releasing new music on her MY IDEAL MUSIC Label.

Debbi was happy with the collection of Festival programs and pictures of Margaret that I gave her. Dick and I enjoyed her company at many musical events during our time in the city. She is delightful, and it has been so wonderful to connect with her.

Jo Ryman Scott

CHAPTER 79

A FESTIVAL SUCCESS STORY
GIACOMO GATES

Giacomo Agostini was an only child. He grew up with his parents in Connecticut, listening to lots of jazz music played on their radio daily. He really liked that music! He learned to play the guitar when he was ten, and he took several years of tap dancing lessons.

Like many other ambitious young men in their twenties, Giacomo made his way to Alaska and worked on the Alaska pipeline. It was the mid-1970s, and there was continuous pipeline work available. He enjoyed singing jazz for fun. A friend of his, Althea St. Martin, who happened to be a friend of mine as well, told Giacomo that with his great singing voice, he should register for the Fairbanks Summer Arts Festival.

In the summer of 1987, Giacomo took her advice, and that's how he ended up in a row of singers on the first day of Chris Calloway's cabaret class that year. Immediately, Chris recognized Giacomo's deep, rich bass voice, and he became a favorite among classmates and the cabaret show audiences.

I had heard a lot about jazz historian, lecturer, and author Grover Sales from San Francisco and invited him to the Festival that summer of 1987.

I enjoyed listening to Sales and learned a lot myself. He was popular with the Festival registrants and spent considerable time mingling with them. Sales had heard Giacomo sing in the cabaret class performances and said he was impressed with his potential. But he also told him that if he really wanted to become a jazz singer, Giacomo needed to move back East, where he could immerse himself in the current jazz scene.

Giacomo shared that, had it not been for his registering for the Festival and getting acquainted with Sales, he would probably never have moved back to the East Coast to pursue his dream.

In a recent email with Giacomo, I was surprised when he described how he learned to sing jazz, saying, "I didn't have a personal singing teacher. My "teachers" were people that I would go to listen to, and then I'd play their recordings over and over again." He listened to singers like Sarah Vaughn, Carmen McRae, and many others.

Giacomo didn't tell me how long it took, but at one point, he was ready to seek professional singing engagements. Before he did this, he believed he had to do something about his last name, Agostini. It was not only difficult to pronounce but challenging to remember. So, he changed his last name, and from then on, he would be billed as Giacomo Gates!

Giacomo had worked hard, and his dreams of becoming a great jazz singer paid off. That talented man is now recognized nationally as a successful, sought-after jazz singer. "I was very fortunate to be accepted by all the musicians and singers I looked up to," he says.

Giacomo has produced several internationally released CDs. He has won numerous national awards and is still getting rave reviews, with one critic saying, "Gates just keeps on getting better and better every year!"

As his popularity and success grew over the years, it was a thrill to invite Giacomo to return to the Festival three times as our Spotlight Guest and guest artist teaching jazz and cabaret.

A true Festival success story!

The link to Giacomo's website can be found in this chapter's Bonus Material.

Jo Ryman Scott

CHAPTER 80

A SMALL h, A BIG HEART, AND A CHERISHED MENTOR

Fairbanks had a unique entrepreneurial businesswoman named helenka Brice. Her hallmark was the small h she used for her first name. When I worked at Ann's Greenhouses in 1976, I saw the unusual name on many of the flower boxes lined up to be filled for customers.

I knew the name, as I'd had several of helenka's grandchildren as students over the years in my Musical Nursery School, my Denali kindergarten classes, and my Junior High Fine Arts Camp. But I had never met her!

A friend encouraged me to contact her, as helenka strongly supported the arts and might be interested in my

Jo Ryman Scott

efforts in establishing the Festival. I called helenka in 1981. She was gracious and interested in my ideas. She became a generous Festival supporter, and beyond that, she became my mentor. She helped me successfully write proposals to many corporations for financial support.

As the matriarch of her family's construction and development business, she had many connections. She encouraged me to write several letters to the current Governor, Bill Sheffield, urging him to support the new Alaska State Council on the Arts, or ASCA, who had given grants to the Festival and other local arts organizations.

On one of his visits to Fairbanks, Governor Sheffield specifically asked to meet "this young lady from Fairbanks who keeps writing to me about the importance of the arts in Alaska." So helenka introduced us, and he thanked me for informing him of the importance of ASCA and the arts in Alaska.

helenka was always coming up with ideas. Her phone calls were funny, quick, and to the point. I can still hear her rather deep, hoarse voice saying, "Jo, be sure to write that proposal to ___," and then she would fill in that blank with the name of an oil company or another big corporation and hang up! No goodbye or any other fluffy words; she had no time for idle chatter.

During one of her visits with me in late 1991, helenka shared that she had been in poor health for several years and was setting aside some financial support for the Festival in her will.

I thanked her and said I would like to use that money for something in her honor. I had often thought about including harp studies in the Festival, but the University didn't own one. I suggested that the Festival use her gift to purchase one. It could be called the Brice Harp. She liked the idea and asked me to go ahead and order the harp right away!

I spoke to Dr. James Johnson, the head of the UAF Music Department, about the harp. He appreciated my offer for the Festival to present the harp to the University someday.

I asked guest clarinetist Gary Bovyer and others from the Los Angeles Philharmonic to recommend a harpist who might be our Festival guest that summer. Everyone suggested Marcia Dickstein. My idea was to have our guest harpist help me pick out the new harp.

I contacted Marcia, and she was delighted to be invited. She would be giving a concert in Chicago in January 1992 and agreed to go to the Lyons & Healey Harp Company to select our harp.

The price was $15,000, including delivery. Dr. Johnson and I were at his office the day the harp was delivered in February 1992.

Around this time, helenka was admitted to a hospital in the Lower 48. I sent her a letter of thanks in care of the hospital with a photograph of the Brice Harp. I'm hoping helenka received that letter. She passed away at the age of 83 shortly afterward. I was sorry to lose my mentor, whose wisdom and guidance had been so important.

I made plans for one of that summer's Festival concerts to honor helenka's memory and her gift of the Brice Harp. I found several musical pieces in our family's record collection that featured the harp. Festival Orchestra conductor Myron Romanul found the orchestra scores for these harp pieces. I sent the music list to Marcia so she could prepare for this special concert.

The plans came together beautifully. I invited helenka's sons and their families to attend as the Festival's special guests.

Shortly before the concert began, something exciting happened: helenka's sons found me in the Festival Office. They had an envelope for me and asked me to open it right away.

Much to my surprise, inside was a check for $15,000 from helenka and the Brice family. I had never shared with them the cost of the harp, but their gift covered the exact amount!

The first thing on the program was the presentation of the Brice Harp to Dr. Johnson and the UAF Music Department.

The highlight of the evening was the Festival Orchestra featuring Marcia performing all those beautiful pieces on the Brice Harp. The audience showed their appreciation of the concert and helenka's gift with a standing ovation and cheers! I will never forget that evening.

Marcia's Festival harp classes became very popular in just a few years. She was a talented teacher, and her students loved her. We advertised that for this area of study, even young music students with no previous harp training could register.

At first, there was only the Brice Harp for Marcia and the students to play on. The only other harp in Fairbanks at the time was owned by a woman affiliated with the UAF Geophysical Institute, who graciously loaned it to us when she heard about our classes.

But in just a few years, students' parents purchased smaller harps, and eventually, some of the more advanced students bought concert harps. By the early 2000s, there were more than eighty harps in the Fairbanks area. I'm deeply grateful to helenka and how her gift made this possible!

"BRILLIANT! CLEVER! HAD THE
AUDIENCE IN STITCHES."
—New York Times

MARVIN
HAMLISCH

"A WONDERFULLY VARIED AND
ENTERTAINING MUSICAL EVENING"
—The Toronto Globe/Mail

CHAPTER 81

A Chorus Line, an EGOT, and a Singularly Sensational Suggestion from Marvin Hamlisch

In the late 1970s, Dick and I had the opportunity to see Marvin Hamlisch's fabulous musical, *A Chorus Line*, in London's West End. We loved it!

We flew home via New York City, and we saw *A Chorus Line* again on Broadway. It was fun comparing the two shows: they were staged identically. Dick and I both enjoyed Hamlisch's catchy tunes and the story they told. From then on, I was a fan of Marvin Hamlisch and enjoyed following his life.

Born in 1944, Marvin was a child prodigy and grew up in Manhattan. He began picking out tunes on the piano before he was five years old. He was admitted to Juilliard's Pre-College Division studies shortly before his seventh birthday!

Hamlisch's first job was as the rehearsal pianist for Barbra Streisand while she was doing *Funny Girl*. She recognized his talent. In the 1970s, his adaptation of Scott Joplin's music for the movie *The Sting*, particularly the movie's theme song, *The Entertainer*, became very popular.

Hamlisch consistently performed, composed, and conducted many shows. He is one of only twenty-seven people to reach EGOT status, having won an Emmy, a Grammy, an Oscar, and a Tony. Hamlisch also won a Pulitzer Prize. I was intrigued by all that he had accomplished.

Much to my surprise, in early 1992, I received a phone call from Marvin Hamlisch's manager. He explained that Marvin had suggested he contact me as he had heard I'd established an excellent arts festival in Fairbanks, Alaska. Marvin had never been to Alaska and wanted to go. His manager asked if he might be the Festival's 1992 Spotlight Guest.

I explained that we had already lined up Mel Tormé, but if Marvin would be interested, he could present a Fairbanks concert in the months before the Festival began. Marvin and his manager liked the idea, and since they had approached us, they charged less than his usual fee. Of course, I extended the invitation to bring his wife along, and this made him even happier. We signed the contract!

Having this special summer concert in addition to our usual two-week Festival was a big undertaking, but it was well worth the extra effort. There was a lot of planning to do. I was grateful to many of my friends who volunteered to help.

First, we needed a warm-up band to open the show. The director of Fort Wainwright's 9th Army Band, Joe Camarda, agreed to put one together. He invited 9th Army Band members and local jazz musicians to be in this pick-up band. They were all faithful Festival registrants.

Thanks to generous help from Alaska Airlines, we booked first class New York to Fairbanks plane tickets for Marvin and his lovely wife, Terre. She was delighted to be included in this trip to Alaska. I wanted to be sure they met some local musical theatre fans while in town, so I asked Shirley Hughes and Dana Hart to help me meet and greet them at the airport. Marvin and Terre were happy with the beautiful Presidential Suite at Sophie Station and the Lincoln Town car Ralph Seekins provided.

The next day, Shirley and Dana took them on a little tour around town and the UAF. Then Shirley and Terre took off in Shirley's car and toured the outskirts of our community. Shirley told me that Terre enjoyed seeing the historic Malemute Saloon in Ester, where Shirley performed at evening shows for tourists during the summer months. The two spent considerable time chatting while hiking in the hills around Ester. They had a great time together that afternoon.

Meanwhile, Dana drove Marvin out the Steese Highway, a few miles from downtown Fairbanks. The main thing Marvin wanted to see was the Trans-Alaska Pipeline! Dana drove to the spot on the Steese where the pipeline is suspended above ground, and there is a slice of the actual 48" pipe that you can walk through. Marvin got a closer look at the pipeline than he had hoped, and Dana said he was delighted!

Thanks to Shirley and Dana, Marvin and Terre had a busy afternoon. Soon, it would be time for the evening's big show, and they returned to the hotel to rest before the show.

Joe's jazz band was the perfect way to open the Hamlisch show. They performed professional renditions of great jazz band music selections, and the crowd loved it!

When Marvin came out onto the Hering Auditorium stage, he was greeted with cheers and applause from the packed house.

He was a polished speaker and performer. His time on stage was entertaining. Much to the delight of his audience, he played *The Entertainer* and selections from *A Chorus Line*. I recall that some of Hamlisch's wit and antics included playing a piano piece while sitting on the floor.

During the show, Marvin shared how much he and Terre had enjoyed the sightseeing adventures in Fairbanks with Shirley and Dana.

It was an enthusiastic crowd that evening. Marvin put on a great show and got a standing ovation and many cheers.

His time on stage performing on Hering's beautiful nine-foot concert grand was about an hour and a half, with no intermission.

After the show, Marvin sold and signed his latest music book in the lobby. It was thrilling for people to chat with him as he graciously wrote dedications on their book's inside cover. My family treasures ours!

When I took Marvin and Terre to the airport the next day, they said what a good time they'd had, and Terre thanked me again for including her.

Every moment of energy needed to make it all happen was worth it. Now, the 1992 Festival was just weeks away.

CHAPTER 82

1992 Fairbanks Summer Arts Festival Mel Tormé

After Marvin Hamlisch's wonderful visit and thrilling concert in June, we kicked off our 1992 Festival just weeks later in July.

Planning for the next Festival started right after the previous one ended. When paying our guests on the last day of the Festival, I wrote a note on the memo line saying, "See you next summer!" to guests who had already accepted our invitation to return.

We had beautiful flyers made that described "a study/performance Festival held on the beautiful University of

Alaska Fairbanks campus." Keeping in mind there was no social media or even email in the late 1980s and early 1990s, promoting the Festival was a challenge. I started actively advertising locally, statewide, and nationally in early November each year when people began looking for summer study opportunities.

Free festival listings were available in many state and national arts magazines. I sent out dozens of letters, and the Festival was listed in every publication I contacted.

Each spring, the *New York Times* published a comprehensive listing of music festivals alphabetically by state. Since Alabama didn't have any, The Fairbanks Summer Arts Festival appeared first! They generously gave us a detailed listing that included dates, names of some guest artists, study and performance opportunities, and who to contact. (There was one other listing for Alaska, violinist Paul Rosenthal's excellent Sitka Music Festival.) We welcomed several registrants thanks to the *New York Times*.

Our guest artists also helped advertise the Festival, many encouraging their students to register and come to Alaska for this unique experience.

The Festival was growing, and it was becoming a year-round job for me to get everything organized. I spent considerable time throughout the year communicating with our guest faculty. It was always my goal to hire all our Festival guests by the middle of January and send out their contracts for them to sign by late February.

From that point on, I compiled all the information on guest artists, classes, and concerts for the paper catalog and registration form stapled in its middle fold. I wanted these printed and distributed by the last week of March. I also typed, photocopied, and mailed monthly newsletters throughout the year to keep guest artists and registrants informed of plans for the upcoming Festival.

With no computer, I had no database of registrants or guest artists. I organized volunteers to come to my home office and hand-address these each month. By the second year, we got a nonprofit postage number, which was printed like a stamp on the address side of the newsletter. That was a huge help. Besides saving money on postage, we didn't have to put stamps on every newsletter like we did the first year!

June Rogers, Debbie Thies Foster, and Dee Lashbrook were the festival office managers from the early years through 1990. Each provided excellent leadership. Debbie became active in the instrumental jazz classes and the Festival Jazz Band. By 1991, the Festival had grown to the point that we needed two people working in the office during the Festival. Delamour Kriley and Patty Roberts joined the list of amazing office managers.

Kathie Jaynes Bungart was a talented local music teacher who also volunteered in the late 1980s and early 1990s. Her experience was especially valuable in planning classes and concerts.

I continued to be open to suggestions for new areas of study. In early 1990, my longtime friend Delamour Kriley participated in the Festival's bassoon classes. Her daughter was an avid ice skater and one day asked if I would consider adding Ice Skating Theatre to the Festival.

I was intrigued with the idea and asked her to propose specific ice-skating classes for students of various ages and levels of experience. I had her prepare a budget for this proposed program's expected revenues and expenses. I advised her to contact Lynn Lashbrook, the head of UAF's Athletic Department, to see if he would approve of the Festival using the UAF ice skating rink for a fee. She completed all of this, and Lashbrook was on board.

We invited a talented ice skating teacher she knew out of Salt Lake City, Stephanie Grosscup, to be the Festival's guest instructor that summer. The ice skating classes were open to skaters with some previous skating lessons. They were popular and successful. Through Delamour's careful planning, the budget was met, and Ice Skating Theatre became a part of the Festival.

I enjoyed visiting the various Festival classes. Dick was fascinated with technology and arranged for me to have a pocket radio pager so I could be reached whenever needed. (Besides there being no computers or email at the time, there were also no cell phones, so this was a big deal!)

Delamour and I had met a woman in Fairbanks who represented a manufacturing company in the Lower 48 that produced beautiful cotton woven blankets with custom designs. If we hurried, a souvenir Festival blanket could be a nice addition to our Gift Shop by opening day. We enjoyed designing the 4' x 5' throw, incorporating images of the Festival's various areas of study, a few bars of music from Mike Monaghan's beautiful song Alaska Is a Rainbow, with a drawing of Mt. McKinley in the center. It featured the Edwin Markham quote that means so much to me:

> There is a destiny that makes us brothers
> None goes his way alone
> All that we give to the lives of others
> Comes back again into our own

We ordered it in several colors, and they arrived just in time to offer them at the 1992 Festival. They were a hot seller in the Festival Gift Shop for many years. I still have mine, and it brings back many happy memories!

Our Spotlight Guest, Mel Tormé, backed by Greg Hopkins' Festival Jazz Band, wrapped up the two weeks with a memorable performance at the final concert. He was warmly received and enjoyed his time in Alaska.

With many returning guest artists and registrants, the Festival began to feel like a family for many.

CHAPTER 83

1993 & 1994 Fairbanks Summer Arts Festivals Maureen McGovern

An essential part of the Fairbanks Summer Arts Festival's mission was to reach out to people who loved music but had yet to have the opportunity to take lessons. To address this mission, we started offering Winter Edition classes in February 1993, with Byron McGilvray for voice and Dean Burris for cabaret. This allowed people who traveled during the summer months to participate, and it was something to look forward to in what was typically the darkest month of winter.

People at all levels of experience were encouraged to register. We were happy to see registrants with little or no training make remarkable advancements.

Like their summer counterparts, the cabaret students performed in venues around Fairbanks, including the UAF Pub, Westmark's Kobuk Room, and a dining hall on Wickersham Street where they would rearrange the seating for live music.

In February 1993, it was more than 40 degrees below zero during the two weeks of Winter Edition classes. The temperature dipped even further on the night of the last show. But in true Alaska style, that didn't keep the audience from showing up! Dean Burris braved the cold and served as the show's emcee, and Wickersham Hall was packed. Winter Edition proved to be a concept people loved, and it is still going on today!

The 1993 Summer Arts Festival opened with violist Raphael Hillyer and pianist Robert McCoy. For "An Evening of Classics," Myron Romanul conducted the Festival Orchestra, with violinist Paul Rosenthal performing *Beethoven's Violin Concerto.* What a magnificent concert!

Hillyer, a founder of the Juilliard String Quartet, was one of our first Honorary Board Members and continued to support the Festival from afar. We were thrilled to have him come back to Alaska as a guest string teacher in 1993.

A fun side note is that years earlier, Hillyer found out that the UAF Music Department was looking for a qualified string teacher with a Doctorate. He recommended his Yale University School of Music student Kathleen Butler, and Music Department head Charlie Davis gave her the job. That same year, John Hopkins came from Iowa and was hired to be the Music Department's voice teacher. John and Kathy met at UAF and ended up getting married! They are still making music together.

Cabaret and pop singer Maureen McGovern was our Spotlight Guest and closed the 1993 Festival "An Evening of Jazz and Cabaret" concert, backed by Greg's Festival Jazz Band at Davis Concert Hall. She was so well-received that we invited her to return as Spotlight Guest for 1994, and she sparkled then as well! Besides her many recordings and hits, such as *The Morning After* from the movie *The Poseidon Adventure*, it's fun to remember that she was also in the classic movie *Airplane* as the singing nun.

The 1993 and 1994 Fairbanks Summer Arts Festivals each had 64 guest artists-in-residence for the two weeks of classes and performances and attracted more registrants with each passing year.

The 1994 Festival opened with the McGilvray Chamber Chorale. What a feat for Byron to coordinate bringing his California choral group to Alaska! The Festival waived all of their registration fees, and they each added a lot to the classes they signed up for.

This concert honored the memory of Charlie Davis, the former head of the Music Department, who had done so much for the program. It was a moving concert, and it was extra meaningful because it was performed in the concert hall bearing his name!

Years later, when Dick and we lived in Manhattan, we were invited to the taping of American Songbook at NJPAC which featured Maureen among others. We were invited backstage and had a wonderful reunion with her. She remembered me immediately and was genuinely happy to see us. She told me how much she loved her time in Fairbanks and said she still has and uses the Festival tote bag and blanket I had given her more than twenty years earlier. She gave me her most recent CD and a big hug.

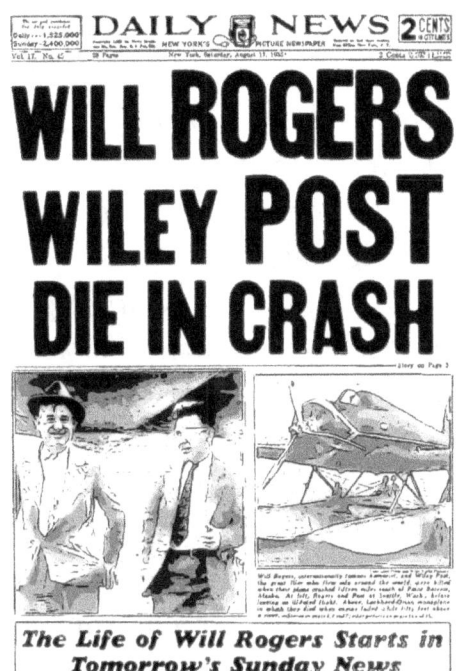

CHAPTER 84

AN ALASKAN ADVENTURE, A PLANE CRASH, AND THE INSPIRATION FOR A PLAY

In the early 1930s, humorist Will Rogers and his pilot friend Wiley Post had been planning for an excursion to Russia, stopping in Alaska en route. On August 12, 1935, their plan took shape when they landed Post's floatplane on the Chena River just a few miles from Fairbanks.

They decided to wait in Fairbanks until the weather up north cleared so they could fly on to their next destination: Point Barrow, the northernmost village civilization of the United States and its territories.

My Fairbanks pioneer friends have told me that their parents met Rogers and Post. The men mingled with Fairbanks and during their unplanned three-day stopover. There were stories of Rogers pulling handfuls of silver dollars out of his pockets and throwing them onto the street for the eager little children to collect!

After a couple of days, Post reportedly became anxious about waiting for the weather to clear. He wouldn't even listen to seasoned Alaska bush pilot Joe Crosson, who advised him not to leave.

Post had flown around the world twice prior to this trip. He had worn out two planes doing that, so he built a hybrid plane with a fuselage and wings salvaged from two different Lockheed aircraft. (Lockheed reportedly refused to make these modifications because the parts weren't compatible.)

Additionally, Post fitted the plane with floats that were reportedly also ill-suited for the already make-shift aircraft. Post's plane was overloaded with fuel, hunting gear, and fishing equipment.

But Post felt he could make the 500-mile trip to Point Barrow, even in foggy weather. Fairbanks was still cloudy and misty on August 15, but Post and Rogers flew out, stopping forty miles away at Harding Lake to refuel, and then heading north.

The plane reportedly performed adequately during the cloudy, misty flight to Point Barrow. However, fog settled in when they got farther north, and visibility was poor. They realized that they were lost.

Post was known to be a good pilot, but he was also known to be a poor navigator! The story goes that while Post piloted the plane, Rogers had his typewriter in his lap and was writing for his syndicated column; his latest column was in his pocket ready to wire to newspapers from Barrow once they arrived.

Post safely landed on a coastal lagoon near a small fish camp called Walakpa, southwest of Point Barrow. Luckily, an Eskimo named Claire Okpeaha and his family were at the camp hunting for walrus. His wife spoke English, so she gave Post directions to Point Barrow, less than fifteen miles away.

Post tinkered with the engine for a few minutes, and Rogers chatted with the Eskimos. Post and Rogers climbed back into the floatplane to depart. Then they started the engine, taxied across the river, and took off in a steep, climbing turn. About fifty feet up, the engine seemed to stop cold; the plane faltered, dragged a wing in the water, and crashed on its back.

Los Angeles Times writer Jerry Belcher interviewed the Okpeahas' daughter Rose in 1985 when she was 61. Rose told the reporter that she witnessed the crash with her family when she was eleven years old. She described the engine stall as sounding like it "coughed."

"I can still see it in my mind. It was very foggy. The plane was red and silver and just went upside down in the water."

She said her father ran the fifteen miles to Point Barrow to report the crash. When Claire got to Point Barrow with the news, several men immediately traveled to the site via motorized whaleboat. The hybrid plane was destroyed. Its fuselage was split, and the right wing was broken.

When they went through the half-submerged wreckage, they recovered two bodies. Big newspaper headlines across the nation spread the news that Will Rogers, age 56, and Wiley Post, age 37, had been killed in the crash. It was a shock to the country.

Rogers' legacy has inspired everything from collections of quotes to newspaper columns, biopics to documentaries, and books to plays. As luck would have it, one of the best-known plays to emerge just happened to be touring when

I was looking for the perfect Spotlight Guest for the 1995 Fairbanks Summer Arts Festival.

Los Angeles Times writer Jerry Belcher believed the Okpeahas to be the only living witnesses to the crash. As it turned out, there was a second family at the camp whose two young sons also saw the plane go down.

CHAPTER 85

1995 FAIRBANKS SUMMER ARTS FESTIVAL JAMES WHITMORE AND HELEN BALDASSARE

One of my favorite Will Rogers quotes embodied how I felt about volunteering my time to keep the Festival momentum going: "If you want to be successful, it's just this simple. Know what you are doing. Love what you are doing. And believe in what you are doing."

I knew, loved, and believed in what I was doing! After the exciting 1994 Festival, I began thinking about who to feature as the Spotlight Guest for 1995. Lists of acts from artist management agencies I had used in the past started arriving.

I came across a listing that intrigued me: It promoted a one-man show called *Will Rogers' USA* featuring well-known actor James Whitmore. As a Rogers fan already, I had just seen the *Will Rogers Follies* on Broadway and visited the Pioneer Air Museum, where parts of Wiley Post's plane and the two crosses that commemorate Rogers and Post are on display.

In 1990, the Festival had opened with Hal Holbrook presenting his one-man show *Mark Twain Tonight!* and the audience loved it. I thought another theatre offering would be well received. When considering this, I realized that 1995 would be the 60th anniversary of the 1935 flight that brought Rogers and Post to Fairbanks.

I called Whitmore's manager, a delightful woman named George Spota. She was fascinated by some ideas I shared with her, and we became phone friends. Whitmore had presented his one-man show for years, but George said he had never been to Alaska. Hearing this, bringing his show to Fairbanks became even more pressing to me.

George confirmed that Whitmore could open the 1995 Festival with *Will Rogers' USA,* and we signed the contract!

I contacted Joe Carter, the director of the Will Rogers Memorial Museum in Claremore, Oklahoma, Rogers' hometown. Joe's wife, Michelle, also worked at the museum. I invited them both to be our guests in Fairbanks to commemorate the anniversary. They were excited about the trip as they had never been to Alaska either. Carter offered to bring some of Will Rogers' saddles and a lariat. George told me that Whitmore was happy that the Carters were coming to Alaska, too, because he had never been to the Will Rogers Museum!

Alaska Airlines helped sponsor the show and provided plane tickets for Whitmore and his wife. Festival supporters donated enough frequent flier miles to buy plane tickets for Michelle and Joe Carter. I arranged for Sophie Station suites, and Ralph Seekins came through once again, providing a Lincoln Town car for each couple.

The Whitmores and the Carters arrived in Fairbanks on the same flight Wednesday afternoon before Friday's show. That evening they rested in preparation for a unique excursion we had planned for them the next day.

Early on Thursday, we got them back to the airport, and Alaska Airlines flew them all above the Arctic Circle to Point Barrow, the northernmost community in the United States. We let them know that a helicopter would take them on a flyover to the crash site, about 12 miles away.

It would be an understatement to say they were simply thrilled with these plans. I was excited, too, and would have loved to accompany them, but there was no way I could leave during the busy days before the Festival opened.

My longtime friend Margie Van Cleve, an Alaskan history buff, would take my place, coordinate plans, and be the guide on this adventure. She had started weeks before to organize the details of the visit, starting with reaching out to the Point Barrow Mayor. She recently recounted the phone conversation she had with the Mayor's secretary:

> *Margie:* Good morning. My name is Margie Van Cleve from Fairbanks. May I please speak with the Mayor?
>
> *Secretary:* I'm sorry. The Mayor isn't in town right now.
>
> *Margie:* May I ask when he will return?
>
> *Secretary:* As soon as he and his party catch a whale.

Margie was amused by this reply. When she called again in a few days, evidently he and his whaling party must have caught a whale because the Mayor was available and ready to help. He volunteered to have a search and rescue helicopter fly the party to the crash site. He warned that if there was an emergency, they would have to respond.

It had been originally believed that Claire Okpeaha's family were the only eyewitnesses to the 1935 crash, but it later came out that two other Eskimo boys from another family at the camp also saw it firsthand. Margie asked about those boys, who must have been in their 70s by then.

The Mayor's secretary connected Margie with the staff at Point Barrow's nursing home, and she found out they were living there! She explained who our guests were and that she wanted to introduce them. The project intrigued the staff member, and she said, "What day? We will invite you all to come for lunch with them!"

When the day came, after landing in Point Barrow, the Whitmores, Carters, and Margie had a delightful lunch with the two Eskimo elders who were the last people still living who had witnessed the crash. Though the boys were young then, they described seeing the plane crash into the lagoon near the fish camp that summer day in 1935.

The Mayor and his secretary had arranged for a school bus to give the visitors a guided tour around Point Barrow. They saw Point Barrow's community college, a pizza parlor, and a Mexican restaurant. They saw where people lived in modest frame homes built on gravel. The area was primarily barren tundra. Margie joked with Whitmore, saying, "I don't think even Miracle-Gro would work here!" He laughed at the reference to his many TV ads promoting the popular gardening product.

The Mayor came through on his offer, and they boarded the search and rescue helicopter and flew to the crash site, as there are still no roads there to this day. They didn't land, but the pilot circled the site several times so they could take pictures of the area and of the monument that had been erected.

A similar monument stands in the lobby of the Point Barrow airport. When the tour was over, exhilarated, they headed back to the airport and were able to take pictures of the monument there. They boarded the 2 o'clock Alaska Airlines flight for the hour and fifteen-minute flight back to Fairbanks. What an eventful few hours!

I appreciated all of Margie's planning for the day, and they did, too. As an Alaskan memento, Margie gave them each handmade zipper pulls that she had crafted out of caribou fur and antlers.

That evening, Dick and I honored them all at dinner in our home. It was a beautiful, warm summer evening for the poolside gathering, and we invited over 30 longtime Fairbanks friends and pioneers.

Whitmore made a point of visiting with each of these pioneers. Some of our guests' parents had been around to meet Will Rogers and Wiley Post in 1935. We all enjoyed a wonderful experience imagining that time 60 years earlier.

The next day, Joe, Michelle, and Mrs. Whitmore enjoyed shopping while Whitmore rested and prepared his mind for that night's performance.

Hering Auditorium was packed. When he came onstage, Whitmore looked just like the pictures we'd all seen of Will Rogers. He put on a fantastic show.

In the lobby after the performance, Joe had Will Rogers' saddles and lariat from the museum on display. He even demonstrated some of Rogers' rope tricks with the lariat. To the joy of the attendees, Whitmore joined us in the lobby and visited with everyone.

It was exciting for the Festival to help commemorate the anniversary, and it was a great way to kick off the two weeks! We had more registrants than ever, many returning and bringing friends. Our guest artists brought fresh and exciting things for their areas of study, so every year, there was something new.

Our delightful guest cabaret artist from New York, Helen Baldassare, again brought her sparkle to the Festival's cabaret classes. With her witty sense of humor, students and audiences loved her. Her classes performed throughout the two weeks in venues all over town.

Helen was the Spotlight Guest for the phenomenal closing concert with pianist Dean Burris and bassist Ernie Provencher. The crowd gave them a rousing standing ovation.

She enjoyed it so much that she invited another New York singer to tag along for fun the following year. That singer was Sue Matsuki, who would return to the Festival many times.

George Spota called me to thank me again on behalf of the Whitmores for all the extra kind things we did, especially Margie Van Cleve's work putting together the day trip to Point Barrow. They were so impressed with their Festival experience that George wrote a letter to the editor of the Fairbanks Daily News-Miner about Whitmore's experience.

I will always be grateful to my many Festival friends in Fairbanks who showed what our small, energetic, creative, and arts-minded community could pull off. It was a group effort, and (besides Alaska Airlines, Sophie Station and Ralph Seekins who I've already mentioned) I would like to acknowledge others whose efforts contributed to the event's success: the Fairbanks Chamber of Commerce members and local residents who volunteered to promote the show; Dirk Tordoff, an award-winning film curator with the UAF Rasmuson Library, who helped find interesting historical information concerning Will Rogers' time in Fairbanks; and Fairbanks pioneer Randy Acord, who was in charge of the Air Museum at Pioneer Park. Finally, many thanks go to the *Fairbanks Daily News-Miner* journalists who wrote various feature stories about the events commemorating the crash's 60th anniversary.

CHAPTER 86

LESSONS, LEGENDS, AND LASTING BONDS

New York singer Sue Matsuki was an enthusiastic Fairbanks Summer Arts Festival Cabaret participant for many years. Though she was already a working jazz and cabaret performer, she fit right into our cabaret classes and was gracious about her professional level. Her fellow registrants appreciated her talent, and she was an example to them that there's always more to learn.

Today, as a multi-award-winning performer on the New York cabaret scene, she is lovingly referred to as The Godmother of Cabaret, as she is a consummate supporter of other singers.

She has come a long way and credits the Festival as part of her trajectory. I asked Sue to share a little about the impact the Festival has had on her life and career. She graciously complied.

I had the honor of attending the Fairbanks Summer Arts Festival for five glorious years. The first year, in 1996, I traveled there with Helen Baldassare and Bobby Peaco, who taught the Cabaret class. Before we arrived in Fairbanks, we visited some wonderful places like Homer, Denali, and Anchorage. We stopped for drinks at places with names like Skinny Dick's, Halfway Inn, The Salty Dawg Saloon, The Howling Dog... well, you get that there's a theme!

My first impression of Alaska can be summed up in one word: *Spendid-for-us*! We saw the two gigantic stuffed bears at the airport, impressive enough, but then we saw a live grizzly and an enormous male moose cross the street right in front of our car. What a welcome to Alaska – I was definitely not in Brooklyn anymore! When we all arrived in Fairbanks, I met Dick and Jo Scott, and my Alaskan adventure began. Who knew that it would last for 5 years and also change my life forever? We were honored to work with Greg Hopkins (brass) and Mike Monaghan (woodwinds) from Boston. That year, I also met two incredible visiting Russian jazz musicians, pianist Evgeny Chernonog and saxophonist Slava Zakharov, who took a shine to my singing and invited me to jam with them at a few of the noontime Lunch Bites concerts held in the Great Hall. They came back in 1997.

I did, too! In my second year, I met the Grand Dame of Cabaret, Miss Julie Wilson. She was 73 at the time. Since I had never met her in New York, when it was announced that she was going to teach the Cabaret class, I literally stalked her to follow her to Fairbanks. This would turn into an almost 18-year gift to me, although I didn't know it at the time. We bonded over a pair of size ten black high heels, but more about that in a minute.

Julie was a renowned movie, TV, Broadway, and Cabaret star. Those of us attending that year were treated to classes taught by a living legend. She was a tough but passionate teacher. She came with Grammy award-winning Musical Director Mark Hummel. We had a blast. Now, what about those size ten high heels? Julie had forgotten her shoes. She had very bad feet, so I ran around town, found a pair in a 2nd hand store, and took them to the cobbler to have them shined up for her. The moment I gave them to her was when we became Friends for Life! Well, dear friends until the end of her life in 2015. She passed at 90. She was the first and best gift that Alaska gave to me, and I will be forever grateful. I was awarded the very first *Julie Wilson Award* by the Mabel Mercer Foundation in 2004, hand-picked by Julie. It remains the most significant honor of my performing career. We just did a show celebrating what would have been her 100th Birthday in New York hosted by her famous actor son Holt McCallany at the Cutting Room. The evening included an all-star cast that, as Julie predicted many years ago, I was now a welcome member of. To think this all started in Alaska!

In my third year, 1998, I met the most adorable and talented West Coast jazz educator, V.J. Singh. He challenged all of us to go outside of our comfort zones to try scatting and improvising. He was an amazing teacher. He was also a part of a world-famous acapella group called "Just 4 Kicks." Every year, attending this Festival brought new colors to my performing paint box, and the gifts just kept coming.

The friends I met there are always in my heart, and thanks to Facebook, most of them are still in my life. Linda Knighten, Susie Doyle, Barbara Schatz-Harris, Linda Marchi,

Lisa Sporleder, and so many more local singers are among those I got to share this experience with for five years.

1999 and 2000 brought amazing musicians into my life, and again, big cats from New York that I would never have met had I not gone to Alaska. Saxophone player Bob Kindred and his wife, the multi-talented Anne Phillips, befriended me. Anne is not only a singer-songwriter, recording artist, and former backup singer for Carole King, Burt Bacharach, and Neil Diamond but also the producer of her show *Bending the Light: A Jazz Nativity*. Also because of Alaska, I got to meet New York jazz guitarist Gene Bertoncini, the sweetest man ever. Another gift was when I called Bob and Gene to sit in on *A New Take*, my first CD in 2001. They both honored me with a few tunes. I also met the talented gent who took over teaching the Cabaret class, Ron Drotos, who, believe it or not, after 24 years, has just recently reconnected with me to do a jazz gig together at the club Jazz on Main.

This music festival, started by a teacher and her supportive husband, is the gift that just keeps on giving even after 28 years. While I was already a working performer when I first attended in 1996, when we stop learning we stop growing. I totally credit my time at this incredible Festival and the support, love, and belief in my talent by Jo and Dick Scott to be the reason I am who I am today, both on and off stage. My gratitude has no boundaries. Thank you, Alaska! Thank you, Fairbanks Summer Arts Festival! Thank you, Dick and Jo!

–Sue Matsuki

The link to Sue's website can be found in this chapter's Bonus Media.

Jo Ryman Scott

CHAPTER 87

1996 Fairbanks Summer Arts Festival Manhattan Rhythm Kings

The 1995 Fairbanks Summer Arts Festival had opened with James Whitmore and closed with Helen Baldassare. Soon, it was time to begin looking for next year's Spotlight Guests. Materials were arriving from the various artist management agencies, and I was excited to see the Manhattan Rhythm Kings in a New York agency's listings. I knew their dynamic renditions of music from the 20s, 30s, and 40s. This, combined with their energetic stage presence, would be perfect for our Festival audiences. The agency was great, the cost was within our budget, and the trio was available for our 1996 concert date! We signed the contract.

Around this time, in the fall of 1995, I met Scott Deal, the new percussion teacher at the UAF Music Department. When I learned that Scott was from Florida, I asked him if he might know something about steel drums. I was taken with their sound when Dick and I heard a steel drum band perform at a conference in Sun Valley earlier that year. They had explained that Trinidadians discovered how to tune empty oil drums left there after World War II by pounding out domes of different sizes, called bosses, on the drums' tops. This fascinated me.

Scott said that he was more than familiar with steel drums, and I was thrilled when he agreed to teach a beginning steel drum class at the 1996 Festival. With help from many friends, I obtained funding for the Festival to purchase a few of those drums for him to use for the new class.

Scott started the steel drum classes with a small but enthusiastic group of registrants. He was an energetic, popular teacher; his students appreciated him, and they had fun in the class. They performed for Lunch Bites and other venues around town during the Festival. Bob Howard, a longtime Fairbanks businessman, enjoyed the class and performing with the class so much that he helped with fundraising so the Festival could purchase even more steel drums, allowing for more participants in the future.

To advertise the class and entice people to register for the following year, Scott had his steel drummers perform in the Great Hall while people were coming to the Davis Concert Hall for the much-anticipated Manhattan Rhythm Kings concert. It was a perfect way to set the tone and welcome people to the festive musical evening. (They were such a hit, I called their agency to book them for the next year right away.)

We had another landmark year with new registrants from all over, many Lunch Bites concerts featuring guests and participants performing, and the popular Festival Art Show, which exhibited the visual arts participants' work in the gallery just off of the Great Hall. There were OMT performances throughout the two weeks as well.

Thanks to Helen Baldassarre, we invited the prominent New York pianist and musical director Bobby Peaco as a new guest artist for the cabaret class. He and Helen made a fun team teaching the Cabaret classes. (He asked, "Why are there no piano bars in Fairbanks?")

Helen and Bobby closed the Festival with a rousing final concert, bringing the house down with their humorous, fast-paced performance. The audience was treated to one song after another, each interpretation sizzling with their unique flair. Fairbanks might not have had piano bars, but we did have Helen Baldassare and Bobby Peaco for an extraordinary evening of cabaret to wrap up the 1986 Festival!

Postscript regarding the wonderful steel drum program: Scott suggested I call Tom Miller, a professional steel drum artist from San Francisco, to teach our Steel Drum classes for the following year, as Scott would be teaching other percussion classes. Tom was just what we needed! He had personality and knowledge and was a master teacher. His classes filled quickly, and Tom continued as the Festival's Steel Drum teacher for several years. Many registrants started purchasing steel drums of their own and began performing beyond the Festival throughout the year.

Local businessman Chris Miller and his wife, Angie Schmidt, were two of these people. In the early 2000s, Chris and Angie purchased Tommy's Elbow Room in downtown Fairbanks, renaming it The Music Room. They turned a portion of the large venue into a rehearsal space for the Festival's steel drum classes, as well as the group that performed year-round. As a bonus, it served as a home for many of the steel drums themselves.

More than twenty years after the first 1996 steel drum classes, I returned to Fairbanks and went to see the steel drummers rehearsing in *The Music Room!* I was thrilled to see how the group had grown, and they sounded better than ever. What a wonderful gift to the community Chris and Angie gave by providing this venue.

Greg Martin Photography 2015

CHAPTER 88

A NEW MILLENNIUM, A TECHIE ANGEL, AND WORLD MUSIC MAGIC

Our guest artists were some of the best master teachers and performers in the nation. Thanks to this, the Festival continued to be recognized nationally for its excellence. Each year we welcomed more out-of-state students.

We again revised our Festival description for mailings and publications and it now read:

"A Unique Study/Performance Festival in the Land of the Midnight Sun. Held on the beautiful University of Alaska Fairbanks campus, the Festival is open to persons ages 18 and older, with opportunities in some areas of study for younger students."

As we neared the new millennium, new technology was helping us reach more people and become more efficient. Kade Mendelowitz of the UAF Theatre Department became our techie angel! I finally got a computer, and Kade generously gave his time to set it up and walk me through using it. The first thing he did was establish the Festival's website. Websites were relatively new at the time, and this was groundbreaking. After this, Kade set up the Festival's mailing list. E-mail made communicating with our guests and registrants a breeze. No more photo-copying a monthly newsletter to be hand-addressed and mailed!

We opened the 1998 Festival in the Davis Concert Hall with the Festival Chamber Chorale directed by Marvilla Davis. (Marvilla's husband, Chip, is the son of Charles W. Davis, for whom the concert hall is named.) We were proud to have Marvilla as one of the Festival's vocal guest artists for several summers. She had many followers throughout Alaska. Her Chamber Chorale concert was an exciting way to open that year's Festival.

During this time, our dance classes diversified in a unique way. Judy Kreith, a dancer from Denver, had found the Festival in an arts magazine listing in 1996 and called me up. She asked many questions about Alaska and casually mentioned that she was considering moving there. I immediately encouraged her to move to Fairbanks. I told her I had ideas for a job for her. By the end of the phone call, she had registered for Festival dance classes and said she would consider moving to Fairbanks. As it turned out, she did!

Once in Fairbanks, she enjoyed the Festival classes she had registered for, and I put her in touch with June Rogers, the Fairbanks Arts Association (FAA) director in Pioneer

Park. Judy was hired that summer to teach FAA dance classes. She was a great teacher and I invited her to join the Festival's dance faculty in 1997.

Steel Drum classes were thriving thanks to Tom Miller, and Scott teamed up with Judy to offer a World Music and Dance class. Percussion and dance registrants enjoyed developing their talents in this collaborative concept.

Over the next two years, that class became very popular! Adults of any age could take it even if they had never played an instrument or studied drumming or dancing. Scott would teach them to play rhythms on various percussion instruments, while Judy would have her dancers interpret the music. By the summer of 1999, it had more than 60 registrants.

The 1999 Festival closed with a fantastic crowd-pleasing "World Music and Dance" performance in the Davis Concert Hall. The dancers and singers wore colorful dresses, and the percussionists wore dark pants and colorful shirts. They were like magic on stage. It was a captivating concert!

It was especially exciting for me to observe what that class was doing in the lives of many registrants with no formal training. They had a natural sense of rhythm and could have fun learning to perform professionally. This was a great example of what made our Festival so appealing to so many. What an exciting time this was!

CHAPTER 89

A GENEROUS GIFT AND A LIFE REMEMBERED

By the year 2000, many of us were concerned that funding for the arts was being cut nationwide. Our Festival budget was kept in the black thanks to our growing number of registrants, our guest artists generously accepting lower fees, and the legions of unpaid helpers. However, funding was always a concern hovering on my mind.

Shortly after the close of the 2000 Festival, I got a phone call from Nancy Marriott. Our outstanding vocal coach, Bob McCoy, had encouraged Nancy to come to the Festival in 1983, and she had been coming every year since! Nancy knew that we wanted to establish an Endowment Fund for the Festival, which would allow the dividends to be used for Festival expenses. She recognized the Festival's positive impact on people and the quality of our Opera and Musical Theatre program, which she loved participating in each year. She has sung many standout roles in OMT performances; she has a beautiful voice.

As it happened, her phone call came when I was working to balance that year's budget. Nancy said that she wanted to contribute $115,000 from her late mother's estate to establish an Endowment Fund for the Festival! This generous donation, a testament to Nancy's belief in our mission, would significantly shape the future of our Festival. I was overwhelmed with gratitude.

Just a short time later, we got the sad news that Bob McCoy had passed away suddenly. Bob had been involved with the Festival since its earliest years and was a driving force in establishing the Opera and Musical Theatre area of study, affectionately called OMT. His talent was only surpassed by his wonderful personality, and he touched hundreds of lives during his many summers in Alaska. His legacy lives on.

I flew to Maryland with Bill and Theresa Reed for the Celebration of Life service in Bob's honor. Nancy and her husband Dick hosted many of Bob's friends at a gathering in their lovely home after the service. That evening, Dick asked me all sorts of questions about the Festival. I appreciated his interest and happily answered whatever he asked. He said he was impressed and that he understood why Nancy had become such a fan.

The Festival is grateful to Bob, who gave so much of himself and brought us Nancy, who believed in the work we were doing and, with her generous gift, helped it get bigger and better.

As of this printing, Nancy has attended the Fairbanks Summer Arts Festival more than 25 times.

THE 2000S

CHAPTER 90

FROM FIRM *NO* TO FIRM *YES* TO FESTIVAL FIXTURES

It was a beautiful summer day in 2001 when I unexpectedly ran into two familiar faces at the post office, Debra Ward Pearson and Yvonne McHenry. I was thrilled to see them after so many years.

I had been the vocal music teacher at their elementary school decades earlier when they were little. I remembered them being good singers even at that age, and I talked to them about participating in the Festival.

They both said they couldn't because they were busy with church work. I mentioned that I was thinking about adding Gospel Choir to the Festival and they both perked up to that idea! They didn't have suggestions for a choir director, but they encouraged me to search for the right person and let them know if I found one.

I called Festival guest artist Ron Drotos, the NYC pianist and vocal coach for cabaret students. He said he would be happy to try to help me. Ron asked his many students and colleagues if they knew of a good Gospel Choir director. He was surprised when they all recommended the same person: Bobby Lewis! One student had Bobby's New York phone number.

I called Bobby and briefly explained that I was calling from Fairbanks, Alaska and that he had been highly recommended as I was looking for a director for our Festival's new Gospel Choir.

Bobby quickly answered, "No, I can't. I'm too busy." But then he said, "Wait a minute. Where did you say you are calling from?" I repeated, "Fairbanks, Alaska." Bobby immediately said, "I can be there!"

I was thrilled!

Bobby needed a professional Gospel pianist, so I also hired his music director, Eustace Johnson. Contracts were signed, and travel arrangements were made. I reached out to Debra and Yvonne, and they were delighted with the news. I was overjoyed when they agreed to be the Gospel Choir's local coordinators. They would be dedicated and dependable volunteers.

Debra, Yvonne, and I worked tirelessly during the winter of 2001-2002, encouraging people to register for the first Gospel Choir. We were committed to keeping the registration fee as low as possible, so we set it at $100 for the two weeks, and offered scholarships for anyone needing one. Our efforts paid off, and we were overjoyed to see more than 90 singers register!

The Gospel Choir not only enriched the lives of its participants but also had a profound impact on the entire community. Many of our Gospel participants took advantage of the Festival registrant benefit, allowing them admission to all the Festival concerts with their Festival ID. It was wonderful to see new faces in the audience at these events.

Bobby was the perfect director. He was personable, energetic, talented, and a master teacher. He worked seamlessly with Eustace, and the Choir members appreciated and loved them both. In July 2002, they made that first year's Gospel Choir concert exciting and inspirational. They performed to a packed house at Davis Concert Hall.

Bobby chuckled when he told me that because he and Eustace had never been to Alaska, they accepted my invitation, thinking they would be a part of our Festival for one year only. But they both had a great experience at the Festival. Everyone loved them so much that I invited them to return in February 2003 for a one-week Winter Edition of Gospel Choir. I suggested that they could create a program to celebrate Black History Month.

They reconsidered their "one year only" thought. They liked my idea, and Bobby wrote a brief story about black history. When he and Eustace arrived in Fairbanks in February, Bobby selected Choir members to read parts of the story, and the Choir would follow up by singing a song related to that story.

At the end of the week of classes, coaching, and rehearsals, the Davis Concert Hall was packed for the Gospel Choir Winter Edition's culmination, the moving evening concert.

Everyone appreciated the inspirational message they received from Bobby, Eustace, and the Choir members that evening. They were amazed at the soloists, the beautiful harmonies, and Bobby's infectious energy. It was beyond anything I had originally imagined!

After their success that first year, Bobby and Eustace realized that there was no way they could quit coming to Fairbanks. With the exception of pandemic years, when everything was canceled, Bobby and Eustace came to Fairbanks twice a year from 2003 on. Their presence not only enriched the Fairbanks community but also has left a lasting impact on the Juneau community. Their Gospel Choir performances are a highly anticipated event, drawing crowds and spreading the joy of Gospel music. Not only did they have a rewarding experience, but they also won the hearts of everyone they met.

They became good friends with UAF Music Department faculty member Jaunelle Celaire. Along with Debra and Yvonne, she was a featured Gospel Choir soloist. Janelle also joined Bobby, Eustace, Yvonne, Debra, Julie Benson, Ron Velez, Diamond Fuller, and others in presenting the MOTOWN Festival Fundraiser held each February during Winter Edition.

When Gospel Choir member Annie Caulfield moved to Juneau, she established a Gospel Choir for that community. Now, every February, Bobby and Eustace add Juneau to their travel plans after leaving Fairbanks' Winter Edition of Gospel Choir.

With Debra and Yvonne's careful planning, Gospel Choir continues to thrive. Choir member Mary Lou Killion gives her time to assist where needed. Another volunteer in those early years was BJ Williams, who spent many hours designing and preparing the concert programs.

For all these years, the Festival has appreciated rehearsing in the lovely sanctuary of the University Community Presbyterian Church. The Gospel Choir concerts are held in various locations on Sunday afternoons in winter and summer. They draw huge crowds.

Debra and Yvonne continue to take care of many Gospel Choir details. They organize Bobby and Eustace's travel, housing, and courtesy cars and oversee getting programs printed. They also arrange for the receptions held immediately following the concerts. Many tables are filled with delicious goodies brought by Choir members, miraculously enough to share with the large audiences! These receptions continue to be a special highlight, and everyone looks forward to them!

Bobby and Eustace have busy year-round schedules. Bobby is the Senior Pastor of the New Light Baptist Church in Harlem, and Eustace is its Music Director. But Bobby and Eustace always make the time to come to Alaska! They are a blessing to the Festival and to the Fairbanks and Juneau communities as they share God's love through Gospel music. They touch the lives of everyone they meet. Who knew, on that beautiful day in 2001, that running into former students from decades earlier at the post office would have set all of this in motion?

CHAPTER 91

2002 & 2003 FAIRBANKS SUMMER ARTS FESTIVALS PONCHO SANCHEZ AND DIANE SHURE

Everything was going very well with the Festival. The first year of Gospel Choir was a hit, and we had good sessions with all of our workshops. The Grammy-winning conguero Poncho Sanchez and his Latin Jazz Band opened the 2002 Festival. Shirley was in town and she welcomed everyone to the concert in Spanish, introducing them as they came onstage, where a packed house at Hering Auditorium welcomed them. The crowd really enjoyed the group and all of their exotic percussion instruments.

About fifty people came to an informal afterparty in our yard, and Poncho and his band joined us. They were fascinated by the fact it was midnight and still light out! We closed the 2002 Festival with West Coast singer Diane Shure at Davis Concert Hall. We had a good crowd, and people appreciated her talent.

The Festival was growing every year. More guest artists and more registrants meant more paperwork! By the end of 2002, I was overwhelmed with all the office work that had to be done, and I was missing my part-time office helper, Audra Tryon. She'd been offered a full-time position, something we couldn't afford to offer her. I needed help desperately.

January 2003 was when Dick and I ran into Judy Divinyi at a "First Friday" art show. I told her I needed to find someone to work year-round with me and our volunteers. Judy had recently sold her business and had quietly said, "Jo, I could do that." I hired Judy on the spot!

We immediately got busy preparing for the 2003 Festival. Judy and I enjoyed working together. I appreciated her wisdom and her business expertise. Having operated her successful business for many years, she quickly understood the Festival's bookkeeping. Thanks to computers, Judy could do much of her work in her home office.

Her arts-minded husband, Carl, also wanted to volunteer to help the Festival. He had an easy-going personality and became a valuable volunteer who helped in all sorts of ways.

After carefully reviewing the budget, Judy and I agreed that the Festival needed to hire a professional to help us organize a community-wide fundraising campaign for its general fund.

Our friend Karen Cedzo had recently retired from UAF University Relations and agreed to organize the campaign. She named it "The Festival for Everyone!" Karen Parr and Jim Holt headed her leadership team of well-known community leaders who were Festival supporters:

Joe Beedle, Mary Binkley, Ed Christiansen, Don Gray, Mark Hamilton, Jim Haselberger, Jim Holm, Rodger Hughes, Patty Kastelic, Lois Lind, Harry Porter, Dan Ramras, John Ringstad, Craig Salsbury, Cherie Solie, Catherine Stevens, Joe Usibelli, Carolyne Wallace, Jinx Whitaker, Jack Williams, and Buki Wright.

The campaign brought in more than $200,000 to the Festival's General Fund!

We forged ahead planning for the 2003 Festival, hiring 80 guest faculty, preparing the registration form and catalog with Lisa Sporleder's help, and planning for all the concerts. We were grateful to have professional photographer Todd Paris continue contributing his time to take pictures of Festival people and events and preserve the Festival's history. We were offering many new things, covering even more interests.

Antoinette Botsford's Storytelling classes gained momentum, attracting a new group of participants. We added a new area of study: Healing Arts Balance and Yoga classes with Jean Couch from Palo Alto, California. Jean's classes became very popular, and additional healing arts classes and guest faculty were added over the years. The local coordinator was Kay Hackney, a well-known Fairbanks yoga teacher who gave considerable time to make those classes succeed. Gianna Drogheo taught a new pedagogy class that was very well-received that year. Gianna had been a dedicated volunteer and active registrant since the Festival began.

Cassy Kelly Bartch worked in the Festival's summer office for ten years. I was so thankful for her people skills and office expertise, and was proud of her for being so proactive and always thinking on her feet.

She did a lot of that during the 2003 Festival, as besides the 80 guest faculty Judy and I had hired, we had over 600 registrants!

Photo courtesy of Fairbanks Summer Arts Festival
DONATION—The J. Willard and Alice S. Marriott Foundation has granted $1 million to establish an endowment for the long-term vitality of the Fairbanks Summer Arts Festival. Festival founder Jo Ryman Scott, left, and board president Theresa Reed, middle, stand with Nancy Peery Marriott in July 2003.

Summer festival gets $1 million endowment

CHAPTER 92

2004 FAIRBANKS SUMMER ARTS FESTIVAL MARRIOTT'S MIRACLE MILLION

I got an exciting phone call in the early summer of 2004. Nancy Marriott phoned with some astounding news. She told me an attorney for the J. Willard and Alice S. Marriott Foundation would be calling regarding preparing paperwork for the Festival to accept a new endowment gift.

It would be in the amount of one million dollars!

I was extremely grateful. Nancy said that she would like to help expand the Festival's Opera and Musical Theatre

(OMT) program by having some of the earnings from that gift be used towards travel scholarships for out-of-state OMT registrants. In her years at the Festival, she had appreciated the experience of taking classes from many of the talented OMT guest artists, including Kathryn Harvey, Carolyn Hague, Michael Pinkerton, Louise McClelland, JT Froelich, and Cindy Oxberry. I told her we would be more than happy to designate the funds for this. I appreciated her wanting more people from outside of Fairbanks to have the opportunity to experience the OMT coaching from our outstanding teachers as she had.

Now, the Festival had two Endowment accounts: One from funds from Nancy Peery Marriott's mother's trust fund and one from the Marriott Foundation. The Festival Board voted to invest these gifts in mutual fund accounts. According to the withdrawal formula, the Festival receives distributions from the two accounts once a year. Each year, the Festival sends a report to the Marriott Foundation outlining how the withdrawals were used.

In the meantime, planning for the 2004 Festival was in full swing. We listened to suggestions for improving the Festival. Part of our mission was to provide Festival audiences with inspirational concerts at affordable prices to enrich their lives.

In preparation for the 2004 Festival, I met with the local coordinators for each area of study. We worked to streamline the course descriptions in our Festival catalog. We also considered how we could attract more registrants and started offering classes by the day or by the week, which appealed to many new registrants. We kept our registration fees as low as possible and offered opportunities for work/study scholarships so registrants could work off their registration fees.

Our classes in each area of study were growing. I was interested in adding Shakespeare classes. I asked Susan Stitham, a high school Shakespeare teacher, to be the local coordinator. She had recently retired from the Fairbanks school district and accepted my offer. Susan's classes were very popular, thanks to her efforts. A few years later, Susan invited a well-known Shakespeare teacher she knew, Graham Watts from London, to join her in teaching. They were both well-liked by the students, and students of all ages enjoyed the classes.

We also added Creative Writing, taught by local published author Peggy Shumaker. Patty Kastelic was the class's local coordinator, and she worked closely with Peggy. This class also attracted many new registrants.

Fairbanksan Christine Upton suggested that we add accordion classes and offered to be the local coordinator. She selected Joe Smiell to teach, and they designed Accordian classes for registrants with various experience levels. These classes brought more new registrants! Joe was a popular performer in the Festival's Lunch Bites noon concerts. He was in his 80s when he came to the Festival, and his energy seemed nonstop. He was a master teacher, and people appreciated him.

Our Visual Arts classes expanded into paper art, fiber art, and more watercolor classes. Several guest artists, including Judi Betts, Rachel Clark, Nikki Kinne, and Vladimir Zhikhartsev, have returned many times. Guest artist Tom Nixon was originally a visual arts student. He kept taking Festival classes each summer and eventually became a watercolor teacher. Tom and his wife, Nelda, spent considerable time as the local coordinators for visual arts, and as a result, their classes continued to grow.

Our Festival Dance classes were also becoming popular, largely thanks to local dance enthusiast Pat Sims. She was a dedicated local coordinator. For several years, Pat worked with local dance teacher Norman Shelburne to add more dance classes and bring the best possible teacher.

The Festival continued expanding its reach, adding diverse areas of study and including more and more people with every new class. Thanks to the generous Marriott gift, our long-established Opera and Musical Theatre area of study would be welcoming new people as well!

CHAPTER 93

2005 FAIRBANKS
SUMMER ARTS FESTIVAL
THE 25TH ANNIVERSARY

There is a story about Winston Churchill telling Parliament to set aside money for the arts. There was pushback, and he said, "Our troops need to have something valuable to come home to."

My first foray into bringing artists to Fairbanks was in 1968 when the Alaska Association for the Arts was able to bring The Canadian Opera Company's The Barber of Seville to Fairbanks. My job of raising funds to do this was made much easier by the fact that the Canadian government highly subsidized the arts. Here we were almost forty years later, in 2005, and the United States was still not prioritizing supporting the arts. The Festival was about to celebrate its twenty-fifth anniversary, and my board and I still had to spend considerable time fundraising before we could even begin to budget what we could afford and then contract the artists.

At the beginning of the year, I spoke with Ruth Burnett, U.S. Senator Ted Stevens' representative for the Fairbanks area. I shared my need for grant funding, emphasizing how important the arts are to society, and expressed that many other countries heavily subsidize them.

Ruth spoke with Senator Stevens, who suggested I write a detailed proposal to the U.S. Department of Education requesting a grant for the Festival. I had written a significant number of proposals over the past twenty-five years requesting grant money, so I used that experience to write the proposal. I detailed the work that many of us were doing as volunteers and noted the large number of people we served. I requested a grant of $150,000 and submitted it.

Within a few weeks, my board and I were thrilled that the grant was approved, but in a different way. The Festival would receive $100,000 per year for two years! However, to receive the actual funds, a lot of paperwork was required. Judy Divinyi was especially helpful in completing the necessary documents, and the funding went through. Receiving this grant was an excellent way to start celebrating the Festival's 25th anniversary!

Karen Cedzo created the colorful 25th Anniversary concert booklet, which lists our financial supporters, guest artists, and registrants covering all twenty-five years. She included engaging comments from several prominent Festival supporters and colorful collages of our Spotlight Guests.

We planned an exciting 2005 Fairbanks Summer Arts Festival that would celebrate all of the year's guest artists and special returning guests from the very first Festival. We brought back our original Boston musicians, whom my co-founder, Eddie Madden, had invited: Fred Buda, drums; Mike Monaghan, saxophone; Bob Winter, piano; Mark Henry, bass; and, of course, Eddie Madden himself!

Greg Hopkins had continued as the director of the Festival Jazz Band every year since the first Festival. Jazz guests for that summer were Josh Davis, bass; Varden Ovsepian, piano; and Ron Veliz, guitar. We were thrilled to have jazz vocalist Chris Calloway return, as well!

The air buzzed with anticipation each evening to sold-out crowds, a vibrant sea of eager faces ready for the magic to unfold. The atmosphere crackled with energy as the audience was thrilled to welcome back the artists they hadn't seen in several years.

Other exciting concerts presented during those two weeks included the Women's Vocal Ensemble, conducted by Marvilla Davis; the Men's Vocal Ensemble, conducted by Byron McGilvray; and the Festival Chorus, conducted by Scott Peterson. These vocal groups were well-received by the crowds at the UAF's Davis Concert Hall.

A highlight was hearing Mike Monaghan sing the beautiful song he wrote, *Alaska is a Rainbow*. He composed this after attending the 1982 Festival.

Russell Guyver conducted the large Festival Orchestra. In addition to the Festival's instrumental registrants, many guest artists performed in the Orchestra, too. It sounded very professional.

String guests were Haroutune Bedelian, David Chew, Minna Rose Chung, Josh Davis, Michael Ferris, Alvaro Gomez, Routa Kroumovitch Gomez, Peter Marsh, Paul

Sharpe, and Linda Wang. Woodwind guests included John Barcellona, Daniel Cathey III, Marc Fink, Dorli McWayne, David Muller, Candy Rydlinski, and George Rydlinski.

Brass guests were James Atkinson, Jane Aspnes, James Michael Bicigo, Peter Brockman, Karen Gustafson, and Kurt Snyder. The Festival's Opera and Musical Theatre (OMT) registrants and guest artists presented popular selections in the UAF Davis Concert Hall.

Some selections were with the Festival Orchestra. Those OMT guest artists included Julia Aubrey, Robert Barefield, Jaunelle Celaire, Eileen Cornett, Richard Crawley, Louise McClelland, Michael Moore, Russell Ryan, and Ken Weiss.

World Music and Dance guests and registrants presented colorful concerts. Guest artists included Scott Deal, Tom Miller, Dom Moio, Valerie Naranjo, Barry Olsen, Lisa Indigo, and Judy Kreith.

Lucas Anderson, Judy Bejarano, Stefani Brown, Jenny Jue Chen, Wei Dongsheng, Suzanne Carlton, and Maria Vegh were the dance teachers. Richard Poland was the ballet pianist. The dancers presented outstanding performances in the UAF Salisbury Theatre.

Staff pianists included Maria Allison, Catherine Pruett, Shari Raynor, and Anita Swearengin. They were kept busy accompanying vocal and instrumental musicians.

Bobby Lewis and Eustace Johnson returned to lead the popular Gospel Choir, culminating in an inspirational UAF Davis Concert Hall concert.

The two weeks of that Festival were packed with concerts, performances, and art exhibits from all areas of study.

Creative Writing guest artists included Peggy Shumaker, Gerri Brightwell, David Lee, and Frank Soos. They performed readings in the Salisbury Theatre.

Rita Baragona, Rachel Kincy Clark, Roseanne Keller, Peter Martin, Tom Nixon, David Rosenthal, and Mark Ross were visual artists, and their students' work was on display.

Ice Skating Theatre guests included Jeff Carstensen, David Nickel, Glenn Patterson, Shanyn Vallon, and Lisa Ware. They presented their program at the UAF skating rink.

Jean Couch, Dana Davis, and Mark Johnson were popular Healing Arts guests. Antoinette Botsford taught Storytelling, an interesting new area of study.

We had many exciting Lunch Bites performances, and the Great Hall was full for these popular mini-concerts.

With 85 guest artists and more than 800 registrants from across the nation, it was an exciting two weeks. We rejoiced that the Festival was in excellent shape, both artistically and financially.

The FAIRBANKS SUMMER ARTS FESTIVAL

Since 1980

CHAPTER 94

2006 – 2008 FAIRBANKS SUMMER ARTS FESTIVALS

We had always worked to keep our registration fees as low as possible every year. We offered talent and work scholarships for students who had financial needs. Thanks to earnings from the Marriott Foundation Endowment, we could provide travel scholarships to out-of-state registrants.

Between 2005 and 2008, I continued to listen when people wanted new areas of study, and we had many new things during that time.

Fairbanks Folk Festival members Jeff Wildridge and Pete Bowers asked us to add American Roots Music workshops. They invited guest musicians and recruited students beginning in 2008. The program is still going strong. We also heeded requests asking for Scrapbooking classes. Leslye Korvola, a local artist, taught those classes.

After potential registrants asked if they could audit Festival classes, we added a Smorgasbord pass! Not only could passholders show their Festival Smorgasbord ID to silently attend any Festival class they wished, they could use it to attend all the concerts, too. It was a great way for even more people to become familiar with the wide variety of classes that we offered.

Every strong organization needs a dedicated board. I was grateful to the following people who served on the Festival Board at various times over these four years: Joe Beedle, Jaunelle Celaire, Sandy Clark, Scott Deal, Celeste Goering and Don Gray, Jim Holt, Patty Kastelic, Doug Lange, Joy McDougall, Karen Parr, Theresa Reed, Jane Sandstrom, David Stephenson, Susan Stitham, and B.J. Williams.

I was humbled when, in early 2008, the board announced a new gifting opportunity in my honor called A Legacy of Love. Festival supporter Mike Powers was the honorary chair, and over $35,000 was received. The Legacy of Love funds would be used as needed for any future Festival expenses.

We were grateful to continue to produce the Festival in partnership with the University of Alaska Fairbanks, and they donated all space for classes and performances.

I appreciated working with Jake Poole, the Vice Chancellor for Advancement at UAF. He helped promote the Festival during this time and was instrumental in helping me make UAF credit for the Festival's classes possible.

Parking on campus had become a challenge. I appreciated the help of Martin Klein, UAF's head of Traffic and Parking. He provided parking permits for our guest artists and the courtesy shuttle buses for the concerts.

The Music Department's office manager, Linda Harriger, and her assistant, Susan Risse, helped to line up UAF music students to work for the Festival. Students Chad Stadig and Lucas Clooten were in charge of the stage crew for our concerts at Davis Concert Hall. They were outstanding helpers. They saved the day shortly before a concert once when they jumped into action to prevent a sudden flow of rainwater pouring down the steps from the parking lot from making its way to the concert hall and flooding the whole stage. I didn't hear about the problem until the next day, and I was so appreciative of their quick response.

Over the years, many dedicated staff members helped with publicity, ads, catalog design, taping concerts, and general help. Those helping included Kathy Jaynes Bungart, Deanna Brandon, Levi Nilsson, Adela Jackson, Catherine Franklin, and Karri VanDeventer Cammack.

James Wardlaw-Bailey was the Festival Orchestra's librarian. He also worked extensively on computers during the Festival and photographed all the Festival posters.

Marcia Boyette organized the volunteer ushers for concerts in UAF's Davis Concert Hall. The Jeglum family and Ruth Knapman were among the Festival's faithful ushers.

I would also like to recognize Tyler Walker, who has been so wonderful in facilitating visitors to the Festival's historical memorabilia at the University Archives, formally known as Arctic and Polar Regions Collections & Archives (APRCA). Appointments can be made at (907) 474-7743. Many of these have been included in each chapter's QR Bonus Media, but there is a lot of Festival history that has been carefully categorized to explore!

I would also like to thank Angie Schmidt, the archivist from the Alaska Film Archives section of APRCA, for her help with the 1967 Fairbanks flood film footage. (She is also an active steel drummer!)

The Festival could never have survived and kept serving so many people had it not been for the literally hundreds of volunteers we had over those thirty years. I thank them all sincerely.

CHAPTER 95

2009 FAIRBANKS SUMMER ARTS FESTIVAL A FAREWELL BOW

All of us who worked to produce the Festival were dedicated to spreading the word about it. In addition to our regular local and statewide advertising, we had free listings in more than twenty arts magazines nationwide and in the *New York Times*.

The last Festival I produced, in 2009, was bigger and better than I had ever dreamed it could be. More than 100 guest artists and close to 1,000 registrants came from around the world. I enjoyed getting acquainted with our guests and registrants and still loved making my rounds to visit classes.

Lunch Bites continued to be a fixture, and the Wednesday editions, especially for children, were very special. I loved those little children and got to know them. One little girl was Sasha Bult-Ito. Her mother started bringing Sasha to Lunch Bites when she was only three. She loved her Wednesday performances! They were her beginnings of sitting to listen to a variety of music. Sasha went on to study music and is now an acclaimed concert pianist, performing across the country!

Our last 2009 Lunch Bites in the Great Hall had hundreds of attendees. Greg Hopkins and his Jazz Band opened with lively favorites, and they were followed by an exceptional lineup of mini performances. It was an emotional afternoon for me, introducing our Lunch Bites performers for the very last time. The large glass doors were open, so the music spilled out to the plaza beyond the music building.

During the final week, the Festival was alive with programs featuring hundreds of our registrants and guest artists.

Bobby Lewis and Eustace Johnson filled the Davis Concert Hall for their inspirational concert on Sunday afternoon, the Festival's last day. The Festival Gospel Choir included over 90 vocalists.

That evening's grand finale concert featured more than 100 registrants in Jazz, World Music, and Dance. The dancers and many other musicians wore colorful costumes. Greg Hopkins' Jazz Band, Tom Miller's steel drums group, Barry Olsen's Latin ensemble, and Valerie Naranjo's Native American instruments all brought the house down. Barry and Valerie, out of NYC, were wonderfully charismatic, and their drumming classes attracted many new registrants to the Festival.

At one point in the program, a line of dancers came onstage with flags of the states I had lived in – South Dakota, California, and Alaska – and called me onstage for a moment, with my family joining as well. I will never forget the warm applause from the crowd and how much love I felt in the Davis Concert Hall at that moment! Then, we returned to our seats to enjoy the final portion of the concert.

For the last number, *all* of the performing registrants and guest artists came out onto the Davis Concert Hall stage for the grand finale. We all cheered with a standing ovation when they finished. Then, a truly exciting surprise happened. After their bows, instead of leaving the stage through the wings, they started singing and playing an encore, filing down the stage side stairs and streaming out into all aisles of the hall through the cheering crowd, stopping to greet people along the way. I got many hugs and cried joyfully as I was swept up with the rest of the throng, joining the performers in a procession up to the entrance, where the overflow audience greeted us when we reached the Great Hall.

What a way to close a concert!

The Festival Board chose Terese Kaptur to be the next Executive Director and, eight years later, James Menaker to replace her when she retired. The Festival successfully navigated the challenges posed by the Covid-19 pandemic in 2020 and is back up and running with many of the offerings we established, plus new and exciting ones. They continue the tradition of the Winter Edition.

I extend my best wishes for the ongoing success of the Festival. I appreciate the opportunity to attend Festival concerts and classes whenever I visit Fairbanks. It is quite refreshing to enjoy these experiences without the responsibilities of leadership!

At eighty, I took my farewell bow at the Festival after thirty rewarding years as Producing Director. I am grateful to everyone who helped make my vision a reality.

The link to sites for The Fairbanks Summer Arts Festival, Paris Photography Festival photos, and the collection of Festival Posters through 2009 can all be found in this chapter's Bonus Media.

CHAPTER 96

A MESSAGE FROM BOBBY LEWIS
FESTIVAL GOSPEL CHOIR CONDUCTOR

A phone call from Jo Scott in the fall of 2001 changed my life. That was the beginning of my decades-long friendship with Jo.

I have been to Alaska more times than I ever imagined I would be. What draws me back is the spirit of the Festival.

I have been to many music Festivals. Jo's vision for the Fairbanks Summer Arts Festival extends beyond simply teaching people how to sing, act, paint, or dance.

The Fairbanks Festival is so special. Jo created such a nurturing atmosphere that was contagious throughout the whole Festival. People truly encouraged each other which took away that spirit of intimidation. Registrants left feeling passionate about their craft and excited about improving their skills.

Jo doesn't talk about the accolades she has received for producing the Festival. So, I will list some of the awards she's received over the thirty years that she produced the Festival:

- The *Fairbanks Daily News-Miner* Community Service Award 1981
- Fairbanks Chamber of Commerce Service Award 1985
- Governor's Award for the Arts for Dedication to the Arts in Alaska 1988
- Delta Kappa Gamma Friends of Education Award 1988
- Rotary Club of Fairbanks Community Volunteer Award 1989
- The Boy Scout Distinguished Citizen Award 1990
- University Alaska Honorary Doctorate of Humane Letters 1990
- The Girl Scout Women of Distinction Award 2005
- The Alaska Women's Hall of Fame 2010
- The University of Alaska William R. Cashen Service Award 2017
- Fairbanks Summer Arts Festival Hall of Fame, with Dick Scott 2019

The trophies and plaques she has received are now in the Arctic and Polar Regions Collections & Archives of the University of Alaska Fairbanks. These awards hint at the impact Jo has had on people's lives.

We also remember Jo's husband, Dick, for his steadfast emotional and financial support of Jo and the Festival.

I think I speak for many people when I say the Festival has changed my life. It has given me a whole new family. I truly thought Eustace and I would come once in the summer of 2002. But we've been coming in winter and summer now for 22 years.

One of the Festival's families moved to Juneau, and they worked to open a door for us to start a Festival Gospel Choir there. For several years now, we've been going there after our Winter Edition of Gospel Choir in Fairbanks.

Jo Scott has been called a passionate educator. She has a gift for igniting a passion for the arts in people's hearts. That passion permeates our culture and gets passed on to the next generation.

Jo's life's work is a blessing to us all.

– Bobby Lewis
Senior Pastor, New Light Baptist Church in Harlem Festival
Gospel Choir Conductor, 2002 - present

CHAPTER 97

FAIRBANKS FAVORITES FROM FROZEN PONDS TO STEAMING SPRINGS

Welcome to Fairbanks, everyone! Whether you're just passing through or you call this charming place home, I want to share some of my must-see attractions that I hope will be enjoyed for many years to come. Fairbanks may be a small town, but it's bursting with a vibrant community full of creative and driven individuals. It's no wonder we have so many unique and exciting spots to explore. Please add these to your bucket list and tell them I said hello!

ICE ALASKA, HOME OF THE WORLD ICE ART CHAMPIONSHIPS

Ice carving was popular in Fairbanks in the 1930s as part of the annual Winter Carnival, but enthusiasm for this event waned.

At a Fairbanks Chamber of Commerce meeting in the late 1980s, some members discussed enhancing tourism by purchasing ice and producing ice carvings. Of course, we all laughed about the idea of buying ice.

However, some visionaries got the idea of starting an ice art competition using ice from local ponds. With help from many volunteers, the World Ice Art Championships were established in Fairbanks in 1990. It is now the largest ice sculpting championship in the world. Ice carvers from all over come to Fairbanks every February, and visitors can watch as they start with chainsaws to begin carving the large pieces of ice and work their way down to shaping intricate small details with heated tools.

Once the judging is complete, prize ribbons are displayed on the winning pieces. Seeing the finished carvings magically illuminated in the dark Alaskan afternoons and evenings is genuinely breathtaking. You can walk or ride the heated van to view the finished entries. It's always exciting to see who won the Grand Champion Ribbon!

Season: Mid-February through March, weather permitting

THE RIVERBOAT DISCOVERY

Jim and Mary Binkley started their tourism business in the early 1950s. They used a small remodeled missionary boat called the Godspeed to take tourists on the rivers around Fairbanks. Everyone liked their tours, so in 1954, Captain Jim built the sternwheeler Discovery I in the family's backyard on University Avenue in Fairbanks. That was around the time I met Jim and Mary. Their tours were very popular!

They had two more ships built on Whidbey Island, Washington. The last one, Discovery III, was finished in 1987 and is still in use today. It has a seating capacity of over 900 passengers. It was no easy feat for the Binkleys to get it from Whidbey Island to the Chena River in Fairbanks! The Riverboat Discovery tour includes a visit to the Chena Village Living Museum and the late Iditarod champion Susan Butcher's Trail Breaker Kennel, among other intriguing things. The Binkley grandchildren are now working in the business as part of their Alaska family legacy.

Season: Mid-May through mid-September

FOUNTAINHEAD ANTIQUE AUTO MUSEUM

Owners Tim and Barb Cerny welcome visitors to The Fountainhead Antique Auto Museum, one of the premier vintage and classic car museums in the United States. The collection includes over 115 beautifully restored and preserved vehicles and thousands of vintage fashions from the 18th to the mid-20th centuries, with 80 of these fashions on display. You'll also find scores of exhibits, artifacts, photographs, and archival videos that tell the story of America's early love affair with the automobile and Alaska's early motoring history. Fairbanks is proud to have this museum.

Season: Open year-round

CHENA HOT SPRINGS RESORT

Located 56 miles north of downtown Fairbanks, nothing else is quite like Chena Hot Springs Resort. With charming cabins and condos available, couples and families can soak in the outdoor hot springs even in the coldest winter weather.

Imagine swimming with snow and ice around you, steam from the hot water mingling with the steam from your breath. With everything from dog mushing to midnight treks to see the Northern Lights to a drink in an ice goblet at an ice bar, there are many activities to choose from between hot spring soaks.

Bernie Karl and Connie Parks-Karl purchased the Chena Hot Springs Resort from the State of Alaska in 1998. Discovered by two brothers in 1905, Chena Hot Springs has had many owners over the years, but none of them had the visions for it that the energetic and intelligent Bernie Karl did. One of his visions was to make the resort more environmentally friendly and to use geothermal technology to power it. He hired an engineer, and they went to work. Patents were issued, new technology was developed, and new business partnerships were formed.

Today, that vision provides heat and electricity for the entire resort and keeps the resort's Aurora Ice Museum a cool 25 degrees Fahrenheit inside year-round. World-famous ice carvers Steve and Heather Brice are the resort's carvers-in-residence. The same vision also heats the resort's greenhouses, where much of the produce is cultivated for the resort's restaurant. Over 45 employees are ready to welcome you.

Season: Open year-round

Pioneer Park

Located on Airport Way and Peger Road, visitors can explore the 44 acres of beautifully landscaped grounds created as part of the celebration marking the 100th year since the United States purchased Alaska from Russia in 1867. In previous chapters, I've documented the vast amount of work involved in creating it and even a 2024 update from Skip Cook, the Manager of the A-67 project from 1965 to 1967.

The charming main street in Pioneer Park is Gold Rush Town, where boardwalks lined with colorful flowers connect little log cabins. Throughout 1965, 29 cabins and a few frame buildings were moved from downtown Fairbanks to the site.

All those buildings must be maintained and that work is constant and costly. A Master Plan was proposed in the last few years, but Skip reports, "This plan has proven to be largely out of reach financially. The time of the anticipated implementation is already past. However, it is still a guideline for ongoing change."

Pioneer Park is a huge asset and essential to the Fairbanks community. Maybe I'm dreaming, but I believe someone out there needs a creative project and the money to put into it! Upkeep of Pioneer Park's enchanting little Gold Rush Town, in a friendly place like Fairbanks, could be just that project! (Do you know that someone?)

Season: Park itself open year-round, attractions vary

THE SALMON BAKE AT PIONEER PARK

The energetic Rick Winther, a fifth-generation Alaskan, opened the Salmon Bake at Pioneer Park in 1979. I've known his daughter Beth since I was her teacher years ago at Denali School. Now, years later, Beth might be at the Salmon Bake as one of three generations working on any given night.

They serve hundreds of people each summer night in beautifully landscaped grounds. Their famous salmon, halibut, cod, prime rib, and even crab main dishes are prepared on huge wood-burning outdoor fire pits, and you'll feel like you're part of a large family barbecue! Then, you'll pick from a variety of salads and sides before heading to your picnic table. The little dessert cabin is your last stop. The choices range from their Sundae Bar, Luigi's Italian

Ice, house-made blueberry apple or strawberry rhubarb cheesecake parfait, and a fan favorite, chocolate "moose"! You will have fun visiting with diners from all over the world.

Season: Mid-May through mid-September

THE PALACE THEATRE AT PIONEER PARK

When the A-67 board needed a pianist who could create a show for the Palace Saloon in 1969, they found Jim Bell. He was in the Army, stationed at Fort Wainwright, but he was free evenings. Finding Jim was a lucky day for all Fairbanks, not just for the A-67 board bit. Jim turned out to be more than just a pianist. He was a gifted composer and singer and knew how to write humorous shows. Jim could have made it big anywhere, but he loved Fairbanks and its people, and he stayed. For years, Jim produced a delightfully entertaining new show for the Palace each summer.

Rick Winther purchased the Palace Saloon in 1985. He hired Richard Ussery, Melinda Mattson, and Bill Arnold to write a new show for the Palace Players using many of Jim's songs and some of the skits from shows he had produced. (No one could fill Jim's shoes when it came to writing a whole new show EVERY summer!) The new show incorporating Jim's music was received by a cheering crowd when it debuted in 1986. That entertaining show, now named *The Golden Heart Revue*, is presented each summer at the Palace Theatre to this day. In the 1990s, when they no longer served drinks, the Palace Saloon was renamed the Palace Theatre.

I'd like to recognize the Palace Players who have performed for five or more years:

Tim Ames, William Arnold, Brian Bennett, Jim Bell, Therisa Bennett, Rob Boyer, Gwendolyn Brazier, Johan Brun, Jaunelle Celaire, Darrell Clark, Dionna Clark, Kit

Cleworth, Cindy Clevenger, Angela Crepeau, Lavanda Davis, Giana Drogheo, Genevieve Elterman, Julie Engfer Jones, Jim Fredette, Dave Fields, Greg Gustafson, Bruce Hanson, Charly Hardage, Gloria Hartzman, Sarah Hoover, Jim Hotchkiss, Shirley Hughes, Bekka Hunter, Cheri Huraux, Abbie Johnson, John Kohler, Millie Link, John Link, Claudia Lively, Melinda Mattson, Bob Miller, Steve Mitchell, Sarah Mitchell, Nicholas Nappo, Alice Nielsen, Connie Oba, Julie Rafferty, Matthew Reckard, Robin Rushing, Carey Seward, Adele States, and Michelle Wazniak. Bravo!

Season: Mid-May through mid-September

WICKERSHAM HOUSE AT PIONEER PARK

When walking through Gold Rush Town, you'll find the Wickersham House next to the little white church. In 1900, Judge Wickersham was appointed to a federal position. He built this house by himself between 1904 and 1906, hoping his wife Deborah would be happy and comfortable in a nice modern house. It was the first milled lumber home in Fairbanks; until then, there were only log structures. This home was originally located on First Avenue and Noble Street in downtown Fairbanks.

If you're lucky, you'll experience the one-man theatre piece and two-minute history lesson, *Judge James Wickersham and a Visit To His Home*. Local professional actor Steve Mitchell takes on the personality of Judge Wickersham as he sits comfortably in the Judge's chair in the Judge's home. He is perfectly dressed in a suit of the day, complete with an elegant gold watch chain across his chest. After his short performance, Steve chats in character with visitors about current events during Wickersham's time.

Every time Dick and I got the chance to see Steve's show, we thoroughly enjoyed it. We felt like we were actually visiting with the Judge, discussing the challenges of the day.

Judge Wickersham spent his last years in Juneau, where he passed in 1939 at 82.

Season: Memorial Day through Labor Day

THE BIG STAMPEDE AT PIONEER PARK

In the early 1960s, C. Rusty Heurlin created 15 gorgeous large-scale paintings that told the story of the Klondike Gold Rush. They form the exhibition *The Big Stampede* at the Pioneer Museum. Visitors sit on a circular platform that rotates and then pauses as a painting is illuminated in front of them. Reuben Gaines' recorded voice tells the story of the painting, then the lights dim, and the platform rotates to the next one. Roger Cotting designed that moving platform. It's a fascinating story, of course, but this moving presentation (pun intended!) gives it even more impact. Fortunately, the paintings were hung high enough that they were above the waterline during the devastating 1967 flood that damaged much of the beautiful A-67 Park.

Season: Memorial Day through Labor Day

SS NENANA AT PIONEER PARK

The *SS Nenana* is a wooden-hulled sternwheeler built in 1933 for Alaska Railroad service on the Yukon, Nenana, and Tanana Rivers. It provided access to interior Alaska long before roads could be built. The ship carried military cargo during World War II, including lend-lease aircraft on their way to Russia. Moved to Pioneer Park in the 1960s, it is one of only three steam-powered passenger sternwheelers of any kind left in the U.S. and the only large wooden sternwheeler. Visitors are welcome to walk through the ship and see the detailed dioramas of some of the villages it served.

Friends of the *SS Nenana* is a non-profit organization that was formed in 2019 and is dedicated to renovating and preserving the historic sternwheeler.

Season: Memorial Day through Labor Day

Enjoy Fairbanks!

Links to these attractions are in this chapter's Bonus Media.

THE 2010S

CHAPTER 98

FROM WINTERIZING TO DOWNSIZING TO MAKING A MOVE

On January 1, 2010, it was great to wake up to a new year with no Festival plans pending, and we had time to concentrate on other things.

It had been almost 40 years since Ed McMorrow had rebuilt our Mason & Hamlin piano, and our piano tuner said it was getting difficult to keep the screw stringers from slipping out of tune. I called Ed to see if he was up for another Alaska project, and he told me he wouldn't have time for several years. I told him I was 80 years old and couldn't wait that long!

Ed told us about a seven-foot Steinway he was rebuilding and suggested a trade. The two pianos crossed paths as the Mason & Hamlin was shipped to Ed in Seattle, and the Steinway made its way to Fairbanks. Ed had done a fantastic job, it looked and sounded beautiful. I enjoyed playing it, and we continued to host concerts at home.

I had so much fun gardening that summer. I enjoyed keeping the large lawn mowed, getting my exercise walking briskly behind the self-propelled mower. When Tom Thumb and Morgan would hear the mower start, they'd whinny like mad. They knew that sound meant clippings were coming, and they loved those clippings!

I loved our home and grounds. I was a farm girl at heart, and this was my mini-farm. Near the end of summer, I was having fun transplanting some ferns by the corral and saw Dick on the pool deck with a legal pad. It was time to list what he needed to do before freeze-up to winterize everything.

Dick saw me, and he graciously suggested that maybe it was time for us to sell and move to a home that had less upkeep. Poor Dick. He tried to discuss this, but I turned him down. A lot was involved to maintain what our family had worked on for nearly 60 years. I told him in no uncertain terms that I didn't want to leave our place until I couldn't wiggle anymore! So he proceeded to finish everything on his winterizing list. I could still wiggle in 2011, and he did it all over again.

In the spring of 2012, Dick and I left slushy, chilly Fairbanks to visit Shirley in New York City. We enjoyed going to museums, shows, operas and concerts. When we were ready to leave, she casually asked if we might like to live in Manhattan someday.

I started thinking about that on the flight home. Dick and I were in our mid-80s, and it began to sink in that it *might* be time for us to sell. I shared my thoughts with Dick, and he loved that I had finally come around to his idea! At that moment, on the plane, we decided to sell our home and move to Manhattan.

Our kids were a huge help getting ready for the sale, which meant going through sixty years of treasures and separating what would be donated from what would be shipped to New York with the piano. Mikey Dewey had been helping Dick with odd jobs and was a delightful worker clearing things out of our dome, continuing the momentum between visits from the kids. Dick had a special pile of tools and hardware that he added to the "ship to New York" category.

When the property was put up for sale, it was bittersweet. In September 2012, the nonprofit Morning Star Ranch purchased the property. We were happy to learn that their mission was to provide learning opportunities for people with disabilities. In a few weeks, we would leave for New York. I was excited and sad at the same time. Dick was happy because this year, he completed his winterizing list for the *last* time as he walked Morning Star's director through each step of the process.

People were surprised to hear that Dick and I would be leaving Fairbanks. There was a delightful farewell party in the Great Hall at UAF. We tearfully said goodbye to many longtime friends that afternoon.

A surprise awaited us at the Fairbanks International Airport. After we checked in for our flight to New York and came up the escalator to security, my dear friend Christine Upton and her accordion band were playing at the top! Passengers stopped to enjoy it, asking if there was always music at this airport.

We landed in Manhattan, ready for new adventures. Shirley had found us a spacious studio apartment with a panoramic view in Midtown West. I loved the name: Symphony House! It was all set up when we arrived, complete with a closet marked "The Dome" for the tools and hardware that Dick had handpicked to ship.

It had windows filling two walls, and a balcony with a little table and a hammock overlooking Central Park. Shirley installed a Murphy Bed on the third wall, and Dick proceeded to mount a sliding covering to hide the bed when it was up during the day. The rest of our things arrived, including the Steinway that Ed had rebuilt. With the bed up and its covering drawn, it felt like a big light-filled living room in the sky. The piano was a cozy addition.

We came to love and adore all of the doormen and building staff, as they would greet us warmly when we passed through the lobby coming in or out. We no longer had a car, but we didn't need one. We could easily walk to most places or catch a bus or subway; we got a kick out of swiping our Senior MetroCards.

Our hearts were still in Fairbanks, but Dick and I were excited to begin our new life in the big city.

CHAPTER 99

A Sailing Ship, a Bullet Train, and a Seaside Retreat

Though Dick and I had traveled a lot, our flight to New York City in September 2012 was the first time we had traveled to a new home. We would never have dreamed we'd be moving to Manhattan!

Dick was born in New York, and his early years were spent in the city. Shirley has lived in Manhattan off and on since going there to take care of Dick's dad in the 1990s. Her airline job afforded us travel that had been hard to take advantage of in Fairbanks. Now we were a hop and a skip from Newark International Airport, a gateway to the world.

In early 2013, a few months after we had arrived, Dick and Shirley looked into going on a sailing trip. Dick did considerable sailing when growing up in California. While living in Fairbanks, he bought two 12-foot Sea Snarks and taught our children the basics of sailing at a gravel pit.

Shirley had previously crewed with Captain Dave Murphy on his boat *Sea Symphony* in Greece, and he had reached out looking to crew an upcoming trip. She was checking with Captain Dave to see about bringing her dad along. I generally don't enjoy boats or the water, but when I heard them talking about sailing in a 52-foot boat through the Greek islands, I wanted to go too!

As a formality, Captain Dave had us register on an Australia-based website called FindaCrew. At ages 84 and 86, Dick and I were the oldest people on the site and FindaCrew mentioned us in a fun piece CNN did on them.

In June 2013, we met up in Athens with Captain Dave and wonderfully fun fellow crew members Flo and Fita. We had a couple days there to explore the ruins, wandering the ancient cobblestone alleyways and stocking the galley. After provisioning the boat, we spent ten lovely days sailing Captain Dave's Formosa 52 from the Piraeus marina in Athens to Lefkada on the west coast of Greece.

We learned a lot about sailing and Greek history from Captain Dave. We had hourly posts to cover while sailing, and Dick and I both got many turns at the helm. Dave is a walking encyclopedia, and he made the trip fun and educational. We docked in villages each night to enjoy Greek salads and fresh fish. A highlight of the trip was going through the Corinth Canal. Captain Dave later sold *Sea Symphony,* and we were part of a reunion in New York where many of his former crew members gathered from around the world!

We barely returned home from that amazing trip when we planned to join Shirley on a six-day layover in Barcelona during the Christmas week. Dick and I would fly standby with the many family members of the rest of the crew. We were getting good at the lingo, and were happy that "the flight looked wide open for standby."

The whole standby gang met at the gate in Newark and our working crew members boarded the flight. As we happily chatted in the gate area, suddenly a flood of young people hurried past us and descended on the podium. Turns out a European soccer team had just been transferred to our flight when another airline canceled! More airline lingo: not only was there no room for standbys, there were "revenue standbys" ahead of us. We were not getting on.

The crew onboard quickly rebooked each of their respective family members to an apparently open flight to Madrid that would leave an hour later! We got the word, and all made our way to the new gate, hoping for the best.

The crew flew to Barcelona as scheduled. Sure enough, an hour later we were seated in first class seats on our way to Madrid! By this time, it was Christmas Eve, and the day Spaniards traditionally celebrate the holiday. All of the trains to Barcelona were full. We had two darling children in our group, Alexander and Shadae, and they were the only ones who spoke Spanish. They took charge in speaking with the ticket agent, and took us to another window, securing all of us bullet train tickets for a few hours later. They felt very proud to do this, and we all enjoyed a nice lunch at the airport while we waited for the departure. That train would only take two and a half hours and Dick was fascinated that it held speeds of over 190 mph. We never would have gotten to ride it had we not been "bumped" in Newark!

We all reunited at the lovely Barcelona crew hotel and planned the Christmas dinner for everyone. We could use the hotel's beautiful restaurant because our dinner time was

6 p.m., and the restaurant wouldn't open to the public until hours later for traditional Spanish dinnertime. Shirley had brought a pre-baked Butterball turkey from the states, kept cool in the plane's galley during the flight, and everyone shopped for local goodies and wine. We had Christmas "crackers" with crowns and prizes, and a fun gift exchange game for the eighteen or so crew and family members present. *Feliz Navidad!*

We had many days to explore and became familiar with the works of artist Antoni Gaudi, visiting both Güell Park and the Sagrada Familia cathedral. After many years, it is still under construction. When it was time to "non-rev" back, it was much less eventful, and we got "cleared" for seats and boarded the plane home.

New York City summers are warm, and Shirley wanted us to have some beach time. Midweek rentals at places on Long Island were considered, but these didn't compare to what she found: a charming five-bedroom villa by the sea on the island of Menorca, off the east coast of Spain in the Mediterranean.

Menorca is smaller and quieter than its neighbor Mallorca, which music history buffs will know is where Frederic Chopin, George Sand, and her two children lived in 1838.

Villa Alegre was staffed with a wonderful Argentinian couple, Marita and Oscar, who spoiled us with delicious food and unforgettable island tours. Oscar was quite a character, and Marita was delightful. Sandra, a beautician from Bogota, Colombia, joined as well and offered beauty and spa services on property in one of the bungalows that opened to the garden. We all loved and appreciated her.

Many friends and family members joined us on and off during our stay. The meals were delicious, and the fellowship was phenomenal. We had such a good time that we arranged to return that fall when Villa Alegre was next available. We returned for another two weeks of fun in Menorca, complete with Marita, Oscar, and Sandra. More friends and family members joined us then as well.

During a visit to the beach, Sandra met her future husband, and a year later, we attended their wedding in Bogota! Dick walked her down the aisle and I played *The Blue Danube* at the reception by special request.

In the five years that Dick and I lived in Manhattan, we took many interesting and educational "space available" trips.

Destinations included Scotland, Ireland, England, Italy, Spain, Panama, Guatemala for a traditional wedding, Colombia for another wedding, Canada for a leaf-peeping cruise on the *Queen Mary II*, and the Bahamas for a Christmas Cruise with our dear friend Teresa and her little Cassandra. Stateside, besides returning to Alaska many times, we also flew to the Florida Keys to visit our sailing friend Flo, where she got us a ride on the original African Queen; Boston, where Linda Marchi picked us up to reconnect with Festival friends and to visit the homes of Ralph Waldo Emerson and Louis May Alcott; and San Diego, to see Bryan and his family.

A particularly fun adventure was getting to go on an Azamara cruise when former Festival registrant Dominique Gagné was its Music Director. With permission from the Captain, she was able to join us for meals, and we got to enjoy her performances with the rest of the guests. Some days at port, she was assigned tours, as were the other ship crew members, so we would sign up for the tours Dominique was leading. When she wasn't assigned a tour, we would take her along and explore the port together. Dominique is like family to us. Shirley was able to work a Dublin trip with a 23-hour layover. We met at Trinity College to see the Book of Kells, then joined up with the airline crew for a glass of wine. Shirley stayed with her crew, and we went back to the ship.

The cruise ended a few days later in Edinburgh, and Shirley worked the flight the night before to fly us back the next morning. We didn't realize that it was the middle of the famous golf tournament there, and suddenly there was only one seat available on Shirley's flight. I told Dick to take the seat, and I stayed with all of the other "bumped non-rev standbys" to try for the next flight.

I didn't get on! But neither did a retiree from Houston that I had become friends with, and we navigated together to get on a train to London. That train trip was remarkable! We could see the countryside, sheep in the fields, and beautiful landscapes. I never would have had that experience without having been "bumped" in Edinburgh. There was wifi on the train and I was able to email Shirley and Dick, who had landed in Newark by that time. They booked us rooms close to London's Gatwick airport. Once we got to London, we made our way from the train to the hotel, and the next day from the hotel to the airport, where we got "cleared" for seats on a flight to New York.

It was exciting to head to the airport with a destination in mind, yet a possibility of ending up somewhere completely unexpected!

CHAPTER 100

MUSIC PARTIES, PARADE BUBBLES, AND A WORLD PREMIERE

My Fairbanks arts connections greatly enhanced our time in New York. The Festival Gospel Choir director, Bobby Lewis, is the pastor of a church in Harlem. Dick and I enjoyed attending his New Light Baptist Church. We love his Gospel choir, and Bobby's messages are always uplifting. Bobby even took us with him on a road trip to Virginia Beach to see his parents, Bishop Rudolph and Lady Maurine, and the rest of his family. It was an inspiring time for us.

We enjoyed going to the morning rehearsals of the Rivera to Lucie Arnaz to Marilyn Maye. Marilyn and I are one year and one day apart in age. I was tickled when she told me she remembered hearing about Maggie's trips to the festival in Alaska, referring to Margaret Whiting. We'd often see performances of our favorite, the iconic Natalie Douglas. We made many interesting friends who became a part of our lives.

We became members of the New York Philharmonic to attend its rehearsals. We liked the daytime aspect of all of these events, as we could easily walk up Broadway to Lincoln Center and catch the bus home with a swipe of our Senior Citizen MetroCards before dark.

Festival World Music guest artists Barry Olsen and Valerie Naranjo gave us the thrill of a lifetime with a backstage tour of Broadway's *Lion King*! Valerie has been its percussionist for many years, and from what I understood, Barry was the only one qualified to sub for her at the time! We also attended Barry's ensemble performances. They are a busy and delightful couple, and we appreciated when they made time for us.

Monday nights in New York City had particularly entertaining options, and no bus or subway needed. For an early night, we could walk to the famed piano bar don't tell mama, on 46th Street's Restaurant Row, to enjoy the amazing Ricky Ritzel at the piano with his weekly curated set list. He is such a wonderful musician, and we loved how he incorporated a theme into each set. Fun and educational!

For a later Monday night, after a disco nap we'd walk down Eighth Avenue to Gianni Valenti's Birdland Jazz Club on 44th Street. Jim Caruso hosts *Jim Caruso's Cast Party* featuring the Cast Party Symphony Orchestra: Billy Stritch, Steve Doyle, and Daniel Glass. Described as an "open mic on steroids" by the *New York Times*, besides our favorite, the iconic Natalie Douglas, we saw everyone from Chita Rivera to Lucie Arnaz to Marilyn Maye. Marilyn and I are one year and one day apart in age. I was tickled when she told me she remembered hearing about "Maggie's trips to the Festival in Alaska," referring to Margaret Whiting.

In February 2014, it would be sixty years since our forty-below-zero wedding in Fairbanks. Our kids organized a beautiful Diamond Anniversary Music Party to celebrate. They rented our building's Starlight Room on the top floor and had the piano moved upstairs for the party. The invitation read, "No gifts, please, but feel free to share a song." We had just met Australian pianist Matt Baker, who'd recently relocated to New York. He was musical directing darling Joan Jaffe's current show, and we were able to hire him for the evening. He was amazing! (We were lucky to have gotten him; soon he became tremendously sought after and hard to book.) It was an evening of nonstop music, from gospel to opera and cabaret to jazz.

The whole evening was such a fun convergence of musicians that we decided to make it an annual event, changing the theme to Music, Friends, and Conversation. We loved this musical tradition. Ari Silverstein and SallyAnn Thibedeau were often emcees. Over the years we were thrilled to host many incredible musicians who shared their talent with our guests. Besides Bobby, Greg, and Valerie's amazing performances, we were treated to music from Natalie Douglas, Eric Comstock, Giacomo Gates, Anne Phillips, Joan Jaffe, Ronnie Whyte, Ben Cassara, Ron Drotos, KT Sullivan, Trudi Mann, Adam Asarnow, Sue Matsuki, Dominique Gagne, Katie Cox, SallyAnn Thibedeau, Andie Tanning, Ruthanne Cunningham, Eric Yves Garcia, and Daryl Sherman, to name just a few.

Each year on Thanksgiving Day, we were delighted to be included in a *Parade & Bubbles* brunch in a lovely apartment overlooking Central Park. Seeing the gigantic balloon figures pass in front of us outside the windows was spectacular! All while sipping champagne with our dear hosts, Gordon and Jessica. Later in the day, I would prepare a non-traditional Thanksgiving dinner in our apartment. We had pescatarians in the group, and crab legs were sometimes served in lieu of turkey. We welcomed friends from all over, and it often turned into a music party as well.

One year, we gathered the group and walked to Radio City Music Hall for the *Christmas Spectacular with the Radio City Rockettes*. Dick remembered going to movies in the beautiful hall as a child in the 1930s and seeing the Rockettes perform before they started the film.

Dick and I were drawn back to Fairbanks for the 2016 Festival when the gifted young Emerson Eads would be premiering his *Mass for the Oppressed*. The story revolves around four young Alaska Native men who had been unjustly held in prison for 18 years for the murder of a teenager named John Hartman. They kept pleading their innocence from prison all those years.

If it hadn't been for UAF Journalism Professor Brian Patrick O'Donoghue and the investigative journalism he and his class undertook, the "Alaska Innocence Project" might never have gotten involved, and the men may have remained in prison.

Emerson said, "When I heard that the Fairbanks Four had just been released in December of 2015, I had just finished my first semester of graduate school at the University of Notre Dame. I was the same age as Marvin Roberts, the only one of the Four I corresponded with. The reality of the injustice of their being held for eighteen years in prison and the joy of their release came out at the piano as my *Agnus Dei*. I took this movement to my late conducting teacher,

Carmen-Helena Tellez, to ask if I could include it in my doctoral conducting recital."

After hearing the story, she said, "Emerson, this is too big a story full of injustice just to be an *Agnus Dei*. You must write the whole Mass."

This encouragement inspired Emerson to write *Mass for the Oppressed*, which would premiere at the Fairbanks Summer Arts Festival in July.

The Festival Orchestra, conducted by Robert Franz, was at its best premiering the dramatic piece to an enthusiastic crowd. Three of the Fairbanks Four were present that evening. When they were introduced, there was a wave of support from the packed house.

Marvin Roberts' mother was there. I can't imagine her emotions. Dick and I were so moved by this concert. We were proud of Emerson and very grateful to have been there.

Links to many of the artists and events above can be found in this chapter's Bonus Media.

CHAPTER 101

ICE AND SNOW, MODEL BOATS, AND A HAVEN IN HAVANA

We were so happy to have so many people visit us when they happened to be in New York. If we didn't host a meal at home, we loved to take them to Apple Jack, our favorite Greek diner on the corner. Spiro and his family always welcomed us warmly.

In February 2017, Karen Ryman Jones, my cousin Bille's daughter, visited with her husband, Michael, on their way to France. I had never met them. Our South Dakota relatives were working on a reunion later that summer, and she knew

534   Jo Ryman Scott

they would still be traveling. It was so special that they made a point of coming to meet us in person.

We returned to Fairbanks again that winter when I received the UAF's William R. Cashen Service Award during the Blue and Gold Gala. It was incredibly touching to receive this award since I'd known Bill Cashen and his family since the 1960s. I admired his leadership then and his continued dedicated service to the University.

We enjoyed reconnecting with Fairbanks friends and seeing the beautiful UAF campus blanketed in snow. Speaking of snow, a month earlier in New York, when Dick and I were walking hand in hand near Carnegie Hall, I slipped on a patch of ice and fell and pulled Dick down with me! We were right in front of Cohen's Optical, my go-to place for putting prescription lenses in my fun decades-old frames. Bonita came running out of the shop, saying, "Mrs. Scott, are you okay?" Friendly people rushed to help us get on our feet.

Fortunately, we hadn't gotten hurt, but this was a wake-up call that perhaps it was time for us to move someplace without icy sidewalks. Julie had a place in Tucson where she would spend time during the winter and suggested we consider moving there. This sounded interesting to us. She'd seen a pretty fountain and signs for a retirement resort community near her place. We expressed interest when she described it, and she went to visit. She was impressed. Dick and I enjoyed viewing their very informative website and decided to make the move at the end of the summer!

We were grateful to be so active at our ages. We had "retired to New York" at 84 and 86 and now planned to "retire to Arizona" at 89 and 91. In the meantime, there was still a lot on our calendar.

In March, a fluke snowstorm threatened to cancel one fun calendar item. We planned a trip to Buffalo to see our actress friend Linda Stein in a play. All flights and even bus options were canceled. So we bundled up, took a subway to Penn Station, and got on a nine-hour Amtrak ride through the snow, getting to see the Hudson Valley along the way. Not only did we make the play and spend precious time with Linda and her husband Carl, but we also traveled to Niagara Falls as an added side trip!

When we returned, Ginger Carroll visited from Fairbanks and invited us to a new Broadway show called *Come From Away*. It was especially exciting as Festival guest Caitlin Warbelow made her Broadway debut with that show.

On my birthday in April, we went to Daryl Sherman's cabaret performance, where she featured Gene Bertoncini, another popular Festival guest in its early years.

In May, Dick and I hosted the world premiere screening of the incredible documentary *Cuba's Forgotten Jewels*, created by Festival world dance guest artist Judy Kreith and filmmaker Robin Truesdale.

The story is about Judy's mother's family and other Jewish families who had escaped Nazi Germany in 1941. When their ship was advised it would be turned away from the New York Harbor, they found refuge in Cuba. What ensues is fascinating.

Several of the 30 guests in our home that day for the screening were the very people who had been in Cuba with Judy's mother at this time. One guest, about 87, got to see footage of herself in Cuba as a teen for the first time.

For Dick's 90th birthday in June, I had fun organizing a gathering of NYC friends and family to celebrate. Lee and Gayle Hazen from Fairbanks were traveling and coordinated the stop in New York to be there. Gayle hadn't told Lee where they were going that evening, so it was a fun surprise.

Dick was King for a Day, and he had people laughing as he told stories of his long life. Dick had a good time. After the party, we went to The Lake at Central Park off Fifth Avenue at 72nd Street. We rented electric model sailboats, and Dick gave us tips on how to maneuver the sails to get across the lake. He had done the same thing 85 years earlier when he was five, only the sailboats had been manual then. He explained how he'd have to set the sail and secure the little line, then let it go, run across the lake, and, hopefully, meet it on the other side. He was happy to share this experience with our grandson, Aydan.

Later that week, we attended the *Swell Party* to commemorate Cole Porter's birthday. In the 30s and 40s, I remember so well when everything was described as swell! That fabulous Ari Silverstein had booked a full evening of music at a private West Village townhouse, and as a surprise, he had birthday cakes for Dick and for Daryl Sherman, another June baby.

Dick loved *Seinfeld* and would often walk the two blocks from our apartment to the famous "Soup Man" for a cup of the Mulligatawny. We booked *Kramer's Reality Tour* tickets for his birthday and met the *real* Kenny Kramer! He got a picture with him in front of Tom's Restaurant on Broadway and 108th Street, the diner shown in the series, and we got to visit many other episode locales. Kenny was charming, and the tour was very entertaining.

One of the last gatherings we hosted at our Symphony House apartment was a lovely concert by Anchorage Steinway Artist Juliana Osinchuk. We were happy she shared her talent with so many people that afternoon.

We were wrapping things up and packing our things, but the South Dakota reunion was shaping up, and I was excited and intrigued about going!

A link to stream Forgotten Jewels can be found in this chapter's Bonus Media.

CHAPTER 102

A SOLO TRIP, AIRPORT FANFARE, AND A WALK DOWN MEMORY LANE

In late June 2017, I set off on a solo trip to Aberdeen, South Dakota, for the *Ryman Family and Friends Reunion.*

The Ryman family ancestry goes back to 1863 when my great-grandparents Melchior and Magdalena Reimann left Switzerland for a three-month boat trip to America. They changed the spelling of their last name from "Reimann" to "Ryman" shortly after they arrived. Also, Melchior's name became Mike.

This reunion was being held in my honor in the farm community of Warner, ten miles south of Aberdeen. I lived there from 1940 to 1950.

I was met at the Aberdeen Airport by a beautiful "Welcome Home" banner and a group of cheering people. What a welcome!

One of them was my talented new-found cousin, Carole Munger Haugh. She was the primary organizer. I had known and loved Carole's three older brothers and their sister many years earlier when they were all little.

Margie Ryman Wiedebush was also at the Airport that day. She was a dear young cousin I loved in the early 1940s, and she was now in her 70s. Also at the airport that day was Margie's niece, Kay Shilman Vikander, who helped Carole with much of the planning for the reunion.

My former Wright School student, Shirley Fuhrman Morgan, was there, too. Shirley graciously hosted me during my stay. She was in her 80s! I wasn't much older than my students when I started teaching at age eighteen in 1947. I loved teaching all those Wright School kids.

The rest of the people at the Airport were cousins whose ancestry goes back to the Reimanns in 1863.

The reunion was to celebrate the 70th anniversary of my first year of teaching at the Wright one-room country School. I'd returned to the Aberdeen area at various times to visit my immediate family. But I hadn't spent much time in Warner since 1950 when I retired from teaching at Wright School and left to finish college.

I hadn't seen many of my former students or high school friends for decades.

It didn't take long for all of us to get acquainted. It was evident that we were related: We all loved to talk. I discovered that my new-found Ryman relatives were not only smart and good-looking, they were also musically creative.

The reunion was wonderful! I was happy to see former students Bonnie Munger Holsing, Keith and Dwayne Rehfeld, and Rodney Schoen. I hadn't seen them for years! Bill Fuhrman was traveling but he called me. Unfortunately, Lois Rehfeld Walters, Mervin Nilsson, Jimmy Rehfeld and Charlean Fuhrman Croxton couldn't be there.

There was a treasured surprise on the first night of the reunion: Dwayne Rehfeld brought his little annual that I had made for him in 1950! I made an annual for each student to help them remember my last year of teaching at Wright School. It was especially fun for them to see pictures of themselves dating back 70 years. I had also included pictures of some of our little visitors who came to our various school parties. It was very touching that Dwayne had saved that annual for all of these years!

I was happy to meet Vickie Breidenbach, whose mother, Aldene Shilman Nelson, was my dear friend at Warner High School. Aldene had passed away and I had never met Vickie.

I was also happy to see my talented niece Karen Angerhofer Mahrt, who was there with her husband, Chuck, and my grandniece Kim. Kim's mother, my late niece Evie Angerhofer Kienow, had married the grandson of my wonderful neighbor, Julia Kienow. (I had written about Julia in an earlier story.)

Of course, everyone at the reunion had questions about my life in Alaska. I had lived there for almost 60 years. They were also curious about my life in Manhattan, where I was still living.

The three-day reunion in the Warner farming community had many wonderful happenings. I met Carole's younger brother, Steve Munger, who was born after I left the Warner community. He and his wife hosted a reception in their beautifully restored 1912 era home which had been built by our great, great uncle, Cap Ryman.

Another highlight for me was when Steve took me on a little road trip back to the farm community of Scatterwood Lake, where I'd lived until 1940. Shirley, Kay and Carole joined us. Scatterwood Lake brought back many memories.

Steve drove us to places I hadn't seen since 1940 when we moved to our new farm a mile west of Warner. He drove us all around Scatterwood Lake, which I remembered as being completely dried up by the late 1930s.

Now, it looked entirely different. It was full of water, and I was shocked to see how huge it had become. But it also looked different because the bandstand was gone, and so were all the beautiful homes I remembered that were around the lake.

Steve drove us around to the north side of the lake. I remembered that little hill going up from the lake. We saw the Bierman's homesite and then we drove to the top of the hill. I knew that area so well that I could point out exactly where our little one-room schoolhouse and the little red barn once stood. Those country schools needed small barns for the ponies. There were no school buses for us in those days; none of us got rides to school. We either walked or rode our ponies.

My little one-room schoolhouse was two miles from our farm home. I saw the little one-lane road where Mike and I walked or rode our pony, Jimmy, to school.

Oh, how I wanted to have Steve drive north on that little dusty road. Steve was so kind. He could tell I really wanted to drive on that road.

So he took that little road north for about a mile. Then we turned west where we saw the large Grass Lake. We continued west for about a half mile, went over a little wooden bridge, and kept watching for a corner driveway.

We found it, and took a left up the little hill. What Mike and I would have seen from here when coming home from school would have been our barn, the barnyard, the chicken coop, the chicken yard, the granary, the garage, and the little forest behind our two-story farmhouse.

What we saw that day when we got to the top of that little hill was that all of those structures were *gone*! Instead, we saw new farm buildings and a charming new farmhouse with flowers all around it. It all looked so beautiful.

I was happy that the forest in the backyard was still there. Mike and I had so much fun there building tree forts.

I knocked on the door, and the lady who presently owned the property graciously welcomed us. She was intrigued that our family had owned the property until 1940 and told me I could look around the grounds. I had fun doing that.

I really wanted to ask if I could go to the barnyard. I wanted to see if the HUGE rock that I used to climb on Jimmy's back was there, but I didn't want to impose. I couldn't imagine anyone trying to move it, but I never found out if it was still there.

I was happy to have seen so much of the place that I'd called home until we moved when I was eleven years old.

As Steve drove back down the little hill to the corner of the driveway, I recognized the spot where Mike and I sat and waited, watching for *A Bad Man in the Green Car*, the first chapter of this book! That corner of land with tall grasses and old trees on the lonely one-lane dirt road looked the same as it did in 1937. What fun memories I had with Mike on that old farm in the 1930s!

Then, Steve drove us north for a few miles to Mina Lake. I was really surprised and happy to see that it had become a beautiful resort community with lovely summer homes on the lake.

This brought us to the end of our road trip. I was so grateful to Steve. Getting to visit where I had lived more than 80 years earlier meant more to me than anyone could know. I'll never forget that day.

The three-day reunion touched my heart. My former student Shirley drove me around Aberdeen the next day. We went past my Uncle Cap's former home on Lincoln Street. Then we went to the Northern State Teachers College campus where I had attended summer school for three years. It is now called Northern State University, and the grounds were beautiful. I was pleased to see how much the campus had grown.

Then we visited the Bethesda Nursing Home, where I got to see my long ago friend Betty Seaman's brother, Chuck, and his wife, Darilyn. Chuck was in the first grade in 1940 when we moved to Warner. He was a smart little kid. Betty had passed away, but Chuck remembered me and we enjoyed our visit!

I had just as warm a sendoff at the airport, and I'll always be grateful to cousins Carole, Kay, Bill, Ollie, and all my new-to-me relatives for so lovingly organizing this memorable reunion.

CHAPTER 103

A Symphony Serenade, a Desert Oasis, and a Jaunt on a *Tin Goose*

Before we left Manhattan for Tucson, Dick and I had fun planning our last annual music party at Symphony House, this time to be called *Music, Friends and Farewells*. Guests came from all over, and I was thrilled that even several of my Ryman relatives made the trip.

I had fun reconnecting with my former piano teacher, Dr. James Johnson, who had recently relocated to New York City. At the farewell party, he performed one of my favorite Chopin Etudes. He had performed the same etude at the first concert on our Mason & Hamlin in 1975 in Alaska!

We'd had five fabulous years in New York. It was a bittersweet time when we packed up in September 2017 and left Symphony House, but we were looking forward to another new chapter in a new place with no ice or snow.

We landed in Tucson on a beautiful fall afternoon, and Julie brought us to our new home. Many places in the area landscape with rock and desert plants, our complex was lush and green with a variety of flowering and fruit trees. While we loved our large studio and balcony in Manhattan, I was excited to have such a large space with two bedrooms, two bathrooms, and a balcony. The second bedroom's large closet held Dick's favorite tools and hardware, and we brought the laminated "Dome" label from Dick's New York hardware closet to carry on the tradition.

Julie had invited five of our floor's neighbors to join us in our apartment for a surprise get -acquainted gathering. It was delightful! Dick and I thoroughly enjoyed meeting our new neighbors.

The complex is billed as a resort community for active seniors and has various planned activities, from Bible study to Bingo. My favorite part about it? Besides the beautifully landscaped grounds, the Dining Hall serves beautiful meals you choose from a menu. Even though we ate out or "ordered in" a lot in New York, I was happy not to be cooking *at all* anymore!

We were also happy to have many people visit as they passed through Tucson. Arizona is a popular retirement and vacation spot. We had a visit from Chris and Denise Akert, whose son Charly is a cellist with UAF's Cynosure Trio. It was great to see our Anchorage Steinway artist Julia Osinchuk again so soon after her concert in our New York home. We also enjoyed visits from Fairbanksans Shirley and Ann DeVries and family, Lynn and Donna Davidson, Jim and Marcia Holm, Becky Anderson, Linda Rosenthal, Karen and Michael Jones, my niece Karen Mahrt, Celeste Goering, Sheryl Frey, and Ann Lackey, among others.

The Dining Hall offers holiday feasts with beautiful decorations, complete with enormous ice sculptures. Dick and I enjoyed the New Year's Eve parties especially. We also attended the frequent live concerts, from accordions to Mariachis, held in the lovely Great Room or the Dining Hall. Dick hung a hummingbird feeder on our balcony, and watching the frenzy of activity through the living room window is entertaining. While I am not a fan of the water, Dick loved going down to the hot tub in our villa. Meanwhile, I enjoyed the landscaping and learned to identify some cacti. There is a flourishing flowering hibiscus plant which always reminds me of the one Ann Dolney gave to Dick in Alaska.

We explored the beautiful Tucson area with Julie. We went to the arts district on South Park Avenue for Cyclovia, though we were walking, not cycling. We took numerous sunset drives through Saguaro National Park East. Julie arranged for Dick to fly in a refurbished Ford Tri-Motor aircraft, as she knew he'd been fascinated with them for decades. Nicknamed the *Tin Goose*, production had started in 1925 and ended in 1933 after only 199 had been made. What a thrill he got out of that plane ride!

While we missed both New York and Alaska, we were making ourselves at home in Tucson.

CHAPTER 104

A Photo Op, *un Polizia Stradale*, and an Unexpected Encounter

In 2018, Bryan and his lovely wife Lyn left their home in California for a trip to Italy.

In addition to seeing all the traditional tourist attractions, they were interested in finding the birthplace of Bryan's great-grandfather, Dick's grandfather, Joseph Fanelli. They knew that he was born in 1862 and his wife, Grace, was born in 1873.

Through their research, they discovered that the Fanelli relatives were from the little mountainous town of Laurenzana in southern Italy, above the arch of the boot on the map.

They got directions from Rome and set out for Laurenzana. It was a stormy day with lots of rain, thunder, and lightning. They had rented a car and carefully followed the directions over the narrow, winding roads through little villages in the storm.

They were relieved when they reached their destination. The rain had let up, and Lyn parked the car briefly to take a picture. She did not realize that she had blocked an access road.

Before long, un polizia stradale, a policeman, drove up behind them. Neither Bryan nor Lyn spoke Italian, but when the officer got out of the car, Lyn gestured to Bryan and exclaimed, "My husband is a Fanelli!"

The policeman was surprised. He showed them his badge. It said *Salvatore Fanelli*. The same exact name as Dick's father, Bryan's grandfather!

Immediately, the Italian charm and friendship came through. Officer Fanelli took Bryan and Lyn on a tour of the beautiful little town. They saw the ruins of the Castle of Laurenzana at the top of the hill, built in the 12th century.

Then, Salvatore Fanelli gathered all available Fanelli's at the Church of the Madonna del Carmine, built in about 1780. There was a religious holiday the next day, and Bryan helped his distant relatives hoist a statue off its perch and mount it on a truck, which would be paraded around town for the grand event. Bryan and Lyn had a delightful time meeting the family. None of them spoke the same language, but they could all communicate with Lyn's bit of Spanish and lots of smiles and gestures. They were invited to stay for the festivities, but sadly had to be in Rome that evening. They were so happy to have shared this special day.

They had succeeded in finding Bryan's great grandfather's homeland, which he and his wife Grace had left 145 years earlier. They felt certain that the Fanellis in Laurenzana were as excited as they were to meet their long-lost cousins.

CHAPTER 105

A Nostalgic Alaska Cruise and a Gospel Celebration of Life

In 2019, Dick and I were notified that we had been selected to be the first recipients of the Fairbanks Summer Arts Festival's Hall of Fame award. Others named in succeeding years include Bobby Lewis, Eustace Johnson, Theresa Reed, Nancy Marriott, Eddie Madden, Greg Hopkins, Ron Drotos, Terese Kaptur, Don Gray, Glenn and Nancy Johnson, and Joy McDougall.

We thought it was fitting to take a cruise to Alaska for the festivities. Dick and I had both taken the Alaska Steamship

Company through the Inside Passage to get to Alaska the first time. Dick ventured up in 1951 and I came in 1953. The vistas were the same, but the luxury of the ship was a fun contrast to our first journeys.

The award was presented during a beautiful gala at the Westmark Hotel Ballroom. It featured the Festival Orchestra conducted by Maestro Robert Franz. It was fun for me to see the Brice harp in the orchestra that evening. They had a beautiful crowd, and we loved seeing many of our long-time friends. Those were happy days for us!

In January 2020 the whole family gathered in Tucson to celebrate Shirley's birthday. Captain Dave from our Greek sailing adventure had since moved to the hills an hour from Tucson and came down for the celebration. We had everyone's favorite, a king crab feast. Dick was in excellent health and we all had a delightful time together.

Just two weeks later, on Tuesday afternoon, February 4th, Dick suffered a sudden massive stroke at home. The ambulance was there in just a few minutes. I was allowed to ride up front with the driver, who suggested that we take Dick to St. Joseph's Hospital, which was closer than the Tucson Medical Center.

When we arrived at St. Joseph's, a team of doctors and nurses was waiting for us. They gave me a little room with a bed to rest after they admitted Dick. Later that evening, the doctor came by to tell me that Dick could never recover.

Our children came, and though he was in and out of sleep, we believed that he recognized them and smiled a bit. He was moved to Pepe's House Hospice on Saturday. We were grateful that Dick wasn't suffering. Our family had dinner together in Dick's hospice room on Sunday. Dick was asleep during that time. The rest of the family had just left for the evening. I was in a recliner in the room with Dick and was resting. I woke when I heard Dick breathing funny. I got up and pressed the button to call a nurse.

In a moment, the nurse came, listened for his pulse and his heart, and she quietly told me that Dick had passed away. The family returned immediately. Dick died peacefully on Sunday, February 9th, 2020.

The next weekend, we were grateful to welcome friends and family at our complex's Great Room to remember Dick's life. Besides our dear neighbors in the community, it was touching to see so many Alaska friends who have retired to Arizona and were able to join us.

That very week, Eustace Johnson and Bobby Lewis were in Fairbanks for the Winter Edition of the Festival. Bobby let us know that he wanted that Gospel Choir concert to be presented in Dick's memory. The next week our family flew to Fairbanks.

There was a warm and loving crowd at Journey Christian Church and Bobby led his choir in a beautiful concert. The last song brought a wonderful surprise. As the choir sang *When The Saints Go Marching In*, they began a processional streaming out of the sanctuary with everyone following behind to the reception and meal the choir had prepared for everyone. I was so touched that so many friends could be present for this moving gospel celebration of Dick's life.

THE 2020S

CHAPTER 106

INTROSPECTION, ISOLATION, AND INSPIRATION

Shortly before Dick's passing, we were starting an amusing project documenting stories of our early years in Alaska. One account involved Dick explaining the monumental task of moving his ten-thousand-pound bachelor cabin from the Richardson Highway to our new lot on College Road after we got married. As he recounted the details, I diligently took notes on my iPad using my trusty Pages app, reading it back to him to ensure everything was captured accurately. The fascinating experiences we shared in Alaska might seem unusual to those from the Lower 48. In another story, Dick vividly described the challenges of locating water on our new property and the process of pounding down a well. Our next collaboration focused on attempting, failing, and finally succeeding in making hundreds of cement blocks for the cabin's foundation. It was remarkable how sharp his memory remained, recalling intricate engineering feats from over sixty years ago.

After Dick's celebration of life in Alaska, our youngest daughter, Shirley, flew me back to Tucson and planned to stay for a couple of weeks. The very next week, however, Covid-19 cases were appearing around the world. Shortly after that, the lockdown was announced, and she ended up staying on so I wouldn't be alone. Her cheery presence kept me from being lonesome after Dick's passing.

My retirement village itself was on lockdown, but we could walk around the beautiful grounds with masks on. The Dining Room was shut down, but meals were delivered. I had TV and internet, but the news was hard to watch. I was busy writing thank-you notes to people who had sent condolence cards and would walk them down to the property's postbox to mail. Facebook kept me connected to others. During the Covid shutdown, lots of people were home learning to make sourdough bread. I already knew how to do that, but I did see a Facebook post about making something unfamiliar: gravlax. Shirley became an expert at making this delicious take on smoked salmon.

I was about to have my ninety-first birthday, and something called a *Zoom* was in the works, rather than an in-person celebration.

Going through my Pages app one afternoon, I happened on the story Dick and I had written about moving the cabin. I thought about putting it on my Facebook page in memory of Dick's ingenuity, but it also got me thinking about my own experiences growing up on our rural farm in South Dakota.

My little brother Mike and I had so many fun adventures in the mid-1930s on that old farm, and Shirley encouraged me to start writing them down.

Instead of trying to tackle a whole book, I could take advantage of social media, share one story at a time, and start immediately! With her techie help, I started a *Facebook Author/Book Page* to keep it separate from my personal Facebook page.

After my "Ninety-First Birthday Zoom Party" on April 11, 2020, I hosted a Facebook Live event announcing and inviting people to follow and share *Jo Ryman Scott – The First Ninety Years*.

I chose the story of Mike and me attempting to catch the bad man with a green car as my first post. I found the 1938 picture of us in my keepsakes and uploaded the story and photo.

During the lockdown, there were likely more people than usual on Facebook, but I was surprised by the instant likes and comments! It was fun for me to reply to people in real time, and I appreciated their encouragement to keep posting.

Thanks to the big print step-by-step manual that Shirley made for me, I was able to publish five stories on my page within just a month and I amassed a few followers. Not only would I publish the transcript along with photos, but also a companion video of me reading the story. At first, I read off of a printed script for the videos, setting up my iPad on a rolling side table that I would put a few feet away from the piano bench. I didn't have to adjust anything for each new video if I just rolled it to the same spot and sat on the piano bench. A creative musician friend, Patrick, suggested I download a teleprompter app like newscasters use. What a game-changer! It made it easier for me to read, and I could still be looking at the camera instead of looking down at my script.

I was already familiar with Pages and could write, edit, print, and even share. Shirley's manual showed me how to export a story from Pages to Dropbox and then download it to Teleprompter. Then, it reminded me what to push to start the recording and get the script scrolling. The last step walked me through uploading it to Facebook.

As the lockdown continued, when I was alone in my apartment after Shirley had to leave, this gave me something meaningful to work on and I found it healing to write. And when I finished each story, I had a reason to pick an outfit, coordinate accessories, choose some glasses, put on lipstick, then get out my manual and set up my video corner by the piano.

The immediate responses I received were incredibly comforting, and I kept writing. Researching background information for my stories online was a joy. I had fun making phone calls and sending emails to Pioneer Alaskans to fill in details on my stories. It connected me with many people by phone and email at a time when we all felt isolated. Another remarkable result was that some of my former students found me there; I loved reconnecting with them after literally decades.

I published a video and a transcript every ten to fifteen days for over three years. When I posted chapter ninety-nine, I thought again about putting my stories into an actual book.

You are holding the result!

A NOTE FROM THE AUTHOR

In this book I've gone from an adventure on a dusty country road in South Dakota to venturing about ancient cobblestone alleyways in Athens. It has been good for my brain to recall the things that have happened in between.

Because of my passion for music and writing, my hope is that my readers will be motivated to embark on their own storytelling journeys. Everyone has a unique and compelling story to share.

The QR I'm including below will bring you to a video tutorial I made describing six steps to jumpstarting your life story. It will be easier than you think!

1. *Capture a Memory.* Jot down some one-sentence memories that stand out in your life. It might be a joyful moment or a challenging experience. If possible, find a photo that relates to the memory.

2. *Highlight Your Story.* Think of a key moment from one memory and start crafting your narrative around it.

3. *Write Authentically.* Use the first-person narrative to share your story. I like to keep my paragraphs short to make the story easy to read.

4. *Practice Your Delivery.* Consider downloading a teleprompter app to practice reading your story aloud. Don't hesitate to seek feedback! Share your draft with a friend who can offer constructive suggestions and encouragement.

5. *Choose Your Platform.* Decide how you want to share your stories. I opted for an Author Page on Facebook, but there are many platforms and options available. Don't be afraid to ask for guidance in this process.

6. *Start Anywhere.* You can begin with any story from any time in your life and allow your creativity to guide you as you write.

Have fun writing your stories. I look forward to reading them!

– Jo

Jo's Tutorial

Jo Ryman Scott

QREATIVE DEEP DIVE

I hope this has sparked your curiosity to do a deep dive into some of what you've just read. Here are some highlights from the Bonus Media to get you started.

Jo's QReative Collection

Jo's QR Tutorial

Facebook Author Page

I'd love to hear from you!

NAME INDEX BY CHAPTER